"What a memoir! Marcus pulls you in with his entertaining and insightful writing. His journey is one to which so many will relate: the search for universal truths, the desire to belong to a cause greater than oneself, the need to be loved. He shares his experience so openly and with such humor, I was sad when it ended. And Grandpa Phil is my hero!"

Marene Emanuel

"One can't help but be caught-up and carried along, page after page, by Jonathan Marcus' new and engrossing memoir. Graduating from college in the waning years of the Vietnam War, he knew he didn't want to get swept up in a fight he didn't believe was his. Instead, in his quest to learn a new way to think about the world and his relationship with it, he was swept up into an almost cult-like group on the same quest. It became a years-long experience he could never have anticipated or imagined for himself. This story of Marcus' times of push and pull and give and take with his fellow seekers and the group's leader will both fascinate and intrigue you."

Mark Terrill

"Sit down to this meaty work for a cosmic dinner. Follow lyrical ribbons that fold on themselves, weaving across decades. Wake up in a story that doesn't end far from where it started. You will find yourself a lifetime from where you began."

Stephanie Bobb

"Wow. What a trip through the time space continuum! I love the easy flow of Marcus' writing, the essence of his years with Jan, the natural dialogue, the aliveness of his memories. I am touched by it as well, both by a sort of wistfulness that I didn't have such an experience, and awed that he did. The tone is flawless, consistent throughout, as if Marcus poured it all on the page in one go. His grandfather's presence is natural yet profound, as is his note to him at the wall, which contains the absolute best prayer ever hidden in a wall ever in the history of hidden notes."

Burnley Hayes

"It's engaging! From the very first sentence I wanted to follow the little bus to see where it would lead. So I did! Excellent read from beginning to end. Thanks Jonathan Marcus you're an amazing writer. I'm looking forward to another entertaining and enlightening book, by you!"

Cynthia Shelley

"I loved this book—it held my interest and kept me wondering how the next adventure would turn out. It was warm and sensitive, unpretentious and enlightening. A great story of a man coming of age, wanting challenges that would nourish his soul. Reading it, mine was nourished as well."

Nancy Terrill

"I very quickly I found myself engaged on a terrific journey. Marcus captivates with the story itself, the saga of a young man in the '70s on a spiritual search with a group of "merry questers" led by Jan Cox. It's Marcus' writing that awes and engages: his pungent, original metaphors; his stunning ability to suck me into the moment; his dialogue with Grandpa Phil; his questions, such as: "What in the hell is all this really about?" with regard to the group; the "Tasks" that Jan Cox assigns. All of this leads to: Everything **is** happening at once. This is a "must read" memoir. If you were in your 20s in the '70s, it's a required read! And if you were born too late and missed it all, then it's a required read!!"

Robert Lytle

"The story is so well focused and I feel like I'm right with Marcus in his perspective and path of discovery."

Jean Pruitt

EVERYTHING IS HAPPENING AT ONCE

A MEMOIR

JONATHAN MARCUS

MARCUS
+
MYER
PUBLISHING

Everything Is Happening At Once
A Memoir
by Jonathan Marcus

Published by
Marcus + Myer Publishing, LLC
PO Box 5662
Richmond, Virginia 23220
Jonathanmarcus.org
© 2018 Marcus + Myer Publishing, LLC

To protect the privacy of certain individuals the names have been changed.

DEDICATION

May the life and memory of Philip Rothenberg be blessed forever.
And may the yearnings he honored in transforming his life be
further honored by his grateful, admiring grandson, that the
yearnings may serve further transformations.

Grandpa's voice. Grandpa's voice is saying, "Yes, I did struggle. And what have you been doing?"

I don't know how to answer the man who came to America all alone at sixteen, never saw his parents again, and sacrificed his youth so we wouldn't have to.

"And what have you been doing?" The question hangs there.

Virgin memories, enfolded since inception. At the sound of his voice, these wrapped-up kernels reanimate. They come alive and pack new punch.

1970

At exactly seven o'clock on Thursday evening, I knock.

The sign over door 220 with that slogan: "Abandon all hope, ye who enter here."

A large man, focused on the papers in front of him, sits behind an ornate desk. With a fancy fountain pen, he scrawls a note. He doesn't look up. He's pudgy and sort of ageless. Maybe late thirties. He wears an impeccable suit. His cheeks are oddly plump, like a child's, but his demeanor—craggy. The room dimly lit by a single lamp. Persian carpets cover the floor. Bookshelves line the walls, packed with books arranged by height. I hate books arranged by height. Books should be arranged by subject. Books should determine their own place on the shelf, based on—

"What do you want from me?" He fires the question right in my eye.

"Want from you?" I'm not ready for that question. I'm

expecting some answers. Is this affiliated with Gurdjieff? Is "The Work" some kind of international organization? How long is the course of study? Does it cost money?

But I look at him and fire back, "I want to see things as they are."

My response surprises him. I like that.

"If I agree to take you on," he says, as if that would be a burden, "you will indeed see things as they are." He snorts. "You will see it all for yourself; you'll see it all as a by-product of your own accelerated evolution. If you can follow that."

I nod and don't say anything.

"You're exceptional," he states impersonally. "Most people come in here and can't stop telling me how much they already know. But you"—he pauses—"you're actually getting some of this already." He says this with utter certainty, even though we have just met. "But that's neither here nor there, really. And there's no way to predict where you will go with this. If anywhere at all. Part of the problem is you're young. You haven't completely fallen asleep yet. You can't wake up until you go to sleep."

I feel naked.

He leans back and folds his hands over his doughy middle. "Sleep" and "awakening" are straight out of Gurdjieff and Ouspensky.

"But if you want to pursue it, then I will let you stay as long as you abide by the rules. We meet here twice a week. It's not optional. If you're doing this, then be on time, or don't bother to come back. Don't get involved with me personally in any way. If you do, you're done here. I'll know it, and I'll throw you out. And express no hostility to me or anyone else involved with this."

He says all this without the trace of a smile. In a rumbling redneck drawl. With rock eyes. Green rock eyes.

"And one more thing," he says. "You can quit anytime."

He snorts again and stands up. He's taller than I am, about six feet. The three-piece suit he wears, I'm sure it was hand-tailored in England. Fits him perfectly. The vest snugs to his big belly like a pillowcase. Then I catch myself. I'm already getting involved with him personally. The fact is, I really don't care where his suit was made.

Before I can utter a formality, he's opened the door, slipped an envelope into my hand, and shown me out without another word.

Bright office building light floods the hallway. The envelope in my hand says OPEN THIS LATER.

≈ ≈ ≈

I walk outside and say out loud, "It's later."

I open the envelope. Two sheets of paper inside. One is a mimeographed sheet listing the meeting times and the rules. The other is handwritten:

You may commence this activity with a real Work group on two conditions:

1. Go to an old-timey barbershop and get a military haircut.

2. Do not explain your haircut to anybody under any circumstances whatsoever.

Or else do not bother to show up here again.

The note is signed in a giant script: *Dr. Cox.*

"Damn it," I say out loud. "Fuck him. To hell with his fancy bullshit and the living dead who follow him."

≈ ≈ ≈

I have pounds of hair. It grows up instead of down, and the longer it gets, the taller and curlier it is. I'm over five foot ten with this hive.

To my surprise, the barber doesn't even blink when I tell him, "A crew cut." He probably thinks I'm joining the military to kill Vietnamese farmers. He's a scissors machine set on *Fast*. Brown steel wool piles up on the floor. Then he picks up the electric trimmer, and when it buzzes my left temple, the word "Task" flashes in my head. "Goddamn, this is a Task!" I say to myself. A Task designed by a teacher for a student to execute, a Task the student would never dream up on his own, a way to catalyze new experience and new perceptions—to crack the limits of self. I want to hug the barber, grab his cheeks, and tell him, "Good God, man! This is a Task!"

It doesn't take long or cost much, but according to the piles of curls on the floor, it should have done both.

Chilly outside the barbershop in March. Still wintertime in Atlanta. Cold clutches my neck, exposed without the blimp of curls. One hand, then the other, up there feeling around. Walking down the street with hands on scalp, fingers wandering like antennae, burnishing this stiff scrub brush where my wire mop used to be.

The physical sensations are shocking and riveting.

But then come the questions.

"What happened?" Friends demand to know.

I shrug. "Nothing. Just got a haircut."

It's the refusal to explain that ratchets the crew cut to another level. I abide by the terms religiously.

"You had a bad trip, didn't you?"

"No, man, I didn't have a bad trip."

"Are you enlisting?"

"Hell, no, I'm not enlisting."

"You got drafted?"

"And I didn't get drafted."

"What the hell? Are you going straight?"

I try to laugh it off.

"Well, what happened to you?"

I abide by the conditions. I don't explain. That makes all the difference.

"What in the hell happened to you?"

A giant crowbar pries open a giant seam between me and all my radical-hippie-anarchic-do-what-you-feel friends. I see gloom in their eyes, which I have never seen before. All I did was *cut my hair*. It shouldn't have mattered much at all. But it matters a lot.

Some of my friends drift away and quit talking to me.

Maybe I drift away from them, too. They're hardly the free thinkers and free spirits I admire if they can't let a haircut go unjustified.

I'm invited to fraternity parties.

All I did was cut my hair and refuse to explain it, and everyone I know gets upset and everything changes. It's a multi-layered shock, and it takes a while to ponder.

I feel like a python swallowing a deer: this is a big lump of cosmic meat, a lot to digest. This is one bellyful of hairy venison.

Everyone fixed in place and one guy gets a goddamn haircut . . . and everyone responds as if to say, "You can't just go and do that. It's not fair. We're all committed to our positions here in life, and you can't just change your bearings without justifying it."

And I never would have thought to do such a thing myself.

Never would I have imagined the equation: Haircut + Silence = Cosmic Meat, a secret excursion behind the walls that contain us.

Like I'm sprung free, a rogue particle, bouncing about to see for the first time how all the other particles are locked in their spheres, all demanding that I get properly locked in a sphere as well and announce exactly what sphere it is I'm confined to.

Astounding.

It's what I have been looking for but couldn't articulate.

A secret opening to what's hidden in plain sight. A tunnel to the other side of the tall walls made of what everyone thinks. Keys to a kingdom.

Travels around the country with my friend Bill come to mind, when I would wake up in the morning and everything new unspools all day long. It wasn't just about driving around. It's about this . . . here I am spooling all over the place . . . relishing strange surprises . . . not because I'm rolling across the continent . . . but because of an unexplained haircut.

Fuckin' haircut. I don't love everything about this. This is not comfortable. I miss my place in the scheme of things. But I wasn't looking for comfort. I was looking for . . . *this*.

Amazing out here in the naked un-formity of it all. Doubly amazing to be transported by something so pedestrian, so nothing-ish.

Breaking news! This just in: nothing changes everything.

The Work has grabbed me by the throat. And mind. I want more.

ONE MONTH EARLIER

Seems miraculous that I stumble into these Dr. Cox readings just weeks after my girlfriend, Madeleine, tells me about a self-proclaimed mystic and teacher from Armenia, G. I. Gurdjieff, who introduced ancient methods to the West—something called the Fourth Way, or simply The Work.

What ancient methods?

She doesn't know. Madeleine is about as well read as anyone under forty could possibly be, and she's twenty. But Gurdjieff is obscure, even for her. Plus she hardly ever speaks, which is mysterious and alluring. She looks like an art deco sylph with huge eyes that don't blink. She says, "Why don't you read the book?"

≈ ≈ ≈

I'd been planning to go to India with my friend Weston in a few months, right after graduation. We'd been chafing for transcendence, and we knew we'd never find anything on the Emory campus or anywhere in Atlanta. We wanted something different, exotic—something other and huge. We knew we would find something there, in India.

We exercise to toughen ourselves for the inevitable hardships ahead and adopt a brutalist menu featuring raw oatmeal, onions with the skin on, sardines straight from the can, and frozen orange juice—frozen. Sort of a self-invented boot camp for hippie seekers, though we'd never call it boot camp because anything that has to do with the war has nothing to do with us.

But in January, before graduation, Weston chants with the Hare Krishnas, and in February he gets the funny pigtailed haircut and joins them. "Chanting makes me happy," he says, "and happiness is all I ever wanted." He doesn't need answers.

Well, good for Weston. But I want more. Sure, I want to be happy, but happiness as a goal sounds kind of mush-minded and vapid. I want something a lot more complicated than a Valium. Something spine-stiffening and challenging and expansive. I want some goddamn answers, too.

Why is our democracy sending teenagers to kill and die in Vietnam?

And besides, what are we all doing here?

What is the highest and best use of the mind?

I devour Gurdjieff's quasi-autobiography, *Meetings with Remarkable Men,* a narrative of his travels all over central Asia and the Middle East during the last of the 1800s, before national boundaries sliced up the vast steppes and windscapes and deserts.

Gurdjieff met with masters of what he called hidden knowledge and determined from them certain bearings about humanity's place in the cosmos, distilled from millennia of prescientific intelligence.

P. D. Ouspensky became Plato to Gurdjieff's Socrates, and Ouspensky penned a thin volume called *The Psychology of Man's Possible Evolution*. Ouspensky states flatly that people are machines and that the ordinary state of consciousness is a state of sleep, severely limited when compared with states of awakening.

Gurdjieff employed many methods to stir students from unwitting slumber; of these, the Tasks intrigue me most. I spend whole days trying to concoct a Task that would liberate me from my limits. But I can't think of what I can't think of.

So I have a new plan. Forget India. I'll find The Work. Something so obscure could not possibly exist in Atlanta, Georgia. But I know it's out there somewhere. Maybe I don't know exactly what it is, but that won't stop me. I'll find it.

≈ ≈ ≈

A few weeks later, a nervous acquaintance at school who knows of my interests and talks to one of my shoes says, "There's a lecture tonight. You might like it. It's about some psychological stuff."

He looks at my other shoe and hands me a mimeographed slip of paper with a time, an address, and one sentence in quotation marks: "Abandon all hope, ye who enter here."

I get there early, to the corner of Fourteenth and Peachtree.

To pass the time, I cross the street and enter a run-down Middle Eastern café in a ramshackle old wooden building of storefronts, a vestige from an earlier, other Atlanta. Funny:

never seen the place before. Only one man works there. He brings me a Turkish coffee.

Amazingly, he resembles the picture of Gurdjieff on the dust jacket of his book: a thick, bald man with Old Testament eyes and a mustache like a weapon from 1880.

A few minutes before meeting time, I enter the squatty Miller Building. The cramped lobby expands into infinite space with mirrored walls reflecting each other. A thousand hands depress the elevator button. Upstairs, about twenty cheap folding chairs fill a room already filled by fluorescent light. The other people there, all older, utter only pleasantries. Hi, how are you? I am fine. How are you? Fine. Hi. How are you? Fine, thank you. Hi. Fine. Hi, already. I was fine until you asked me how I am. Jesus, don't ask me again.

A woman I'd seen around campus strides to the lectern. Room gets quiet. She reads a short announcement from the guy behind all this. It says don't think about the guy behind all this. She unseals an envelope. She shuffles the papers, and she starts reading solemnly.

"Everything you know is incorrect," she proclaims. "Everything you know is incorrect because the apparatus of you is just that, an apparatus, and not a fully formed free-thinking conscious being. The apparatus is by nature, by design, by necessity, flawed.

"That essential flaw in each of you is, by the way, the reality behind the concept of original sin. Of course, this is not understood at the ordinary level of religion, but all religious precepts reflect something real, whether that reality is understood by the practitioners or not. Most often it is not, not at all."

Man, I could wrestle with every sentence. Who wrote this stuff? Where did it come from? Who is he to interpret all religion? Who does he think he is? But some of it grabs me. And some of it I can't stand.

"Each of you remains fractured and incomplete, and what you call self-knowledge is nothing but a dream of knowledge because it is filtered through the accidental, self-reflexive prism of you, and in most cases, it is primarily a litany of your flaws and excuses. But it's so noisy down there in your apparatus that you can hardly hear my words."

She calls it The Work. Could this be affiliated with Gurdjieff? As obscure as Gurdjieff is, it would be astounding to discover a group dedicated to him—right here in Atlanta—only weeks after being captivated by some of his books.

No, everything I know is not incorrect. That's ridiculous. She keeps reading. I keep rejecting. But the words are sticking whether I want them to or not.

"Everything is just as it should be," she reads. "You think there is something drastically wrong in the world. But that's merely the output of your mechanical mind. Such automatic responses do not qualify as conscious thought."

Everything is as it should be? That's preposterous. What about racism and locking people up for smoking a joint and sending my friends to slaughter Asian farmers who never did anything to us? You call that *just as it should be*? Certainly, obviously, irrefutably, everything is not just as it should be.

Gurdjieff would intentionally irritate newcomers to qualify and test them, to see if they had the mettle for the undertaking. He would schedule meetings in parts of town where people were afraid to go. He would offend their sensibilities by maligning every sacred cow. He relished the accusation of blasphemy.

Knowing this, though, does not insulate me from irritation with what she's reading. Partly it's the tone. The arrogance is enough to choke a CEO. And the haughty certainty clashes with the nonjudgmental, love-and-let-live, do-your-own-thing spirit of the times—which I embrace completely. But sandwiched between obvious fallacies are some startling new thoughts that just might be worth exploring.

I'm gonna find out who and what is behind all this. Right now, as soon as she's done reading.

But she concludes by reading, "It is perfectly appropriate that you should never return here and never think about any of this again. However, if you wish to find out what reality thrives beyond these mere words, then you must attend a total of four of these readings, and we shall see what we shall see."

Damn it, I am not going to sit through three more of these.

Everyone stands up. Some people leave right away, and some people stand around. I ask one of the guys who was arranging chairs when I got there, "Who's behind all this?" He doesn't say anything and smiles as if one of us is lobotomized.

I ask the woman at the lectern. She fakes a smile and says, "You'll have to come back if you're interested."

I get out of there and start driving down Fourteenth Street. Shit, I'm never going back to that shit.

≈ ≈ ≈

For the goddamn second, third, and fourth lecture, because I have to find out what this royal pain in the ass is all about, the same woman stands at the lectern. She reads, "You have long ago plumbed the depths of the rational mind."

Okay, true. Whoever wrote this stuff has me there. I know I can't reason my way past reasoning, but I get lost in the futility of thinking about thinking before I realize she's on another subject entirely.

The harsh tone of it all appeals to me. I appreciate it, the way you appreciate a splash of cold water. A demanding coach. Or what a rich kid gets by joining the Army.

The harshness of it magnifies the cloying, pleading appeals of most other "spiritual paths" and alternative religions, all rampant in the late Sixties. As if they're all saying, "Come with us! We make sense! We are nice! We are good! We will save you! We are reasonable and holy and we serve God and we will make you whole and happy . . . we promise! Please believe us!"

But whatever this is says, "Go away if you want to go away. We don't need you. We're not promising anything. The question is: Do you need this? The question is: What can *you* promise? If you need this badly enough, then you must rise to unnecessary challenges."

Yes, I do want unnecessary challenges. I've got an urge to sacrifice for something larger and higher. The same elemental urge that drives soldiers to apply for Special Forces. I'm soldier age, with soldier urges. But my urges point the other way, away from war in Asia to the invisible war with the ramparts of self. *Fight your own war. That's where the peace is.*

At the end of the fourth reading, one of the boring people hands me a note: "If you want to pursue the unnecessary, then show up here at seven o'clock sharp on Thursday evening and knock on door 220."

On Thursday evening, the sign over door 220 with that slogan again: "Abandon all hope, ye who enter here."

≈ ≈ ≈

How much of this can I tell Grandpa? That is, if I were able to tell him anything at all.

I want to tell him all of it. But I'm afraid to tell him anything. How would this business with The Work stack up against his elemental struggle? He came alone to make a new life in the New World. To escape piercing poverty and religious persecution.

But Grandpa wasn't one of those grumpy self-made men from the old country, pissed off because we have it too easy. He wanted us to have it easier than he did.

Maybe, somehow, he would get the seriousness of all this.

≈ ≈ ≈

So after I meet Dr. Cox and plunge into new dimensions by way of an unjustified crew cut, I want more. I go to the meetings. I respect the rules: show up on time twice a week and pay the modest fee for The Work, which amounts to the cost of a couple of lunches a week.

At the meetings, twelve or fifteen of us in folding chairs squeeze around Dr. Cox's fancy desk. He displays hand-drawn charts of consciousness. Drawn on poster paper with magic marker. He dots his capital *I*s. I hate dots over a capital *I*. There is no dot above a capital *I*. This is exactly as annoying as arranging books by height.

The charts he's using are straight out of Gurdjieff, with circles representing the three circuits: the physical, the emotional, and the intellectual. I get what he's talking about. General habits of mind function like physical habits of the body, and this is essentially the sleeping state of consciousness. You don't *decide* to tap your fingers a certain way any more than you *decide* to be a certain height or *decide* to hold certain opinions.

Many such habits of the body and mind burble up randomly and ossify over time without a person's conscious intent. In such a condition, people are only dimly aware of themselves, and through these pathways—these habits of body and mind— energy is transferred unwittingly.

I look around the group. Everyone's face scrunches up at Dr. Cox's charts and circles. These people look befuddled, but I get these charts in a second.

I feel ferocious sitting there.

These people are boring. They are nice and polite and boring, but they seem about as interested in change as mashed potatoes. I want something fresher and meatier and bloodier. I want another confounding lump of cosmic meat. And this hunger only intensifies as the weeks go by.

These meetings pale in the shadow of my life-changing haircut. The haircut is worth decades of charts and words. The haircut is a rocket ship to new spheres. The charts and descriptions are just theories of motion.

After three weeks, I drive over to the Miller Building one afternoon and knock on door 220, unannounced. After a long interval the door opens, and it's obvious from the look on Dr. Cox's face that people don't just drop in.

His eyebrows rise.

I announce, "I'm going to do this on my own for a while." I reach out and shake his hand before he can react. I look him in the eye and leave.

≈ ≈ ≈

And damn it, I am gonna do this on my own for a while. A

while, like the rest of my life. Because. This is what I gotta do. Even if I don't know exactly what it is. Yes, I do. I do know. At least I know this: I gotta do this, and I'll change as I do it, and as I change, it will change. The process will change. That's what The Work is. A process. A change process that changes as the process expands. For people with this urge. This hunger. Hunger for what's not on the menu.

But. Graduation's coming. Then what?

The wannabe doctors are diagnosing the med schools and the wannabe lawyers argue over law schools. But this curriculum I'm pursuing is not in any grad-school syllabus. All that stuff is boring compared to The Work.

Like I'm a junkie all of a sudden. Yeah, a junkie for my next hit. I got hooked immediately. The air has weight. The days and the faces are magnified. It is a river.

I need another hit of cosmic haircut venison. Jawing for another dimension fresh for chewing.

One afternoon after class I'm on my bed, holding P. D. Ouspensky's small volume upright on my chest. Book is closed. Can't take my eyes off the cover. Bright fuchsia letters on a black background: *The Psychology of Man's Possible Evolution*.

I'm deconstructing the title, the combination of words: *psychology + possible + evolution*.

I never would have imagined it that way. I never would have put these words together.

I flip open the book randomly and read:

Our fundamental idea shall be that man as we know him is not a completed being; that nature develops him only up to a certain point, and then it leaves him, either to develop further, by his own efforts and devices, or to live and die such as he was born, or to degenerate and lose capacity for development.

I close the book and ogle the words in the title again.

Psychology of.

Possible.

Evolution.

Imagine levels of development beyond mere adulthood, beyond recognized professionalism and craft-level mastery . . . it all points at *something else*, something new: that you can participate in your own development beyond present limits, the way a species develops wings or eyes or artistic impulses where none existed. Imagine a third eye. Wonder what it might see . . . something huge and bright and confounding, like apprehending sunlight.

And then, a little before my very last term paper is due, Madeleine quits college in Florida and announces that she's coming to Atlanta to live with me. Perfect. Yes. Come on. And it's all lined up with the next book I read about The Work, another thin volume, this one by a physician in England who studied with Gurdjieff. His name is A. R. Orage, and the title is *On Love.*

Orage says that another form of love, ordinarily beyond the purview of human beings, can be cultivated under rare circumstances. It will never happen automatically. He calls it conscious love, wherein the lover will anticipate the desires of the beloved even before the desire is manifest.

I want to do this. I want to apply myself to this goal.

Madeleine. I should be able to do this with Madeleine.

Orage says conscious love always returns itself. He says you can see a simple representation of this in what may develop between some people and their dogs. Or between some people and their plants. The plant lover is able to anticipate what the plant needs before the plant knows what it wants. And the plant returns this love, if you will, in the way that a plant can, with flowers, fruit, and beauty. These exchanges are low-level reflections of what may emerge between people making extraordinary efforts.

I'm fascinated, starting with these names, these words: The Work. Conscious. Love. Fascinated with all of it. Extraordinary. All that and more. *Extra*ordinary.

I want to sacrifice for some greater good, some greater sensibility and greater knowledge.

And conscious love seems measurable: if I do this, Madeleine will return my love. So I will know. By my connection to Madeleine, I will know if I am really getting anywhere with this. I like the idea of measurability. I don't wanna bullshit my way into imagining how wonderfully awake I have become.

Plus I just really like that name. *The Work.*

≈ ≈ ≈

But everything in the literature says you can't do this on your own. You need a teacher, a teacher who can see beyond your limits in a way that you can't. But so what? Gurdjieff himself learned from various masters, and *his* efforts and explorations and discoveries were self-directed. Why can't I do that? I will learn from rich experience + raw desire.

I determine to stay the course, even as conditions, commitments, and the unpredictable converge and diverge after graduation.

The course is set with my earnest commitment to conscious love.

But beyond that, who knows what form this will take?

A decision emerges one night from random forces, including beer, when I walk up to Emory Village with my close friend from high school, Byron, to celebrate—again—DeKalb County's legalization of alcoholic beverages. Jagger's is the first bar in the neighborhood. The beer goes down easy, and we plunge into the giant issues: What are we going to do when the Selective Service orders us to Vietnam to kill farmers? How will we get out of it? And assuming we survive the war, what are we going to do with our lives?

I mention some money, extra money I saved from my summer job working as a cook with a demanding chef in Florida, plus the sum Grandma Rose left each grandchild.

"Money," he says. "If I had some money, I'd be outta here. You could go somewhere, man. You could leave the country."

The thought had never occurred to me. I figured I would use the money for something grown-up someday, maybe to help with a down payment on a house in the remote future. But his words hurry over me like a wave that won't stop.

Inevitability hovers: the Selective Service will soon demand that I kill Vietnamese farmers. Without a college deferment or bad health or a high lottery number, I'll soon be a citizen of interest to the war machine. Maybe leaving the country will help them forget me.

≈ ≈ ≈

I put only two books in the backpack when Madeleine and I find a cheap one-way charter flight from New York to Glasgow. One is a hitchhiker's guide to Europe, and the other is *On Love* by A. R. Orage.

Gurdjieff talked about the importance of Aim when pursuing The Work. So did Dr. Cox. Especially while living life as you find it—as opposed to pursuing this kind of work in a monastery or retreat of some kind, where impressions and habits are quite controlled. Well, yeah, I got Aim: I'm gonna continue my work in The Work, and I am going to practice the art of conscious love.

Late November. The plane lands. We're in Scotland. We follow the people in front of us. Madeleine and I might be more educated and better read than the average American, but right now we don't know anything about anything in the whole world.

In Zen Buddhism, it's called *shoshin*: beginner's mind. As if we are English garden orbs absorbing the world anew. As if all our neurons got a crew cut and are starting over.

So we follow the people in front of us. We get through customs and change some money. We're staring at shillings and pounds and pence and crowns. She hates math, and I'm trying to divide everything by 2.4 because one pound sterling is worth two dollars and forty cents and I am acutely aware that while these bills look like fancy play money with pretty pastel etchings of the queen, it is very real money, a lot of which came from Grandma Rose, which came from Grandpa Phil, who sacrificed his youth for his family's future so that . . . so that his Jewish grandson could go to Europe with a shiksa? So: I better make something out of whatever it is we're doing.

We follow people outside the airport. We think it's supposed to be afternoon, but it's dark outside. We don't know how many time zones we crossed. Don't know how long we were flying. We're about a million miles east and a million miles north of New York. Never been this far north. Days get short up here, this close to the winter pole.

We stand at a sign that reads Town Center. A bus stops. People get on. We get on. It goes a while and then we're at "town center," and the doors open. People get off. We get off. They disappear. We're alone.

This is downtown Glasgow? It's empty and dark. We

thought Glasgow would be a major world city, like New York, with cafés and bars and waves of people and traffic. But we might as well be in Valdosta, Georgia. Except in Valdosta, the pool hall would be open. Here, nothing is.

We're next to one of those handsome red British phone booths that makes each call seem worthy. A sign inside reads FOR LODGING GUIDANCE, RING US. We don't know what coins to put in the phone, so we insert some coins and hope for the best. I dial the number. It rings. A woman answers. I cannot understand a single word she is saying. Nothing. Isn't this supposed to be English? In Scotland? She keeps talking. I hand the phone to Madeleine. The woman is still talking. Madeleine holds it up to her ear, gives me her deadpan look, which right at this moment means, "I don't have a clue." She hands the receiver back to me, and I, with regret, while the woman is still talking, hang up.

Outside the phone booth with our backpacks, looking around. The buildings are well proportioned and old, probably a lot older than anything we've ever seen. Even in the darkness, the facades teem with detail and formality. So very formal. The correct buildings make me stand a little straighter. But we don't know what to do. Madeleine is looking at me for an answer, but I don't even know what question comes first or whom to ask—if we could find anyone to ask anything. We're comparing crowns and shillings, as if understanding the coins might somehow help.

I look up from my palmful of coins, because now a few people are right next to us. They're about our age. They're from here, you can just tell. One of them speaks first.

"You can stay with us."

We are both stunned.

"No, it's quite all right. We just saw you are American, and we don't often see Yanks without money to toss about. You can stay with us."

We walk with them, a group of four students at the university, for a few blocks. We have no idea where we are. We follow them up two flights of stairs to a very large, very old, very chilly loft with beds and tables and dim lamps scattered in far corners. They show us to a bed and say, "It's a featherbed. You don't mind a featherbed?" We are exhausted and would have paid for a bed of leaves, sure, no problem, even though we have no idea what a featherbed might be.

"With a feather comforter," he says.

Within seconds, we are floating on feathers. Reality is a cloud, and we are aloft.

≈ ≈ ≈

I don't think about conscious love or my Aim all day every day because we are out here hitchhiking into the unknown and getting to know it, delicious bit by delicious bit. Because you don't need to think about expanding your mind when your mind is expanding, and you don't need to conjure a life-changing haircut when your life is a rising tide. The hours peel off the days and the days bloom and time is fruit.

What could be more *conscious love* than wide eyes, a new old world, and indelibility?

Or so I think.

Late December. Madeleine and I are hitchhiking through Ancona, on the Adriatic Sea. Who knew a port town in Italy would be colder than Scotland? We're dodging piles of slush on the main drag, the air heavy with sleet, the sky darkening with weather or evening or both. My thumb is outstretched. Cars zip by. I glance over at Madeleine. Tears are streaming down her cheeks. With one hand I pull her closer. The other hand is still hitchhiking.

"What? What's the matter?" As if wet feet and sleet needles aren't enough to bring tears to Floridian eyes.

It's all she can do to say, "It's Christmas Eve."

Christmas Eve. It never crossed my mind. I had no idea when Chanukah might have been, either. Maybe because I'm getting a new brain. Because every day everything is fresh and strange and different, and the old markers, like religious holidays, just seem like, well, old markers—and who cares about any of that anymore? But Madeleine's dad is a Methodist minister. From Florida. She's a third-generation native. I wonder if she's ever seen snow before.

Suddenly I hardly know her. We've been traveling together, but are we having the same experiences? Has she been continuously amazed as the curtains framing the world keep receding?

For a second, I wish she were my old traveling companion Bill.

Even though she dismisses her dad's religion as form without content, I can see her cozying up to the decorated tree in toasty sunny Florida.

"We'll find a place to stay," I tell her.

Silence. Her face says she doesn't believe me.

I elongate my shoulder and extend my thumb. As if it's possible to hitchhike harder.

"How will we find a cheap hotel on Christmas Eve?" She wants to know. It's a fair question.

I have no idea. We don't speak Italian. It's a Catholic country. I don't know anything about anything. Do all the hotels close and everyone goes home in the afternoon, like right about now, maybe?

One more glance at her and it hits me: I have failed. *Conscious love*: I should have figured out how to anticipate the desires of the beloved, as Orage puts it. But I have failed completely, at least right now, and this sloppy, cold Christmas Eve is proof. I didn't know it was Christmas Eve, and I had no idea that Madeleine would care about it.

A Fiat peels out of the traffic and splashes to an abrupt stop a few yards ahead of us. The passenger door falls open. We hurry over and pile in. It's one of those tiny blobs of a car that would fit in the back of Dad's Chevy Nomad. With our backpacks, we feel like clowns stuffing a Volkswagen.

"Augusto," he says.

"Augusto?" I answer.

"Si, si, Augusto Golfarelli," he says proudly. He extends his hand.

"Buon Natale," he continues in Italian. "Lei viene alla mia casa."

The syllables fly too fast, but I can pick out a few that correspond to French or Spanish.

"Su casa?" I ask in Spanish.

"Si, si, per Natale," he says.

Madeleine says to me, "Natale must be Christmas."

"Si, si, Krees-moss," he says.

He takes us to his home and won't discuss any other possibilities. "Insisto," he says firmly. Not that we are protesting.

He opens the door to a simple, clean, and cozy apartment, fires off a cluster of Italian syllables, and his wife, Carmela, appears. She welcomes us as though we were long-lost family. Our dirty backpacks stick out like Conestoga wagons in this tidy Italian home. They show us to the guest bedroom. Handmade pasta is drying on the bed. Augusto and Carmela think this is hilarious. Tears gather in Madeleine's eyes again. It's dry in here. And warm. And Christmas. Tears of joy.

Wine and blessings and antipasti follow day into darkness, and the conversation flows easily in a pidgin vocabulary tossed together on the fly from bits of Italian, English, Spanish, French, international pantomime, and some mystical scaffolding that supports it all. After two kinds of pasta, then roasted fish and roasted vegetables, with wine and stories and laughter to accompany each course, a sentence out of Gurdjieff pops into my head: *A person's consciousness attracts his life.* Well, to judge by the joy at this dining table, it looks like our consciousness must be pretty robust. I whisper under my breath, "Hell, yeah, Gurdjieff!" and fill my mouth with more wine. Augusto and Carmela glow in the candlelight, and I love them.

They're our European parents for a day. It's a dream. Rescued from the slush on Christmas by angels who drink and cook. And rescued by grace from utter failure to maintain my Aim: conscious love.

1971

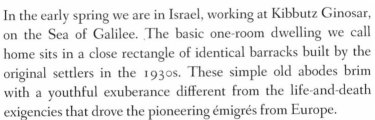

In the early spring we are in Israel, working at Kibbutz Ginosar, on the Sea of Galilee. The basic one-room dwelling we call home sits in a close rectangle of identical barracks built by the original settlers in the 1930s. These simple old abodes brim with a youthful exuberance different from the life-and-death exigencies that drove the pioneering émigrés from Europe.

Mick, the chipper, beery Irishman, bounces around like the offspring of a bean stalk and a leprechaun. Ann and George, the blond and beautiful surfers sent by central casting from Redondo Beach, play against type by studying a hardbound copy of something called *The Urantia Book*, which they have lugged with them in their travels around the world. The book probably weighs six pounds: every night they thumb its fine pages, which purport to explicate the true nature of God and the hierarchies of life in the universe. The brawny bronze Manolo from Portugal, with his innocent vanity, lies in the sun on cloudless days after work with a collarbone mirror canted just so to ensure that the tint of the skin under his chin will match the tint of his cheeks. And the kind, shambling giant Hugh from Scotland towers over everyone but is more like a fog than a functioning human. He is most notable for his name, the first letter of which the Israelis cannot comprehend, so he is universally known as You.

And then John Califano lands at Ginosar. Italian, from a working-class Jewish-Italian neighborhood in Brooklyn. He grew up around more Jews than I did in Florida, but they were all cops and plumbers and teachers and bus drivers and auto mechanics, so the blunt, burly, earthy kibbutzniks make more sense to Italian John than they do to most American Jews.

His shiny black eyes bore into life, same as Picasso's did. He points at me and says to Madeleine, "What's a preacher's kid like you doin' with a hippie rabbi like him?"

She tosses her blond hair, and her green eyes bore right back at him. "Don't call me a preacher's kid." She tries to snarl but starts laughing.

"So you are one!" John lights up.

She hates being called a preacher's kid.

John looks at me and says, "What do you believe in?"

Belief. Dr. Cox lumps belief in with faith, and I picture the words on his office door, "Abandon all hope, ye who enter here."

"It's not about belief," I announce.

So John says, "Okay, then, what's it about, wise man?"

He drills into what drives people, and he's curious about The Work and Dr. Cox and the possibility of conscious love, even though he's not buying any of it. Madeleine and I talk openly to him about it all in a way we've barely done even with each other.

I tell him, "You can't attain these states of awakening or whatever you want to call them without someone who got there, who knows how to get there. You need instruction from someone who knows how it's done. Like a recipe from a chef."

John says, "That sounds nice, but you can't give one guy all the power. Every time you do that, something bad happens." He refuses to buy any of the premises that I deem a priori bedrock.

≈ ≈ ≈

My job at Ginosar is harvesting bananas—hard, heavy work in the muddy Galilee fields. But it happens that I'm quick and handy with the banana knife. It's a small machete with a curved blade. Banana leaves come at your face like wet laundry, and you juke through them, all floppy and slapping, and grab a stem. It fills your palm like a baseball bat. Cut the stem with one hand while holding it with the other, and a bunch—consisting of multiple tiers of what they call hands—comes free. Feels like a hundred pounds. You sag under it. You lug it to the wagon and hoist it atop the pile.

We work side by side with the *sabras*, the native Israelis. Proud and brusque, they grudgingly admit I'm the rare American who can maintain the pace. The work agrees with me, and I like plunging in every morning.

One afternoon when I come in from the fields, someone hands me a letter. From the Selective Service System, forwarded from Mom and Dad's house in Florida. The envelope is fat. And official. This can't be good.

I open it.

Shit. They want me to go to war. They want to fly me to Asia to kill villagers. Makes me sick, even though I knew this was coming.

But they are giving me a choice. I must either show up for my physical at the Selective Service System on Walton Street in Jacksonville in twenty-one days or fill out the attached forms and declare myself a conscientious objector to war, a status the board may or may not recognize after proper review of my religious beliefs.

Madeleine and I excuse ourselves from Kibbutz Ginosar for a few days and hole up at a youth hostel down the road near the south end of the Sea of Galilee so I can concentrate on filling out these forms. Pages of questions. Did a supreme being tell me not to kill farmers in the jungle twelve time zones away? What religious authorities have led to my beliefs? What religious organizations will certify my beliefs?

The government says that pacifism can't just be your opinion. It has to be a religious belief, and you have to substantiate how this belief is integral to your religion. So I mention God in the forms. This war was not His idea. He won't mind if I bend the rules to get out of a war that the government bent the rules to get into. After God, I cite Rabbi Lefkowitz from the temple in Jacksonville as a formative influence in my pacifism, even though he doesn't give a hoot about either pacifism or me. But he does like my dad. And Dad hates the war, too. So Rabbi Lefkowitz will say that I have always been opposed to war. Even though The Old Testament is largely a vortex of war, bloodshed, and mayhem—and it hardly mentions pacifism.

Madeleine curls up in the corner. She reads while I write. I like the way she sits. I like the way she reads.

She helps me without knowing it. She doesn't see me wink at her.

One of the term-paper trances that got me through college starts to roll. I slam paragraphs at the questions and get on a jag about karma, a concept from Hinduism that has yet to penetrate American popular culture. As another formative influence on my pacifism, I throw in Don Bender, a Quaker back in Atlanta. He helps draft dodgers sift their options. I know he'll testify as to the solemnity and profundity of my beliefs.

I save Dr. Cox for last. Because . . . well, I'm not sure why— or why I even put him down as a reference. I have enough names without him. Maybe I want to let him know I'm out here and I trust him on some level. At the very least, I do trust that he will write a damn good letter to the draft board on my behalf, no matter what he or The Work might have to say about war in general or this bullshit war in particular.

I answer every question they ask, and assume the Selective Service System will weigh every word.

I mail the letter, plastered with a bunch of Israeli stamps— olive branches. Nice touch, in my opinion. Not that the Israelis are pacifists. Hardly.

The letter I send them is fatter than the letter they sent me. So there. Hah. Take that, Selective Service System!

$$\approx \approx \approx$$

A couple of weeks later, I'm startled to find a telegram with my name on it at the Ginosar mailroom.

This can't be good.

It's a single piece of paper. The words jump at me. I read and reread these few lines of telegraph font, all caps, spread out across the page:

WE ARE SORRY TO TELL YOU THAT GRANDPA PHILIP PASSED AWAY PEACEFULLY IN HIS SLEEP. WE WILL HAVE A CEREMONY IN DAYTONA BEACH AND THEN WE WILL BURY HIM NEXT TO

GRANDMA ROSE IN WESTCHESTER COUNTY ON FRIDAY THE 18TH.

YOU WILL BE WITH US IN SPIRIT. CALL US WHEN YOU CAN.

WE LOVE YOU, MOM AND DAD.

Grandpa. He had been declining ever since Grandma Rose died almost ten years ago. The last few years he was hardly even present anymore. But that's not how I think of him.

Grandpa Philip Rothenberg. The arc of his life seems impossibly huge, all the way from a medieval shtetl in Poland to Manhattan wealth and retirement in Florida. But . . . of all the relatives, Grandpa is the one I know least. I never realized this before. Not until his death. This telegram.

I go to Jerusalem for a couple of days. Alone. To observe Grandpa's passage. To honor him and ponder him and his life and maybe somehow to get to know him better. So on the day they're all hoisting dirt at the cemetery in Westchester County, I'm trying to see the invisible at the Wailing Wall.

This is all I have to do today, to be with Grandpa and the family from the other side of the world, and there's a kind of forever circling the ceremony.

About half the people visiting the wall are Orthodox Jews in the traditional black garb. And half are everyone else in the world, from pink to ebony. Cycles of people come and go, like cycles of lifetimes. They mouth prayers, as God is the air. And according to tradition, each supplicant then folds a handwritten prayer into a crack between the ancient stones of the long-gone temple. Late in the forever day, in the presence of Grandpa, I pull paper from my journal. My pen pours out a small stream of words:

May the life and memory of Philip Rothenberg be blessed forever. And may the yearnings he honored in transforming his life be further honored by his grateful, admiring grandson, that the yearnings may serve further transformations.

≈ ≈ ≈

During this yearlong odyssey across Europe and into Israel and back across Europe, each border crossing and passport stamp from customs hurls me into a new culture, and I bounce. New royal faces on the money. New ways to divide a dollar. New cadences of conversation, squeezing new hollows in the mouth. New flavors, like colors you never imagined. People are whiter or browner or thicker or richer or louder or slower. Every border crossing exhilarates completely. Except one. The last one. The return to the United States.

It's jarring.

The surprises are instant. The sound of American speech. Haven't been enveloped by American for a year. Love the sound of American speech. Didn't know that. The vowels roll in soft ovals and the consonants, weatherworn.

The cars are so big. The new Chevy Impala could be a bus. Acres of sheet metal and fat whitewall tires. Bus tires.

The green lawns. The front yard and the backyard. I never knew what luxuries they are.

And the miles. I really like miles. Kilometers seem puny and fussy, plus we got more miles here than they got kilometers there, even though miles are a lot bigger.

How crazy did it look to Grandpa Phil when he climbed out of steerage in 1896?

I love America.

But I worry about it the way you worry about a gifted, passionate friend who always manages to screw things up.

The sadness. The wealth. The poverty. The wealth.

It all seems unfinished. Messy and exciting with reckless gaping gaps.

The lack of pauses. Why is everyone rushing through dinner? So they can go and . . . and what?

More speed and more possibility and more edges in America.

And that crazy goddamn war. Any idiot can see the war is crazy. Batshit crazy. What sick culture sends an army clear across the Pacific to kill farmers?

Madeleine and I visit our families. Mom and Dad can tell I got something during all these travels, and maybe they want some of it. But they don't know how to ask. I don't know how to offer or even how to think about it.

We wind up back in Atlanta. Late in the autumn. I love the way scarlet and tangerine leaves swirl on the streets.

Nothing bad happens. Everything is all right. Isn't it?

I call my high school friend Byron and tell him, "You're the one who said go, just go and go. I gotta tell ya about it."

We're going to meet for a beer at Manuel's Tavern. I feel like Marco Polo, as if I've been gone for a generation. I have to ask him how to get there. Even though it's just three turns from Emory Village.

Surely he'll want to know about all of it, every day, so I jump right in to tell him about Christmas dinner at the Golfarellis' and the featherbed in Glasgow and how we were so ignorant that in Barcelona we didn't see the Sagrada Familia, plus I worked for a sabra on a cattle ranch on a bluff above the Jordan River, but he interrupts to tell me about what happened at work today and then I try to tell him about the artichoke omelet in Florence that was like eating a breath of creation and crossing the Adriatic from Italy to Greece, when the seas flop from glass to chaos, but he says half the staff is crazy, and it hits me. He doesn't want to know any of it. The beer tastes good, and I drink it. For a second it's like I never left.

Scary.

1972

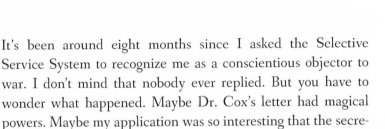

It's been around eight months since I asked the Selective Service System to recognize me as a conscientious objector to war. I don't mind that nobody ever replied. But you have to wonder what happened. Maybe Dr. Cox's letter had magical powers. Maybe my application was so interesting that the secretary of defense, Melvin Laird, had to talk to Nixon about it. Maybe they stuck me in a file labeled "Annoying College Hippie Chickenshit Smartasses We Will Deal with Later."

But just as I am about to find some kind of job back in Atlanta, the Selective Service System decides I should get a job that serves the national interest. How will they define their terms? How selective is the Selective Service System? Will I have to work in an Agent Orange factory? Or drill for oil? Is that "national interest" enough? I'm dreading the argument with a soulless bureaucrat. But the soulless bureaucrat doesn't utter the words "conscientious objector application." Amazingly, the soulless bureaucrat seems to like me.

All I say is, "Do you have any suggestions?"

I am allowed to serve the national interest at the Georgia Mental Health Institute, as a psychiatric aide on Unit 9, Alcoholism. Unit 9 is located in the old mansion of Asa Candler, Jr., on Briarcliff Road, about a mile from Emory University. His dad, Asa senior, started the "Co-Cola" company. Junior got rich being born, then spent his life wrestling with demon booze and mostly lost. So he donated his estate to the cause. As if to say from the grave, *I couldn't get clean, so here's my mansion. Maybe you can.* My job is to spend time with the patients and to affirm their existence. The nursing staff says I'm really good at it. The psychiatrists don't say anything. The patients teach me how to shoot pool, and one day I run the table.

Sometimes on the night shift I wander around the old mansion. The ballroom, big as a banana field. The front porch columns, probably thirty feet tall. The place feels haunted. The director is a nun, Jane Chadwick. She's about the same age as Dr. Cox, and she's bright and smart and she's married to Jesus. (He's Jewish.) She and I connect on some level somehow and really like each other. And considering that it's a lot better than slaughtering farmers in the jungle, I like my job.

Madeleine gets a job working for a veterinarian. She wants to maintain our connection to the natural world.

I delve into the *Whole Earth Catalog* and order a book, *Breaking and Training the Stock Horse,* and dream of the white Arabian stallion I met in Jericho. He's on springs. He has the power. When he canters, dust squirts from the earth like steam from a locomotive. Because I want to maintain my connection to the natural world, too. Maybe I'll breed horses after serving the national interest.

I devour every word of *Breaking and Training the Stock*

Horse as if it's Gurdjieff, because, like Gurdjieff, this book speeds my entrée into an unknown world. But just as with Gurdjieff, you can't really learn it from a book. You need to grapple with the world you're involved with and get some feedback.

Madeleine and I rent a little house in Decatur. It's in a forest, under towering oaks, right next to the Agnes Scott College campus. Late autumn leaves fly, and it's thrilling outside. We are treating each other well. But I can't fill my lungs.

≈ ≈ ≈

Every day I struggle to keep and hold everything from the travels . . . to nurture this larger sense of being. Whatever I can do to capture it. Distill it. Hold it on my tongue.

I picture myself as a tiny shiny spine on the earth.

I trace the crazy line we followed from Glasgow to Fishguard, Bath, London, Dover, Calais, Bordeaux, Burgos, Madrid, Barcelona, Genoa, Florence, Ancona, Brindisi, Patras, Haifa, Jerusalem, Kibbutz Ginosar.

I try whatever I can to retain and hug it all, the whole globe . . . borders transform, and transformation is what I need, so I render everything a border. Passages from the grocery store to the car are grand transformations of experience. Post office planet smells different from barbershop planet. Every breath a possibility. Inhale deeply.

Mostly I try to practice Gurdjieff's self-observation. It's subtle. You shift your attention: hold a slice of awareness apart while you're doing . . . well, anything. That's really it: holding a bit of attention aside so that you maintain a separate, objective viewpoint. Sometimes Gurdjieff called it impartial observation. It sounds like nothing. It kind of is nothing. But atoms are mostly nothing, too, and they comprise our world. So this subtle practice—like prayer if you break it down—is mainly a shift in attention, and whoa! It provides a new view, a clearer perspective, on everything you're immersed in. So a new sense of living comes from, well, anything. Putting the dishes away or painting a wall or turning left onto Lullwater Road.

These efforts, these practices, are instantly rewarding every time I do them. But they are not enough. Or maybe it's that I can't do them enough to escape my ordinary self.

So now, boundaries are fixed by what I've done instead of being stretched by what I'm doing.

Feels like I'm sinking below a horizon.

The days have no shape, no grains, and no definition. Slippery. Nothing glitters. And clutching past experiences more tightly doesn't help.

Losing momentum.

Stuck.

Not that I'm walking around complaining all the time. At least no more than everyone else.

Half my brain knows everything is okay.

Isn't it? A warm, safe place to sleep. A job that serves the national interest. Or at least keeps me out of the war and flips a paycheck my way. And living with Madeleine. We're doing well, aren't we? We know what we're doing. Don't we?

The other half of my brain knows that nothing is okay.

Grandpa Phil would probably dismiss all this as nonsense. Fussiness. *"This might sound crazy,"* I would tell him.

"No, son," he would say. *"It doesn't sound crazy. It is crazy."*

But dousing this flame doesn't extinguish it. I try that, too.

≈ ≈ ≈

One day we argue, Madeleine and I. Sure, I know, people argue. It's part of the deal, and then you apologize and get over it.

But this time it's nasty. Really bitter. And what's it about? Nothing. Absolutely nothing. It starts when I ask her, "What's wrong?" With that face of hers, inscrutable, you never know. Sometimes she wants me to ask what's wrong, and sometimes she doesn't. This time she doesn't, so I get that icy stare, like I'm the enemy. That's how it starts, with nothing. From nothing to really nasty really quick, like a tiny spark ignites a cloud of gas— random rage gas, they should call it on the emotional periodic table—and I tell her to quit looking at me like I'm the goddamn enemy for asking a little question, and I grab her arm and I don't know how strong I am. I hurt her arm. I let go. She slices me with her ice-cold rage stare. She looks grotesque. Everything goes red. I say something worse, words you can't remember even as they spew.

I feel sick. Sick at what comes out of my mouth and betrayed by what she says, which I also can't remember, except it's cruel and ridiculously intelligent.

It's a colossal failure. *It*: the entirety of my endeavor. My endeavor: a devotion to higher consciousness. Meaning yes, I just got a measurement on my progress, the gauge I've been asking for. Am I pursuing my Aim? No. Complete failure. I'm nowhere with this higher-consciousness crap. This is not a hobby. This is my life's work. And my report card reads: IRREFUTABLE! QUANTIFIABLE! FAILURE!

Conscious love my ass. I'm no closer to conscious love than I am to God or a billion dollars. I'm not even attaining ordinary decency here, let alone conscious love. Complete, utter failure.

I don't know what the hell the fight's about. Like wondering what a tornado is about.

A horrible daytime argument is worse than a horrible night-time argument, because the day won't budge and you can't start drinking yet. Hours of day remain to be endured. The sun, brilliant, and the trees eager to bud. But I hate the sunshine and I hate the coming springtime because I hate myself for failing, and I can't deny the ugly truth now. Whatever I'm doing isn't working.

Desire alone isn't enough.

And it hits me: I can't get there on my own. Unless I'm traveling around, getting amazed. But I can't spend my life just traveling around.

Shit.

I can't get there on my own.

I gotta do something, and messing around with more futile self-direction isn't good enough. Only one place I know to turn. Almost exactly two years since I shook his hand and walked out of his office saying, "I'm gonna do this on my own for a while."

I pull out a piece of paper and compose a letter in less than a minute:

Dear Dr. Cox,

I have returned from my travels and am living and working in Atlanta.

I am now ready to begin The Work.

I look forward to your reply.

I sign my name, seal the envelope, and walk to the post office.

≈ ≈ ≈

The reply to my letter comes in the mail four days later, handwritten.

The Work is not something you can just start or stop from

time to time on a whim. You either undertake The Work or you don't.

If this is something you absolutely need, then here is what you must do: gather a group of twelve to fifteen like-minded people who also are willing to commit to this endeavor. If you do this, I will meet with you and your group, and then we shall see what we shall see.

The signature is huge, flamboyant, one name: *Jan.* Jan? What happened to *Dr. Cox?*

But never mind his name. This is ridiculous. And impossible. If he can't double the size of his old group, then how can he expect me to? What an asshole. He acts like I don't know what The Work is. Then he says go find a bunch of people who want to do it. What a jerk.

≈ ≈ ≈

Madeleine says, "Of course I'm part of it."

She's insulted that I even ask. We never really make up after our fathomless fight. Fight over nothing. Which is damn near everything. Only thing for sure is I'm not going to bring it up. Apparently neither is she. I guess we tacitly agree to avoid the subject.

The next day I grab my old friend Byron.

"You know how we've always been looking for something?"

He nods, but he nods weakly.

"All through high school and even before that—you know how we were searching for something?"

He nods, a little more oomph this time.

"How we were always . . . well, there was always a yardstick, and we were measuring things against some better standard of the way things ought to be."

"Yeah?"

"And all the hours we spent laughing at grown-ups?"

He knows, and he laughs a little.

"Well, this is it. This is what we were looking for. It's a way to get to the way we ought to be."

Byron says, "Well, yeah, all right. I get it. I'm in. Go find the rest of the people."

Byron's like that. A switch flips, and he's all in.

Three of us, counting me. Nine to go.

I call friends from college and old hippie friends and friends from the Atlanta College of Art, part of the High Museum right on Peachtree Street, where I took some classes, and talk my way through the list. I tell each of them the truth about my experiences in all this. About the exhilaration of fresh preverbal perception. And the enervation of living in a rote, self-referential loop. The haircut as a step in liberation, and how I never would have imagined it for myself. That's a critical part. That's why you need a teacher.

I drop by Jagger's Pizza right across from the Emory campus, owned by my old friend Bill Jagger, to resume our ongoing debates about the nature of reality, peppered with a sideshow argument about what might happen to all the capitalists after the revolution. So I tell him this is it: this is the thing we've been looking for.

And he says, "What thing we've been looking for?"

"Jagger, I thought you were a seeker. How many times did we wrestle with 'higher consciousness' before they wore the words out? You can't get there on your own. You need someone who can see the limits of your personality because you can't rely on yourself if you wanna be more than your self. It's teacher-based—"

"So you're one of those wannabe enlightened hippies, huh?" He puts on his PhD face and says, "Before you march in some pseudo-mystic's parade, have you exhausted your own Judeo-Christian tradition? Have you even scratched the surface? What about William Blake? He was a world-class mystic. And our American Transcendentalists. Of course, from your tradition you know that the word 'rabbi' means teacher. Or do I need to specify Teacher with a capital *T*?"

The conversation with Jagger reminds me of the feisty wrangling with John Califano at Kibbutz Ginosar. I actually like the wrangling, and welcome the pushback. But I need about nine more people, and Jagger's not going to be one of them.

Conversations with others are easier.

Through a friend of a friend, I meet Mara, who's living in a windowless basement near Emory packed with books, and she nods at every statement as I tell her about this teacher who told me to simply get a haircut and how it ripped a seam in the continuous fabric of everything. I take a breath to say more, but she cuts me off and says, "Tell me when to be there."

Mara leads me to Ross, one of those collegiate boy wonders who graduates early and knows so much that you can't tell when he's making stuff up. He nods dismissively no matter what I say, as if to make clear that I couldn't possibly know anything he doesn't. He reminds me of Ouspensky: alive from the neck up. In the mildest way, he says yes, I'll see what this Dr. Cox has to offer. Not sure if I should count on him for Dr. Cox's group or not.

Ed Webber from psychology class pays most of his own way through college with poker winnings. Poker is not a game, Ed says. Poker is life. That's his lens. When I get my military haircut, Ed's easy smile and cool eye remain the same, and he's probably thinking, "Is this dude bluffing?" So I tell Ed what the haircut was really about, but I can't tell if it piques his curiosity or not. Poker face. Then Ed says, "If you like it that much, yeah, man, I'll check it out."

After about five weeks I have nine people, counting Ross the boy wonder.

Byron's getting impatient, and he insists it's time to tell Dr. Cox. "You never even replied to his letter. He doesn't know if you're doing this or not. Maybe he's finding someone else to find the people. You need to tell him what you're up to."

Byron's a convert. He can't wait to start.

My next letter to Dr. Cox is almost as short as the previous one. I tell him I have nine people and will keep him apprised of my progress.

This time his reply comes back in three days. Like he was sitting there waiting for it. Like he's eager to see what I got.

If this is still something you wish to pursue, knowing it is unnecessary, then here are the names of some others who may have an interest in joining your group. Contact them if you wish.

It's a list of five names. I call them all. Someone likes it, someone doesn't, someone else does, and someone knows someone who might.

Two weeks later, sixteen people are ready to meet.

≈ ≈ ≈

"And what have you been doing?"

Grandpa. Philip Rothenberg. He made his fortune in the fur trade, as a middleman buying pelts from trappers out West and selling the goods to furriers in New York.

Grandpa Phil. Lived ninety years. Can picture him vividly. Short and dark with brilliant green eyes. With his erect spine and confident gestures, he always seemed physically powerful. Grandpa made people laugh. He sat at the head of the table. He would sing opera with no prompting. Mom always spoke solemnly of the poverty he suffered in childhood. But Grandpa Phil never said a word to us about it, and Grandpa is the one I know least of all the relatives.

So I whisper, "You came to America, alone, as a teenager, and you struggled . . . you became wealthy . . . but did you get what you came here for?"

And right away I hear Grandpa's voice.

The hair on my neck stands up.

He says, "I did struggle. And what have you been doing?"

≈ ≈ ≈

I have the luxury of choosing my troubles.

I'm the same age as Grandpa was when he opened his own fur brokerage, after saving coins from meager wages during five years of medieval-style servitude to his abusive brother-in-law.

And Jesus, I'm choosing Dr. Cox.

Like a rich kid who joins the military: Richard Kidd III. He doesn't have to do this. His parents could buy him out of the draft and land him a fat job with Wall Street warmongers. But instead Rich Kidd enlists. In the Army. He wants to be a Green Beret.

But if Rich Kidd wants that fierce challenge—the drill sergeant screaming in his face and the goddamn sweat and burn and humiliation that he's never going to get in a high-back executive throne on silent casters—then how much choice does he have? If it's about what you're drawn to, no matter the range of reasons, then how much choice does Rich Kidd really have?

Not much.

Neither do I.

You see it coming like a new year, and there's no way to stop it. And then you seek it out. Rich Kidd has to enlist. So do I.

But I'm nervous. John Califano's words ring in my ears: *Don't give one guy all the power.*

But I'm desperate for a working knowledge of how to optimize my brain and being, and if Dr. Cox has some kind of manual, then I'll eat it. Memorize it. Master it. Marry it. Whatever I gotta do. But I don't know about Jan Cox's moral compass. And I don't want to become a lifer in any group. So in a moment of fear about all my good intentions going bad, while Madeleine is asleep, in a private ceremony in the bathroom, with all the solemnity I have, I look at myself hard in the mirror, one shiny black galactic pupil to another, and I write a promise to myself:

I will stay true to the vertebral roots that sprang me here, roots to ancestral souls. I promise to abide by the truths I know now, and I promise to use new knowledge wisely and to complete the internal edifice already under construction.

I'm thinking of Grandpa's odyssey and the uniquely human urge to be more than human, while folding the vow corner to corner with sharp origami creases.

I want to tuck it between ancient blocks of the Wailing Wall.

Then I hear that voice.

Grandpa.

The hair on my head stands up, just as it did last year in Jerusalem.

He says, *Thinking takes time.*

That's all he says. *Thinking takes time.* Does he mean I

should slow down with my urge? Don't know that I can. And now all these people are ready to meet Dr. Cox.

≈ ≈ ≈

Fifteen of the sixteen people show up at the meeting—at 7:30 *sharp*, according to a guy with a corporate voice who calls on the phone. It's not at the Miller Building anymore. It's at someone's house, off Northside Drive, in the fancy part of town. But the house is a simple ranch in a neighborhood of pricier properties. We newbies gather in the carport. We're crackling. Life is about to change. I start introducing people. Byron glows, and Madeleine is frosty.

The front door opens. It's people I recognize from two years ago. Almost two years exactly since I went to those meetings and got a freaking crew cut. They are friendlier now and introduce themselves. Sam and Knoxie. They actually say hello, good to see you.

Then Dwayne appears. He's the guy on the phone who said 7:30 *sharp*, like he's Mr. Pompous Drill Sergeant. Dwayne herds us into the basement. He thinks we're a 747 and he's air traffic control. He announces with way more decibels than necessary that we're going to meet Jan one at a time. Then, if a group remains, we'll all meet with Jan.

I'm first.

I walk upstairs, and Dwayne shows me into a room dimly lit by candles. Dr. Cox—or Jan—sits in a puffy faux leather chair. The finely tailored British suit from two years ago is gone. He's wearing a polyester disco shirt open to his hefty bronze belly, and he says, "Call me Jan, world traveler."

I don't say anything. I wonder if he's going to say anything about my big hair. It grew back. I extend my hand, as I did the last time I saw him, when I went to the Miller Building to say good-bye. He seems just as surprised now. But we do shake hands, and then he says, "That's it. I know what you've done." He nods at my eyes, and he means it. "I just wanted to greet you first, before meeting the others. I'll say more later."

And I leave.

One by one, the people go upstairs, and fourteen of us wait. Dwayne calls names. Someone trudges upstairs. We wait. Everyone who goes up comes down. Madeleine and Byron and Mara and Ross the boy wonder and Ed the cardsharp and James the architect and Judith the artist.

After an hour or so, we're all still here. Fifteen out of fifteen.

Jan comes downstairs. He sits in the big chair. He looks straight at me but announces to everyone, "I gave him a nearly impossible Task, and he did it. All of you—and by that I mean you collectively, as an organic unit—have the potential to become a real Work group. You have the necessary mix of types, that is the main thing. You are not all one type. In addition, you all have a basic sanity. That's absolutely essential."

He pauses and points at me. "And he did it."

The way he says it makes me wonder if he'd been trying to attract new people and new energy to his group. Trying and failing?

But Jan—I'm not used to the name; I'm still thinking Dr. Cox, and I wonder if he's really a doctor of anything—is not going to linger on the accolades, and he continues, "But whatever he told you to get you here, forget it. It served a purpose, but as of right now it's immaterial. I am responsible for what we do here, and I'll see to it that we will move quickly so that those who need to benefit will benefit, and those who do not belong here in The Work will leave posthaste."

I had forgotten how he throws overblown words into his

deeply southern speech. Can't tell if he's just trying to show off his vocabulary. Who goes around saying "posthaste"? In a redneck accent?

He continues. "None of this is necessary, and in that regard —among others—this is the opposite of religion, in which everyone says the gods demand that you be religious. They say, 'You have got to do this! Be the perfect Christian, Jew, or Muslim, or else you'll burn in hell!' But while The Work is the fount of all religions, it is also the diametric opposite of what all the ordinary religions inevitably become, and so I tell you directly that all this is absolutely unnecessary, and if you do not need it, then don't waste your time here. If you don't feel the tug of it, go ahead and leave now, because you'll be leaving soon enough anyway, either by your own boredom or by me throwing you out.

"In the interest of feeding those of you who are truly hungry for this, and in the simultaneous interest of boring those who don't truly need it, I will leave you with a question and a Task. The Task is simply this: for one week, until we meet again, do not say the word 'there.' That's the Task. Just abide by it. Don't say 'there,' and don't talk about not saying 'there.' That's all you have to do."

But he doesn't spell it, so really it's three words: "there," "their," and "they're." Wow: that'll be a mess.

"And the question for you to ponder," he says, "is simply this: What is the first word in the dictionary?"

He stands up, strides in large, heavy steps across the room, and withdraws his attention so completely that he's gone before he's gone. He disappears without saying good-bye.

Dwayne, the air traffic controller, walks to the front of the room, copying Jan's ponderous steps, but they don't fit his skinny, knock-kneed legs. He opens an envelope, unfolds the paper, and reads the rules, unchanged from two years ago. No hostility. No drugs. Don't get involved with me personally. Be on time at the weekly meetings. And pay your weekly dues. It amounts to the cost of a couple of lunches a week, just as it did two years ago.

≈ ≈ ≈

What is the first word in the dictionary? I get Dr. Cox's—I mean Jan's—question right away when I think about it the next day.

Simple. There is no first word in the dictionary. That's the answer.

Language, like everything it represents, is nonlinear and interconnected and, just like atoms, it's made of practically nothing.

Plus there is no word "here" without the word "there," because all the words are in it together, supporting each other in a superstructure. There can't be a first word. Because it doesn't go from one word to two words. It goes from no words to language, and the language is all the words pushing and pulling each other into a wobbly, shimmering, unstable whole, and the language mutates into many forms and dimensions, one of which is a dictionary, which is only a snapshot of the language on *a day*, a single day in all of evolving language time.

I'm chewing on an answer I don't know I have until I have it, and *the only reason I have it is because this guy Jan Cox asks a question.*

Whispering to myself, "This is worth a lot more than two lunches."

I'm having a great time blasting around with the nonexistent first word in the dictionary Task. More fun than lunch.

Then I'm wondering, well, if there's no first word in the dictionary, then there's no last word. Language spins on and on. And then "zygote" pops into my brain. Ha-ha, what if it's the last word on the last page of my dictionary? I look it up. "Zygote: Any cell formed by the union of two gametes." That fits: I got a zygote in my head right now, spawned by his question + my answer = a new embryo of no first words, no last words. New knowledge, gestating.

≈ ≈ ≈

The there/their/they're Task—well, I take it seriously, but it's a bumpy ride. I actually get through the first day without saying the words that shall not be spoken.

But removing these three words from conversation really messes up the whole language, because it messes with the whole invisible structure and energy flow that culminates in words pouring out of your mouth. I feel words backing up in different parts of my brain and body as I try to snare three of them at the spillway of my lips.

It all blows up in my face at the staff meeting that week, on Wednesday morning, with the head nurse, a recovering alcoholic named Smitty; the unit director and nun, Jane Chadwick; and Dr. Hans Schiller and Dr. Regina Knowles, the he-and-she psychiatrists at Unit 9, Alcoholism. The four of them and me. That's the staff meeting.

On my way into the meeting, Unit 9 inpatient Bruce Abingdon, a jaded, gossipy, and brilliant Virginia aristocrat, one of the patients I get praised for connecting with because nobody else can, pulled me aside and whispered, "*Entre nous,*

Dr. Knowles is carrying Dr. Schiller's balls around in her purse." When Bruce saw me do a double take, he nodded, leaned in closer, and whispered, "That's right. His gonads. In her handbag."

It is now impossible to look at either psychiatrist without thinking about his balls in her purse.

In the meeting, we're reviewing each of the inpatients, one by one. I'm not saying much, but usually I'll have an answer when they ask about someone in particular, because I spend a lot of time with patients "out on the floor."

Bruce Abingdon. How is Bruce doing this week?

Nobody answers.

They all look at me.

Have you seen Bruce?

"Sure," I tell them, looking at the he-and-she psychiatrists, the corners of my mouth curling inappropriately. "He's been holding court . . ." I'm about to say, "down *there* in the billiard room," but as the-word-that-shall-not-be-spoken is forming and my tongue peels off the back of my eyeteeth to form a *th* sound, I try to abort the word but it's too late, and I have no other substitute on such short notice, so what comes out is a mutilated, vaguely Julia Child-ish sort of "they-aaaah." A voice so ridiculous that none of them wants to look at me, but they can't help it.

With eight eyeballs on me, I start laughing. And the more they stare, the harder my laughter. I can't stop. Shaking with laughter. Way the other side of appropriate. The he-psychiatrist looks at the she-psychiatrist. First she clears her throat. Then he clears his. This doesn't help.

For a moment during the spasms of laughter, Jane Chadwick catches my eye and smiles. She's a nun, for chrissakes, and the embodiment of Christian good cheer and piety, and in some incomprehensible way she's okay with me cracking up like this.

I don't know why, but it helps calm me down. Eventually. And we do get on with the meeting.

None of them says a word about it then, and they never mention it again, as if it never happened.

Jan's Tasks seem so subtle. Eliminating a word from conversation. Pondering the first word in the dictionary. But when you deploy them in the grit of daily life, they're about as subtle as atomic energy.

≈ ≈ ≈

We meet once a week at Sam and Knoxie's house. Jan breaks it all down—how to become extraordinary rather than the ordinary beings we are, the bones of it straight out of Gurdjieff. But he spins it with his own spiky, bristling, rude, boiling intelligence in loopy run-on redneck genius sentences packed with digression inside of digression. And his blasphemous humor melts everyone's freeze on all that's sacredly, brow-crunchingly serious.

Grab the tiller of your own sprawling messy hazy wobbly ship of self and *do something* with your attention. Do something newer better bigger smarter quicker crazier, sharper fresher. Focus! Remember! Remember everything! Splice your foamy life with a sharper knife. Don't sit there with your mental thumb up your mental ass! He doesn't say it exactly that way, but that's the way it's charged.

At the conclusion of each talk, Jan specifies a Task for the coming week. For me, at least, this is the critical part. Tasks are the power cord. Plug me in, please.

The Tasks part curtains you didn't know were drawn. The

Tasks are all over the place. He says just keep your eyes open and see what you can see.

He says go to a public place and preach, as if you're a street evangelist.

Oh, shit. This certainly qualifies as an activity I would never pick for myself, never even imagine for myself. Like getting a military haircut. I wanna do this about as much as I wanna pay a stranger to make me bald.

He says just stand out there and preach. Only you will know that you don't belong out there. Nobody else will pay you much attention at all. And he says, "Remember your aim here: to see what you can see."

A wave of nausea slaps me in the belly. Goddamn him for coming up with something so dreadful. I really, *really* do not want to do this.

Sure I want to step out of myself, beyond myself, and embark on the unknown. But I don't want to waste my time on ridiculous bullshit. This is supposed to be the pursuit of enlightenment, not clowning around in a dumpy city park.

Then, without expecting to, I'm laughing. I hate to admit it, but if I'm so unnerved by, well, what is really just *reading out loud*, then, um, this is quite a rigid, small, dictatorial self boxing me in. Hmm.

Jan sliced it up in a meeting by saying, "The ordinary mind will say, 'Limits?' The limits themselves look around, see no limits, and declare, 'Limits! I don't have any limits!' But it's only the limits speaking."

So limits or no limits, he says do it. That's why I'm here—to do what I don't want to do and what I never would have imagined doing. So I'm going to do it and see what happens.

But still, I really, *really* do not want to do this.

Clutching my Bible as a shield, I approach Hurt Park, in

downtown Atlanta. Near the bus station. Before the word "homeless" replaces the word "bum."

I open up to the book of Ezekiel. At least it's the Old Testament, small comfort for a Jewish kid masquerading as a Holy Roller.

But as I stand with perfect posture, with open text, next to old wooden benches and two gnarled oaks at the corner of the one-block-square city park, the pressure against doing this overwhelms me, and no words will clear my oval mouth. So I dally weakly around the perimeter while a few real Pentecostals shout, "Jesus This!" and "Jesus That!" and "Revelations! Revelations!" and one guy shouts, "It is easier for a camel to pass through the eye of a needle than for a rich man to enter into the kingdom of God!"

This is good enough, right? I'm here; I get what it's like. I should leave it to them—the real street preachers. They'll know I'm a phony, anyway.

I feel a little sick in the belly. Sick with fear. I want to go home.

Fear of what? Fear of reading? Out loud? To strangers? Really? You're afraid of *reading?*

No, I am not going to leave this place a chickenshit failure. And I am not going to walk away from Hurt Park mute.

So I grab the tiller of my own sprawling messy hazy wobbly chickenshit ship of self and anchor myself on a piece of pavement in the shabby downtown park. The book opens again, my spine telescopes upward, and words fly. Louder than I expected. "Now it came to pass in the thirtieth year, in the fourth month, in the fifth day of the month, as I was among the captives by the river of Chebar, that the heavens were opened, and I saw visions of God," and now, as if skydiving, I have jumped out of the airplane and *I'm really doing this,* and it's not about the preaching, because neither the passersby nor I care about that. It's about the liberation: the liberation from being encased in a personality that could never do exactly what I'm doing right now.

I keep reading. It's thrilling. I make eye contact with someone. As if I really am a street preacher howling the word of God. And in a crazy, upside-down way, I really am. I hold the stranger's gaze, an older guy in his thirties in a blue shirt. We both feel something. It's not about the words. The Bible is, among other things, about a kind of expansion. About stepping beyond yourself, deferring to something higher and larger and binding to the higher and larger. The guy looks away and moves on. But we exchange something, a little spark. Because at Hurt Park, I am flying outside my brain, outside the country, without a passport. Or a flight plan.

Chapter 2 of Ezekiel. It's a great chapter. So is chapter 3. Not that I know what they're about. The words are not about the words. The words are the deed, and the deed flows from torso and breath.

At the end of chapter 6, I click the Good Book shut with a nifty flick of the forearm and float from Hurt Park without a hurt in the world, twenty feet tall and punching the air.

Later I wonder where all that energy came from. Because I didn't really do anything other than read out loud.

A wild frontier. A lot of color. A lot of light. No curtains, no walls.

≈ ≈ ≈

"Walls," Grandpa repeats. "The only thing that set me free from the basement walls, from the endless workdays of my youth, was a

fistful of double eagles. I saved my nickels and dimes for more than a year until I had my first twenty-dollar gold coin. American gold. It was empowering. I was crawling through a tunnel of dark, boring labor, and the double eagles were my light at the end. My fingers knew the face of liberty on one side of the coin and the wings of the mighty eagle on the other. These coins were my dreams coming true, and I could hold them. I was going to leave my brother-in-law Louis Rabinowitz and start my own business. But it was going to take a while.

"I would go to sleep holding these coins."

≈ ≈ ≈

"Spend a day without complaining," Jan says at the end of one meeting. "Just one day. Any day you want in the next week. That's it. That's all there is to it. The other six days of the week, complain all you want, all day long. But on the day you pick: no complaining whatsoever, no matter what, no exceptions. All right, one exception: if for any reason you're in the hospital emergency room, complain all you want, the louder and more hysterical the better. I'll come down and complain with you if you're loud enough."

He gets a chuckle out of the room.

I figure this one Task will be easy. I'm just not that much of a complainer. Plus, he's got to be exaggerating. He says people complain all the time, that nearly all human conversation is just one form of complaining after another. C'mon, Jan. That's a little simplistic, isn't it?

I set aside Wednesday, and on Tuesday at midnight I fire a final complaint of the day at the alarm clock just to clear my system: I hate the alarm clock. Okay, even if I do complain a bit, how hard can it be to quit for a day?

Wednesday. Good morning. You call this good? Shit, it's hot again. Shit, we're almost out of coffee. Shit, I gotta get to work. Shit, the traffic. I wish we lived closer. Shit, no—I wish we lived farther away, so far that I couldn't work there. Shit, I hate my job. Shit, you call this *the national interest?* Shooting pool and shooting the shit with a bunch of drunks who aren't drinking? How national-interest is that? Shit, I miss the Galilee and pounding fence posts into the rocky slopes. Shit, if I were doing that, I wouldn't be thinking all this crap. Plus, cigarettes. I hate 'em. I hate 'em 'cause I can't stop smoking the bastards. This is disgusting. Shit, I don't care if Jan Cox smokes like a chimney. It still sucks. Plus, shit, he chain-smokes Pall Mall Gold 100s. Disgusting. In a shiny gold pack. Same shitty color as one of his garish disco shirts.

Later, I wonder whether I really know anything about anything, because I thought it would be easy. Because *I'm not the complaining type.*

How little can one know about oneself? Astoundingly little. Or worse: the little bit one does know about oneself is mostly wrong.

≈ ≈ ≈

A few weeks later Jan says, "The Task for this week is what I'll call Not Staring. For the next week, at the top of every hour, as long as you're awake, for a duration of five minutes, do not stare. By that I mean, specifically, do not let your eyes stop on any one thing. Not on any anything. Keep your eyes moving for five

minutes at the top of the hour. That's it. That's all there is to it."
He lets it sink in for a moment, how simple this is. "The hard
part," he says to himself with half a laugh, "is remembering to
do it."

I can't wait to try it, so I try it right here right there in Sam
and Knoxie's basement while he's talking, and I hold it for long
seconds.

Immediately, the room expands, and everything becomes
rather splendid and freshly fascinating.

Then he adds, "This is not about drawing attention to yourself. You'll find that you can move your eyes subtly, almost like
shifting your weight from one foot to the other. Suffice it to say
that no one should ever notice you doing it. There is no wrong
way to do it, by the way, except by drawing unnecessary attention to yourself. Of course, that applies to everything we're
doing here." He snorts, enjoying another private joke.

And then he says, "One thing you'll learn, if you can
remember to do this, is how lazy your eyes are. And another
thing you'll learn is how hard it is to remember to do this. Top of
the hour, every waking hour, every day, all week."

I get it right away. I get it sitting in the room while he's still
explaining it. For whatever reason, Jan usually explains everything three times. Probably because of his dim assessment of
ordinary human consciousness. Sometimes I wish he'd shut
up, at least for a little while. We get it already. He says, again,
that it's really hard to remember to keep your eyes moving.
Then I realize—oh, yeah, he's right, I did forget, right now, to
keep doing it, it is hard to remember, and then I do move my
eyes again while he's talking, and the room becomes, well,
splendid all over again, and I can see everyone's face, mostly
looking at Jan. An amalgam of tilted eyebrows and lips curling
up and down and telltale yawns and itches that must be
scratched immediately. My eyes keep moving, and it's a feast,

and I don't care if he repeats himself straight through to next month.

I would never in a million years think to do this.

≈ ≈ ≈

Sounds so simple. Once an hour for five minutes. So easy to pour through the day, though, and miss the mark by twenty minutes or two hours. So it's hit or miss. But more often than not, I hit the mark right at the top of the hour. I do remember to simply keep my eyes moving.

Wall. Window. Ah, yes. This feels good. Sky. Head. Hair on head. Leaves outside the window. Ceiling. Lamp. Side of lamp. Pencils, very yellow, on well-worn desktop. Back to pencils. I linger on yellow but remember again and jump back to wall.

It's not about the objects in your field of vision. It's about a domed awareness of everything happening at once. The longer you maintain it, the grander it gets.

≈ ≈ ≈

I get high from it and am thrilled and gush to Grandpa, "It's the extension of the arc, the urge, the same longing that pulled you here, to America, for something more. Isn't it? You know, the big IT."

I'm afraid I may have disrespected his struggle. Because his

*youth did not afford the luxury of such efforts. But Grandpa
surprises me with questions, with specificity.*

*"It seems like a very nervous activity. The eyes jumping
around all over the place. If you wanted to focus, wouldn't you
keep your eyes still?"*

*"Maybe the description sounds nervous, but in actual prac-
tice it's the opposite. It's meditative and hyper-alert combined."*

"Hmm," he says. "Everything comes from somewhere."

≈ ≈ ≈

Jan says, "Spend a day smiling." Simple as that. Nothing mysterious or difficult about it. Sounds like a picnic in the park
compared to most of the other hoops and loops he throws
our way.

So I pick a day and slide a smile across my face. And every
time it fades I ease it back—against a heretofore unrecognized
sideways gravity pressing in on the corners of my mouth—and
hold the happy lips.

Sometime midmorning, the smile isn't fake anymore. I'm
really smiling. It hits me that *I'm really happy*, and the reason is
stupefying: just because I'm smiling. Astounding that you can
induce happiness by faking a smile instead of waiting for happiness to deliver the smile.

Mid-afternoon, the whole enterprise of *higher consciousness*
turns silly. All that tonnage of serious thought about this
goddamn serious endeavor washes away by simply holding a
smile that was fake this morning! Dr. Fenton, the professor of
Asian religion in college, would be shocked to discover that I
learn more in six hours of intentional smiling than I did in the

entire semester I spent under his serious tutelage. Which I loved at the time.

Jan doesn't ever ask in the meetings who did what, Task-wise. But you can tell during this first golden age of Jan's group that people are *doing things*. Plowing different brain furrows. So those furrowed brows everyone brought to the first meeting about goddamn Serious Higher Consciousness kinda dissolve. Looks like everyone got blood flowing where it wasn't before. People laugh a lot. And the deep stated-and-unstated promises of it all from the very beginning—to keep you off guard, to demand the unnecessary, and to spark development beyond the ordinary—are all being fulfilled.

It's the Tasks that get me addicted, and it automatically follows in my mind that if the Tasks are this good, then everything Jan says must be this good.

So when he says, "I'm never wrong," sure, it's arrogant. But so far, the statement seems true.

≈ ≈ ≈

Even as Madeleine and I become immersed in The Work, we still abide by the pursuit of excellence in what Jan would refer to as our "ordinary lives."

We don't want to live like everyone else. We want to live the way we want to live. *Young and frothing when your culture is young.* That's how Grandpa would say it.

We move far away from town, to an old farmhouse with a barn, a smokehouse, and an orchard on a hundred and twenty acres of rolling pasture and woods. It's a long way from anywhere, outside the country town of Alpharetta, one of the southernmost fingers of Appalachia, stretching within thirty miles of downtown Atlanta. Northern Fulton County could easily be the hollers of West Virginia.

Holiday season rolls up. We've been going to Jan's meetings since spring. It's the last week of the year, and, on impulse, I suggest to Madeleine that we should invite everyone to our place for a party. To my surprise, she immediately says, "Yeah, good idea." She's not exactly a party animal.

But who would venture way out to northern Fulton County for a party?

The answer is: they all do. Practically everyone in the old group and everyone in the new group makes the trek. Maybe The Work has become enveloping in a way we didn't realize, riveting with challenge, and the raw edge of it all supplanting old friendships. So maybe we all quit talking to old friends and have no other party to go to. But maybe it's also because Jan embraced the party idea with such gusto. He was the first to say he'd be there. But Jan doesn't show up, and, to my surprise, nobody seems to miss him. Is everyone more relaxed without Jan around?

Cold outside, and a fire blazes in the old farmhouse kitchen, which is really the original one-room cabin from the 1800s homestead. People are asking about the place. Yes, it did have an outhouse. The bedrooms and indoor plumbing came later. We painted the rooms and cleaned up the apple trees and put in a garden. People are talking as they never talk when Jan is around. So I get to know some of them in a new way.

I ask Sam and Knoxie about the speedboat parked in their garage when we go there for meetings. It's never come up in conversation before because we all find value in Jan's stricture against talking about yourself.

"Tell us when you want to go for a spin on Lake Lanier.

Sam will try to make you seasick," Knoxie says with a giggle. She's squeezable and sexy.

Sam hardly looks the daredevil. He's old, more than forty, a skinny computer engineer, but a gleam in his eye betrays something wilder. They were high school sweethearts from the Sequatchie Valley. She doesn't look that old. Sam says Sequatchie is the Shenandoah of Tennessee, running in a straight line northeast from Chattanooga. He takes a swig of bourbon and says, "It's a lush valley where everything grows except the people. A redneck Eden."

Knoxie adds, "After the fall." She giggles again.

James, the architect, almost didn't make it tonight because he's cramming for his licensing exam in a few weeks. His wife, Judith, says, "Doctor's orders."

"Yeah," he says, "Doctor Judith."

"Drink up, dear," she tells him. "It's good for me."

Even Dwayne, the Pompous Announcer, responds like a normal human being. The booze does him good. I ask him what kind of work he does. Instead of trying to evade the question, as people in the group usually do, he answers directly. He works for Ronnie and Rachel, at their commercial photography studio downtown.

What? Ronnie's an engineer at Lockheed, father to two kids, and a he runs this business on the side?

Dwayne says, "I run it for him."

I'm not so sure. But I don't say anything.

I tell Dwayne I know a bit about photography. He's actually interested. It's the first real conversation we've had.

I'm having a blast. Euphoria zaps the winter air leaking in through the old farmhouse windows. The fire helps a little. The booze helps more. But the people heat the room.

Sometime after ten the door opens, and Jan walks in with a swirl of cold. Says he's been driving all over. Couldn't find the place. He pierces me with his hard green eyes, saying I gave bad directions.

But I'm not buying it. I know how to give directions. I gesture to the roomful of red-faced partiers. Same directions they got, I tell him.

Everyone freezes for a second. Seems these people never disagree with Jan.

The hardness leaves his eyes. He shrugs and says, all right, then, where's the beer?

He cracks open a bottle and swallows half in one gulp.

Knoxie takes my arm and whispers, "You're so brave to have us all here."

Brave? What does she mean by that? What does she know that I don't?

The center of gravity in the room shifts to Jan.

He's impressed that I have the triple album *Will the Circle Be Unbroken* by the Nitty Gritty Dirt Band. Maybe he thinks with my big hair it's Led Zeppelin for breakfast every morning. But no. I prefer these valley twangs, mountain echoes. I just nod and say, yeah, this is a good album, and he puts it on the turntable.

But before the first cut, somebody lifts the needle off the LP and hands Jan my old guitar, leaning in the corner as a piece of sculpture. He shrugs, sits down as his body cradles the guitar, tunes it in no time—to a key I never heard before—and his right hand strums a chord. In the wake of the chord, his ramrod posture melts. He abdicates his throne. He's all about harmonies on the strings. He's not trying to teach the guitar anything. His fret fingers shift as he strums another chord and then another and his foot taps and his face eases, and elemental, hard-driving blues fills the room.

Never imagined he plays guitar. Not like this. Ancient and

urgent. Like one of the Mississippi Delta bluesmen. Braiding pain with yearning.

He lets the last chord linger, then slaps the strings one time and puts the guitar down. He tilts his head at the turntable and somebody lowers the needle onto "Keep on the Sunny Side" by Ma Carter.

Jan stands up. The musician drains out of his body, and he stiffens. But something about him—what is it? He's not dowdy enough to fit with the people who have been with him since the Miller Building from three years ago, and he wears way too much polyester to fit with the new people I brought. And even though he sometimes talks like a bricklayer, it's never convincing. What is it? I'm looking him up and down.

The words "baby fat" pop into my head. Dominator dude Jan and baby fat, hilariously incongruous. I laugh to myself. But that's it. He's so heavy on his feet, they thud when he walks. Heavy and formal in his bearing, like an older person, but damn, he's got a big baby belly and a fat unlined face, and it's impossible to know his age.

Mountain music keeps playing, but the pitch of the room keeps winding up, like that crescendo on "A Day in the Life" by the Beatles.

Tim Smith, one of the old Miller Building people, positions a dinner plate half off the table, lowers his palm close to the floor, and slaps the plate with the back of his hand toward the ceiling. The plate flips up in the air. Everyone gathers around. He says, okay, the deal is who can knock the plate good and hard up from the table and grab it out of the air before it touches anything. Tim tries again, and the plate spanks the table on the way to banging the floor. Good thing it's plastic. So Sam and Byron and Ronnie and Dwayne try it. The plate makes a racket falling on the table, pounding on the plastic silverware that somebody brought, and then clattering on the old pine plank floor. The plate is a one-man band. Jan says, "Let some women try it," but nobody can catch the plate once it flips into the air. We're running out of people, and all eyes fall on me.

So I say, okay, sure, I'll try it. But instead of one plate, I position two of them side by side, half off the edge of the table. One for each hand. I relax my knees just enough to feel coiled. The drunk room gets quiet. Two plates hanging over the edge of the table are all I see. My knuckles poised in the shadow below. I wait for the moment, then smack both plates up in the air. They rotate end over end in the farmhouse kitchen, all slow motion, and it's easy. For this one instant, I'm perfectly sober. Grab one flipping plate with my left hand, and damn, I already got the other in my right.

The room erupts, and raw energy rips around. I've never been at a party like this. The music loud, everyone packed close and vibrating. Nothing like the spacey, sedate, pot-smoking marathons in college.

People are dancing with undone hips in our farmhouse kitchen, carving curved space with their butts where none existed before. And then Tim Smith and his luscious, doe-eyed wife, Phyllis, are clogging like mountain hillbillies to one of the cuts on *Will the Circle Be Unbroken*. And they keep the beat through the silent break between songs, everyone clapping in a circle around them, as they seamlessly find the beat on the next cut, "Losing You Might Be the Best Thing Yet."

Then I glance in the dark corner of the farmhouse kitchen.

Jan is dancing to the same song, but he's found some geologic bass beat, down at sonar levels. Whoa—never seen anyone dance like that. That is some *slow* dancin'. Right there is why Baptists forbid dancing. All I can see is his backside. A woman's hand draped over his shoulder. Even in the dark corner, that hand looks familiar. His body rotates around, way too slowly, because he's dancing way too slowly. He's all hips on skinny legs. Disturbing, because I can't see the woman's hand anymore, but damn it, it's riveting, and I can't stop looking.

My eyes race around the room, looking for Madeleine. Can't find her.

Some inner Puritan I'd never heard in my head before scolds, "A Teacher shouldn't behave this way."

I gulp some beer. And remember how outrageous they all said Gurdjieff was.

Gurdjieff would poke your weak spot. It seemed like a wonderful, even amusing, technique for spurring growth when I read about it. The Work is not supposed to be a place of comfort, like a church or a synagogue. Gurdjieff didn't want a bunch of acolytes gumming up the works. The Work plays for keeps, and if you get boiled out in the process, then you didn't have what it takes and you best get out of the way. So I'm thinking, yeah, whatever it takes . . .

But in the next second, she is pressed into his chest and hips, my belly is churning, and I hate it.

And the next second . . . if it's about him fucking her, then I hate the whole goddamn sham.

I imagine flying across the farmhouse kitchen like a monster middle linebacker and pounding Jan's knees so hard his head pops off.

I take a breath and snap out of it, but still twitching on titanium legs I look around to see if anyone realizes, ahem, that I'm "all et up," as they say in Alpharetta, because after all, we don't express any hostility, and I don't want to violate the tribal maxims or sacrifice my good standing in the community.

I gulp some more beer. And my gaze snaps back to the corner. Jan and Madeleine. Okay, they still have their clothes on. Because without the clothes, they'd be regaling us with a live sex show. Okay, I remind myself, they're wearing clothes. They are not having sex. They are just dancing. If you want to call that dancing. But I am going to make it through this song, which I cannot hear, and then they will stop dancing. I'm going to will that they stop dancing, and everything will be okay. Maybe.

I can make it through the song. None of the cuts on this album is longer than three minutes. And this one song has already been spinning and spinning and spinning.

The next song is "You Don't Know My Mind," so I swill some more beer and realize that the song title could be funny in other circumstances.

But goddamn it, the fuckers are *dancing* again, if you want to call humping dancing, and I think, well, I made it through one song, I can make it through another. Yes, I can really do this, the way Rich Kidd follows his tour of duty in the Army by volunteering for the Green Berets because they're not hurting him enough for his country, for his longing.

But before I draw another breath, my legs take off, and I'm zinging through the swaying happy bodies, and in one gesture my grip finds her bicep and pulls. She's away from him. I stand there. This much is good: they're not dancing anymore.

But we're just looking at each other, the three of us.

All eyes in the room on us now. Nobody's breathing.

Absurdly, "You Don't Know My Mind" keeps playing. Jan and I are staring at each other.

"What are you doing?"

He's asking what *I'm* doing? This seems like a stupid question.

He's really pissed off.

What happened to Jan's cardinal rule—that no hostility can be directed toward anyone in the group? Now that he's pissed off, is the rule suspended?

Madeleine's eyes are wide open. For no reason, I want to protect her. From what? From this ferocious energy. She didn't know. Or did she?

Jan growls, "You're out."

The room is a tomb.

"You're out of the group."

He strides in his big heavy steps toward the door, grabs his suede cowboy coat. It's got miles of fringe. Each tassel shimmies in his overwrought grip. He slams the door behind him.

It's an ice sculpture in the farmhouse kitchen. Nobody moves.

Except me.

Instinct and desire are quicker than thought. I open the kitchen door and slam it behind me, same as he did.

I catch him at his car door and grab the handle so he can't get in. He's sizing me up. My mind is afraid of him, but my body isn't. I've got him for a second. He doesn't know what to do. Then my mind's not afraid, either.

And I say to his left eye, without any modulation, "Now, you listen to me." People don't bark at him like that. But he is listening.

Atlanta freezes your bones in the wintertime. It's really cold out here. But my bones are hot.

"I didn't do all this just to get thrown out of the group. I'm not done."

I am up to my eyeballs in the activity. And I'm gonna get what I'm gonna get whether either of us likes it or not. So he's stuck with me. And I'm stuck with him.

The icy air feels really good now.

Jan's got a force field.

But so do I. I'm not backing down from his glare.

"Well, then," he says with the hint of a smile. "Let's go back inside."

I follow him back in the house.

The ice sculpture of what used to be a party hasn't budged, and the music is stopped.

"Couldn't get rid of him," Jan announces cheerfully. "Is this a party or a wake? Crank up the music! Hell, let's make some goddamn noise, people!"

But just before the tone arm settles onto the record, he interrupts with a wave of his hand, catches everyone's attention with a forefinger pointed at the ceiling, and proclaims, "Everything to excess! Nothing in moderation!"

Everyone's laughing as though they just remembered how. The music and the tribe fill all available space in the farmhouse kitchen.

Jan takes me aside and talks right into my ear.

"The Work is in life, but it doesn't operate the same way. In ordinary life, if you are thrown out of something, whatever it is— the army, a club, a job, whatever—and reinstated, you're on some kind of automatic probation, as if you're almost still out, or halfway in at best. Not here, not in The Work. When you were out, you were completely, totally out. You were over. Kaput. History. Forgotten. Do you hear me? Forgotten. And now, you're unconditionally, completely here, maybe even more than you were just thirty minutes ago."

He takes a breath and pulls me closer, his deep voice sunk to a whisper.

"I like you," he says. "Not that it matters. But I like you. I don't like most of these people. But I like you," he repeats. Lifts his head from my ear, catches me with his gaze, and returns to my ear. "I really like you." He repeats it again. "But it doesn't matter. The Work is not a popularity contest. It's not about who you like. The Work is about what it is about, and that's all it's about. But I thought you might want to know. I like you. You are absolutely exceptional. You are one of the main reasons I have decided to stay in Atlanta."

Leaving Atlanta? News to me. Staying here for me?

I'm laughing. I could say the same to him.

And laughing because Knoxie was right. I am brave to host this party. Jan is outrageous. But his completely focused, unabashed affirmation washes over me and draws me in. He stands too close, and he smells clean.

≈ ≈ ≈

"He's not lazy, though." Grandpa is talking too loudly.

Maybe he's talking to someone else. Grandpa sounds worried.

"Some of the grandkids are lazy."

Yeah, true, I can think of a couple and hope he names them.

Grandpa continues. "But Jonathan is not lazy at all. He's got some energy, and he'll engage it." Sounds like he's proud of this. "He just refuses to grow up. He doesn't want to work."

Not sure he knows I'm here, the way he's referring to me in the third person.

"No, that's not true." He corrects himself.

Who else is here with Grandpa?

Grandpa continues. "He works. He really does. He works at the wound, the yearning, as he calls it. He just doesn't work for pay."

Someone answers back in a Yiddish-accented singsong sort of chant from the Lower East Side. "So? He works but not for pay? Is the boy even Jewish?"

Grandpa Phil continues. "You know, if he worked for pay, he'd learn a few things. I'd call that a Task for the boy. He'd learn the value of his endless minutes in life. And the value of a dollar. The value of a dime. The boy has no idea."

"So good, he has no idea. But is he Jewish or goy already?"

Grandpa speaks slowly. "He might have made a good rabbi back in Augostowa. It just came to me. He might have made us dance a little bit. But he's interested in this cockamamie enlightenment business with some know-it-all."

"Philip, were you at the boy's bris?"

"The boy himself, he can't dance, but I would bet—"

"You're not listening to me!"

"Bris? Why are we talking about a bris?"

"Is the boy Jewish already?"

"Yes, I was there at the boy's bris!"

"Oy."

"Oy, what? I think he's a good boy. Of course we are related. He's my grandson. I'm just a little worried about him."

1973

More in now than before. After the bond of booze until 4:00 a.m. and the roller-coaster ride with Jan and everyone dancing their butts off, tribal connections are forged. Nobody is a rookie any more. We're all in, we're all one group, Maybe the way Rich Kidd bonds with his platoon, new recruits and veterans alike, after live fire.

Not that our basic training, so to speak, is over. Jan has quickened the pace, upped the ante. A new blast at every weekly meeting, and I can't get enough of it all.

And I'm freshly curious about the older people who have been there for years.

I finagle an invitation to visit a pair of the silent stalwarts—Ronnie, who works for Lockheed, and his wife, Rachel, who manages Dwayne as he manages the photo studio. I want to see what's going on with these people.

They live on a hundred acres in Lost Mountain, out in

western Cobb County, about twenty-five miles from downtown Atlanta. This is before the whole region metamorphosed into suburbia. I follow their directions, through the old Marietta Square, and then west on State Road 120. At the Lost Mountain Store, turn right.

But I have to stop at this crossroads country store. A weather-beaten cornerstone reads "1880."

1880. Damn. The year Grandpa Phil was born in Augostowa, Poland. Fifteen years after the Civil War.

Finely figured heart-pine siding. Gray now. Amber then, when Grandpa was an infant and the lumber was fresh-outta-the-sawmill clapboard, as aromatic and wiggly as life. I have to go in.

More space than store; beadboard ceiling at maybe twenty feet. Fine, kinda-parallel lines wobble into unity at the back of the building. The shelves hardly above my belt.

At the worn countertop one ancient pink man mumbles to another ancient pink man, both in faded overalls.

Despite their pinkness, they remind me of the leathery sheikh with the white stallion I saw in Jericho and the cocoa-colored people I saw on Crete tending olive trees. Gurdjieff says people who live close to the land tend to be propelled by the force and truth of Essence, whereas in modern, urban life, Personality has mushroomed as the operative force in humanity.

I find the icebox—that's what they call it—grab a Coke, and approach the counter.

"Fifteen."

I look up. Fifteen what?

The pink man behind the counter. "That'll be fifteen cents. For the Co-Cola."

"I'm just on my way to the Cavanaugh place." That's Ronnie's last name.

"Well, then, it'll be a quarter."

This is hilarious, south-of-the-Mason-Dixon-line funny, and neither of the overalls can stop laughing.

Finally, the first pink man takes my fifteen cents and tells me that Mr. Ronnie is a fine man and Mrs. Rachel is a fine lady.

I want to tell them about Grandpa Phil—he was born the same year as your building—but I don't want to explain a shtetl to these guys or Judaism or fur brokerage or the yearning so I just thank them and turn up Lost Mountain Road and follow their directions: left into the first gravel driveway; you might not see it, and it'll be a little ways.

"We're so glad to have a guest," Rachel says. "We don't get too many." She takes care of the hundred acres and their two kids and her violin, which she calls a fiddle. Ronnie's barn has one of everything. Tools I never heard of.

I think he could build a spaceship.

He says maybe, as long as it's mostly wood.

Rachel says sure he could, as long as NASA's not in a hurry.

We don't mention Jan's name. It's one of the major rules: "Don't get involved with me personally, never speak my name, and don't get tangled up in discussions about what this is."

But we talk about it without talking about it. And Ronnie laughs a lot. I bet more than all the engineers at Lockheed combined. Lockheed, a military contractor. I probably marched against them a few years ago.

Rachel is radiant when she cradles imaginary tomatoes from this year's garden.

A 1960 Chevy Impala two-door hardtop sits in the side yard, red and white with the V-8 badge on the hood. I tell them we had two '60 Chevys when I was in high school. One was a four-door sedan with a 283 that we bought from the next-door neighbor, and the other was a Nomad station wagon with the 348-cubic-inch V-8, and Ronnie's eyes get wide.

"And I wrecked 'em both."

This makes us all very happy.

Ronnie gets a faraway look in his eye. "My favorite motor—" he begins, then Rachel finishes his sentence. "It was his Vespa."

Ronnie's nodding and says 125 cc's, a two-stroke motor. Burns gas and oil. Spews smoke, well, yes, but it'll go over forty!

Makes my old hippie Microbus seem like a Ferrari.

How many cubic inches is 125 cc's?

Ronnie frowns for a few beats, calculates in his head, and says about eight.

Eight cubic inches? How far can eight inches get you?

They both laugh.

Then Ronnie says, real matter-of-fact: California.

You rode that thing to California?

His eyes glow. Riding that Vespa to California in 1952. Ronnie's version of my year in Europe and Israel. Quaffing from the infinite jug. Our universes bind.

On the way home, some of Jan's words circle my mind: "A real Work group requires different types . . . normally, people are attracted to only their own types, so you have Holy Roller churches with mainly physical people, and you have cerebral groups like the Unitarians. A real Work group requires that you benefit from the efforts of all the types."

I don't try to crack exactly what he means by "types." I simply get it in one fat gulp that neither Ronnie nor Rachel is *my type*, and I am enriched by getting to know them this way, as comrades pursuing the ineffable. The yearning we share allows me a whiff of their talents, goodness, and accomplishments. I fill my lungs.

≈ ≈ ≈

We're all revolving on a Ferris wheel at the county fair, or the planetary fair, and Jan is the cosmic barker, cranking the apparatus faster and faster.

One night during our weekly meeting at Sam and Knoxie's house, Jan says, "Everything is happening at once."

This sticks in my head like a pushpin.

This is a startling statement, no matter how simple it sounds.

So simple. But . . .

Everything *is* happening at once. These words peel back horizons. Way, way past the edges of the mind and the bits that rattle in it.

Everything: it's a big planet, with billions of people. No, everything. It's a very small planet in a very big universe. Everything.

Jan leaves it hanging for a moment, and for once he doesn't repeat it three different ways. And now he's already talking about the Task for this week, and for once I'm not listening.

I'm busy: *everything is happening at once.*

Everything is happening at once in the universe.

The solar system, with all the planets, more than a hundred moons, all those asteroids, and Halley's Comet blazing around and around. Each celestial body a concentration of mass hurling through a trillion trillion trillion cubic miles of *absolutely nothing*, the entirety of which is a completely expendable wisp of a giant galaxy that is itself a completely expendable wisp of our local family of galaxies, all of which are tugging us with their own gravitational fields so that we're rotating in probably umpteen hundred different arcs simultaneously all the time so that we will never be *right here* ever again.

Meanwhile Jan keeps talking about something important that I'm not listening to because *everything is happening at once,* and if you're busy attending to everything, then why listen to him?

People stay longer than usual at Sam and Knoxie's house after the meeting.

Madeleine and I are in separate cars, because we each drove from work, so I'm driving home alone late in the evening.

Right now, close to midnight here, it's near dawn in Galilee, where I built fences on rugged round hills above the Jordan River.

Right now is tomorrow there.

Right now is middle of the night in Augostowa, where the ghosts of Grandpa's long-gone shtetl hover over ruined hovels and a shul.

Everything is happening at once.

Everything.

All the brains of all the mammals and all the cellular transactions of all the microbes and the water cycle and the nitrogen cycle and evolution and the dark side of the moon and birth and death and the S&P 500 and the expansion of the universe.

On these empty streets. Glazed with night light. Cool air riffles like caffeine in my bloodstream.

As I approach the corner of Northside Drive and Collier Road, the light turns red. Nobody around. I could run the light, easy.

But right now I don't want to. Because everything is happening at once at the intersection where nothing is happening, and I don't want to miss a single frame.

The asphalt, sparkly in streetlamps. Asphalt violet in the shifty leafprint shadows. Forest canopy rustles. Distant hum of the city. Intimate hum of the motor. Slices of sky between giant oak tops. Slices of Orion's belt.

Now is a million light years ago up there beyond the boughs.

I hope the light never changes. I'm good right here.

I could turn either way at this intersection and get home. Because if all roads lead to Rome, then all roads lead away from Rome, and all roads lead to Jerusalem, too, and all roads lead home.

The intersection passes right though my head.

I can go either way. I can go either way and get there. The Way of the Red Light. My new religion. Pursue traffic to enlightenment. Especially when there's no traffic. Because if there were traffic, someone would be honking at me now: the light is green.

≈ ≈ ≈

A letter arrives from The Selective Service System. Another letter. Oh, no. But this time, amazingly, it's welcome news. They say that I have fulfilled my service to my country. They thank me. I am no longer obligated to serve.

So the next day—propelled by some ancient urge, emboldened by Jan's declarations that different kinds of work accelerate a person's progress in The Work—I quit my job at Unit 9, Georgia Mental Health Institute. But first I share a heartfelt good-bye with Jane Chadwick. The nun. My boss. We share a surprising, unspoken communion that connects our separate worlds. When she says she'll miss me, all I can do is nod.

The next week, through a friend of our farm landlord in Alpharetta, I wind up filling orders at State Road Steel, out on Buford Highway.

A thousand profiles of steel in here. T profiles, U profiles, Z profiles, L profiles, H profiles, flat bars, tubes, sheet stock, all sorted under a two-acre steel shed according to thickness, dimension, and type—such as galvanized or stainless or Corten or high-tensile. You have to decipher the triplicate order sheet and wrap cables around the exact quantity of specified stock so the conveyor will hoist each order precisely. Once you count how many pieces get cabled, you need the strength to lift the pile and snake the cable through. Elbert, the supervisor, says to me, "How'd ya get so stout, son?" "Stout" is country for "strong." But you need more than brawn to work at State Road Steel. What's on the sheet is one language. The monochrome geometries of steel in the shed are another language.

People think work like this is for simple people, just as they think working on the line at the Quick n Tasty in Ormond Beach, Florida, with Ralph Sawyer, as I did in college, is for simple people. But it's not. None of my friends could keep up with Ralph Sawyer. With his beefy forearms and giant torso, bulbous nose and porcine eyes, he looked like a lumbering dullard. But Ralph was quick on his feet, with defensive-tackle strength, and he kept a hundred dinners in his head, in sequence—including which five had no onions—and one night as he's shaking the grease off fifty pounds of hot fry baskets he says, without looking my way, "Get those snapper steaks out of the broiler." The broiler is on my side of the line. I'm supposed to know when they're done. How can he know that before I do? His end of the line is busier than mine, and he keeps his orders in his head—plus my orders? Eleven hours a day, six days a week, trying to keep up with Ralph. I got really good at my job, but even on the best days, when I got everything right and nailed one order after another for the entire dinner rush, like an athlete in the zone—even then I never got as good as Ralph Sawyer.

But as soon as I get good at something, boredom follows.

While scanning these acres of steel profiles, a new word boils up out of my mouth: carpentry.

≈ ≈ ≈

"Carpentry?" Grandpa Phil says. "What the hell do you know about carpentry?"

Well, nothing.

Carpentry seems impossible.

In our house, when I was growing up, Dad had a hammer. But he never used it. Changing a light bulb called for a family discussion. Do it now? Later? Wattage? Rotation direction? The discussion did not generally end in agreement.

Grandpa agrees that it was hard to get anything done at our house.

If it's possible, then why bother? Anyone can do what's possible.

So I buy a big, lavishly illustrated trade-school textbook entitled Carpentry.

But Grandpa Phil isn't buying any of it.

Grandpa puts his hand up like a cop in traffic and says just hold on a minute here. Carpentry?

So I start to explain. "Everything is wide open in The Work and the world, and all these new—"

"No. Wait a minute here," Grandpa repeats. "For a man like you, carpentry would make an admirable hobby. But hobbies must be secondary to your security in the world. And I do mean financial security." He pauses for a moment and says, "A favorite old folk proverb says it well: 'Wisdom begins with a roof.' I urge you to secure a roof before you indulge your fancier ruminations."

Grandpa doesn't seem to understand that, well, maybe this smorgasbord is my career.

But Grandpa says, "Consider that there is a lot you don't understand. I have told you that I had no native interest in being a furrier. But you might consider that doing the business of the world is worthy, and it doesn't really matter if you love the product or not, because engaging in the world is its own reward.

"In order to succeed, you must respond to the chaotic flow of events and be attuned to the vagaries of human nature. If worldly conditions and your decisions align, you will be rewarded for your good judgment with profits. You will find vitality in success."

And then he says, "Still, I remain most interested in your otherworldly pursuits. I trust that, before you are done, you will attend to worldly matters and earn worldly rewards as well. All beings must earn their place among the living, and those who cheat pay the price. Whether they know it or not."

≈ ≈ ≈

In any case, I'm doing this business with Jan, and I can't stop. Don't want to stop. I am happily addicted to all of it.

The Tasks become portable tool kits to pack in your central nervous system. So even though Jan rarely mentions not staring after that first time, I practice it all the time—the way a musician practices. Strumming the chords of perception. Do I do it every day? I don't know. But I do it enough to know that moving your eyes intentionally changes the moments.

The more direct impressions you dial into a unit of time, the longer that unit of time lasts. If you want to slow time, perceive more. Time is a function of impressions.

I hear Grandpa's voice. He repeats: *"Time is a function of impressions!"*

He repeats it again, and he makes it a question. *"Time is a function of impressions? Is that what Jan Cox said?"*

No, Jan never said that. Those words came from the practice. The practice of moving my eyes the way he told us to.

What if I could do this without Jan? Doing it on my own is what I always wanted.

My vow. The night before we met at Sam and Knoxie's house. My written vow, whispered in the wee hours, eye to eye with the mirror. I promised. I never wanted to be a lifer in any group.

So why can't I just do this? Why can't I apply all these bombastic recipes and crazy vectors and inhabit prisms of brilliant stopped time? Damn, I want to absorb all Jan's admonitions to remember everything and drop nothing—never break a glass—and determine to rise to his ongoing challenge: *"What if you could be as alive all the time as you are a little bit of the time?"*

So what am I waiting for? Why should I wait a whole week to devour—with relish—another of Jan's Tasks? Oh, I'll wrestle and have sex with anything he throws our way, but why wait for him? I should invent some of my own Tasks, whirl myself around the Ferris-wheel week with more centrifugal force. I'll make up my own stuff. I'll be my own dealer.

Jan spins these Tasks with ease and confidence, but I, too, have experience with this. I ought to be able to run with it. So I'll do it myself. I'll invent my own catapult.

But hmm, wait a second. It's not so easy to come up with something, something with raw joltage. Where creation meets control. An action widget that converts potential energy to kinetic energy.

What could do that? I'm squeezing my brain. Not coming up with much of anything.

Okay, then, something outrageous, just to shake up the old habitual self. But what's outrageous? That I can do?

So I think about the power in human relationships, the social contract, how strong that is, maybe like the strong force that binds subatomic particles. So how about breaking that contract with somebody I know? Just somebody ordinary.

Jan draws a clear line between the *extraordinary*—those of us pursuing this unnecessary Work—and the *ordinary*, which is everyone else. He says ordinary people do not experience real emotion, and because Jan says, "I'm never wrong," I accept this statement as truth, at face value.

The longer I try to invent my own Task, the angrier I get. Angry at myself. *Why can't I do this? I should be able to do this!* I feel the limits Jan often talks about, as if I'm locked in the federal pen. It's dark in here. Where is the light? Can I hurl a grappling hook over these walls to escape?

The power of the social contract comes to mind again—the glue that binds those knots. The name Jane Chadwick pops up. The nun, my former supervisor, my unlikely friend and kindred spirit. In this desperation to invent my own Task, I leap to the outrageous: I will tell Jane that I have a drinking problem. Yes. Outrageous. Scary. That is surely something I would not ordinarily do. As far from what I would normally do as, well, preaching the Gospel in a shabby city park. Without any further critical thought, I commit.

Later in the week, wearing wrinkled clothes and days of stubble to hide my robust good health, I walk into her office. She welcomes me with a grin, a laugh, and hug, and sings, "So good to see you! Thank you for this surprise! How *are* you?"

I swallow hard. Long pause. I feel sick over what I'm about to say. I know it's not right, but the words are already formed in my mouth, and they won't stop. The words fall out. I've been rehearsing them. "I've been drinking."

In slow motion, her smile dissolves into shock and disbelief and pain, but because Jane is a counselor she recovers professionally. Her spine straightens in the chair.

I dread what's coming next, whatever it is, because now it's done. The words can't be reeled in.

"Well. I'm so sorry. What are you prepared to do about it?"

The friendship is over. That fast. I'm a client now.

I feel awful. I tell her that I will stop drinking just to get out of there because I can't fix what I broke. I can't tell her that I don't have a drinking problem, that this was a misbegotten Task, that I still want to be friends and that I will cherish her forever, especially now that I have ruined it . . . it all now sounds like a bunch of garbage even to me, so what in hell would it sound like to her?

≈ ≈ ≈

I slink away from the clinic like a shamed priest. Sit in the car. Spent. Queasy. The opposite of what is supposed to happen. Which does happen in every Task of Jan's. The unfolding of the worlds. Falling walls. Acceleration. Gathering in. And expanding out.

Now I just feel like crap.

Disgusted that I wrecked a friendship. So stupid. You call this extraordinary? I'm an ass. What an ass.

And I'm disgusted that Jan was wrong. First time wrong. Big wrong. As obvious as sunshine: ordinary people *do* have emotions. I don't care what Jan says, she and I just exchanged a large charge, for better or for worse—well, all worse, for sure—and if you tell me that wasn't real emotion then you don't know what real emotion is.

But goddamn, forget that, true as it may be. It's a bullshit complaint compared to the mess I made of a seriously attempted

Task . . . Shit, you call that a *Task*? I call that a mess, made by an idiot who's a lot dumber than I ever imagined. I sit there and cringe. I'm supposed to be better—wiser—than this.

Jan's Tasks always hit the mark. I am freshly appreciative, and jealous, of these nifty elegant potent aerodynamic arrows Jan draws from his quiver week in and week out. He supplies the arrows. If we draw and shoot them, they will hit the mark.

Shit. I can't make arrows like that. I'm sticking with him for a while.

≈ ≈ ≈

My well-worn copy of Orage's *On Love* sits on the bookshelf. I feel affection for it, the affection you feel for an old scrapbook or a song that changed your life thirty changes ago.

Not that I have mastered the practice of conscious love. But Madeleine and I are together, and close. We have a garden in the country and a big-chested handsome German shepherd "son" named Zulu, after the rancher I worked for when we were in Israel.

But the focus has changed. Our shared experience is now all these amazing revelatory forays into corners of rooms you never knew existed, and ultimately, such experience is not really shared. It is private by nature, and the inherent privacy is sharpened by Jan's rules: don't talk about it. Talking bleeds energy from consciousness.

She takes acting classes.

Her posture changes.

She dresses differently.

One night, Jan asks Madeleine and me to meet him in the

bar of the old Parisian-inspired Georgian Terrace Hotel, at the corner of Peachtree and Ponce de Leon, and the place to see and be seen for fifty years. Right across the street from the Moorish fantasy known as the Fabulous Fox Theater, Atlanta's premier architectural treasure. But the old Georgian Terrace is a relic now, not a place we would ever imagine going. The doorman tries to gesture grandly, but it's all he can do to open the door. Looks like he's been there since opening day, in 1911. A jagged crack slices the intricate lobby floor mosaic. Latin music pours from the bar. Feels like a slice of crumbling old Havana right here on Peachtree Street.

Jan is already on his second beer. Monday night. We're the only ones there. Maybe a crowd will show up later. But who cares? The five piece group plays with abandon, as if Jan has arranged a private concert. He doesn't say anything. Madeleine keeps the beat with her hips. Jan tilts his head at us. We get the message: "Dance."

Dancing is not my best sport. Trying harder doesn't help. I'm stiff as a robot.

Madeleine liquefies the claves and brass.

After a few minutes, Jan motions us to him and pulls me in close. He pours words right into my ear, as if to bypass mentation and mainline the message. His attention is saturated, like a primary pigment, and I dote on it. He says stop moving your head to the music. Don't listen with your head. Find the beat with your hips. Jan's hips rotate subtly, right on the syncopation. The horn section throws in some accents, and for a second it seems easy.

Out on the dance floor again, Madeleine pours around the floor, seamless with the sassy band. I am actually, um, dancing to the beat in a new way. I'm not what anyone would call *good*, but I'm doing it like I never have before. "But I'd rather be playing football," I whisper to myself and laugh out loud. The laughing helps. I'm laughing in my butt to the music, and it helps.

The band takes a break. The three of us sip our beers and speculate about the ghosts lurking in this ornate old ballroom. I ask them, "You think Tallulah Bankhead did something here in this room to get a highway named after her?" They laugh. Bankhead Highway runs west from downtown into a rough neighborhood.

With no warm-up notes, no tuning, the band resumes full speed ahead and steamrolls our banter.

With his eyes, Jan draws Madeleine onto the dance floor.

Oh, no. Here we go again. The two of them dancing.

But I like watching them. She's completely, harmonically enmeshed, as she never is in social situations. She shines in her element. And Jan finds the deepest, slowest part of the beat, which I can't hear until his gyrations point it up.

But oh, shit. Here we go again. My little reverie is shattered when they're all wrapped up, hips glued together. If they were strangers, I'd love watching them. But they're not, and I don't. I hate it. Hate it. I don't give a shit if Jan is trying to teach me a lesson or test my limits or keep me off guard the way he always keeps everyone off guard or if he's just trying to make me squirm, which I am. So what's he trying to do? That's easy: he's trying to fuck her. He makes a big deal out of group rules forbidding casual sex between any of us. But what about him? He always says, "Don't get involved with me personally." Well, all right, then don't get involved with me personally, either. Because sex with Madeleine is exactly where this is rolling between the two of them, and I would call that getting involved personally. With both of us.

Abruptly, while the band jams on, Jan stops dancing. He walks straight to the table. I'm getting ready for whatever is coming. He walks up, grabs his beer, chugs what's left, and stomps out, his face twisted with an Elvis Presley scowl.

What the hell? Mr. Omniscient, who admonishes us to "be of good cheer," is now pissed off—over what? Pissed at me, because I don't him want to fuck her? At life, because he can't take her with him right this second? What the hell?

Madeleine and I ride home to Alpharetta in silence.

1974

"Charisma?" I ask Grandpa when he asks me about Jan's charisma.

I never wondered about Jan's charisma before.

I guess Grandpa is wondering why a guy would put up with him. Jan must have some powerful magnetism, no?

This multifaceted process Jan orchestrates keeps poking me in places I'd never know to poke. The bracing challenges keep coming. I ride a tide that keeps rising, and these moments of arrest and wonder and surprise arise with increasing frequency, and when Jan talks on meeting nights he always delivers. He's on his game. He speaks fluently on a wide range of subjects, from sports to music to business to astrophysics to hard-boiled insight into human attention. He speaks without notes or hand gestures but with simmering passion and weaves together eclectic threads in giant run-on sentences that loop back to the original idea after double digressions lasting twenty minutes, and it all culminates after about an hour of bobbing and weaving in a splendidly constructive combination punch that lands square in your brain. I guess all that adds up to a form of charisma.

And oh, yeah: he's sacrilegious. And he has a biting sense of humor.

But let's be clear: a lot of people find him not only without charisma but also actually repellent. A lot of people don't like him on sight.

This becomes wildly obvious when, at Jan's direction, we all break into smaller groups of six or eight so we can invite new people into the process. Jan doesn't say so directly, but it seems obvious: it forces each person to engage, which would not happen if all forty-odd of us worked on one presentation.

Jan says, "This Work group is growing, and like anything else in the universe, from Andromeda to General Motors to the corner saloon, you're either growing or dying. There is no stasis anywhere. And because this group is growing, it needs new blood, in the form of conscious effort. Such efforts are the lifeblood of a real Work group. Conscious effort is the only food we have here."

"Some will show up, listen to you people, and think this is wonderful—until they meet me. Some will then disappear immediately. Some will become a part of this for a little while and leave. This is all exactly as it should be. And some will stay and benefit, maybe even more than some of you. And then some of you will leave. All the parts of the process, including all the parts you consider extraneous or disturbing, are absolutely necessary."

Jan specifies that we must refrain from mentioning his name, his words, The Work, and Gurdjieff. Speak from your own experience, he says. Don't lie. Talk about what you understand.

These rules make sense to me. If the whole thing is going to grow organically, then it should build on our own understanding rather than on parroted repetitions of someone else's declarations.

The spirit of the Sixties is still rampant, so people are still openly looking for *something*. The small group I'm in gets permission to use a free meeting room at the Unity Church on South Ponce de Leon.

We get a handbill printed on startling, heavy orange stock. Judith the artist draws a logo. An eagle in flight, wings forming a sphere into which the eagle is flying. Below the image, a question: "Do you envy the freedom of the eagle?"

The rest of the page is empty startling orange stock. You have to turn it over: "Flight instructions available for the Few."

And a time, date, and place.

We pass out the handbills at movie theaters, the student centers at Georgia Tech, Georgia State, and Emory, and on Tenth Street, between Piedmont Park and Peachtree Street, where some of the hippies still hang out. We post them at health food stores and bookstores and anywhere else we can think of.

The first night, people do show up to hear what we have to say, about fifteen of them. During the weeks that follow, sometimes twenty or more show up regularly.

Based on our own experiences, we tell them what it's not: a place of refuge and comfort. You won't find palliatives like *God is within you* and *We need to be nice to ourselves so we can be nice to each other*.

Instead it's for those who function well enough in life but itch because *this isn't enough*. It's for those who find benefit in constructive irritation, which fosters the growth and expansion a few people need. The kind of growth that is unnecessary for people in general but crucial for the Hungry Few.

Without talking about myself directly, I describe the shock and benefits of my life-altering crew cut.

I tell them that time is a function of impressions and that, among other things, this path provides the tools for expanding your ingestion of impressions. And fresh, new impressions provide the nourishment on which consciousness grows. As a by-product, your sense of time, your experience of time, expands.

New ways to say it pop up as I wonder what to say:

You don't want to just spend the rest of life just *you-ing*, do you? Just being *you* all the time for a lifetime? Doesn't that get stale after a few decades?

If you'd rather laugh at yourself than explain yourself, then yeah, you might want to see where all this leads.

This is where opposites, such as freedom and responsibility, meet. Silly and sublime. Effort and effortless.

All this resides beyond pure reason and forms a more startling life.

Between fifteen and thirty people show up to hear what we have to say, every Tuesday, week after week.

And then, after more than a month, everyone is invited to meet "the guy behind all this."

So most of these new invitees show up, and the entire group itself shows up. The room hums with expectation. Time to meet the Man.

Jan lumbers to the podium wearing sharply creased polyester slacks. Cowboy boots broadcast his large strides and heavy footfalls. A wild paisley polyester shirt opens to his big belly. He is not smiling.

A couple of the new people leave immediately, before he says a word.

He says this is not for everyone. With a different delivery, and a gesture toward those leaving, it could have been a punch line. But his face is stone, and nobody's laughing. He continues: this is for the Few. The Few who can't scratch the itch and sate the hunger.

He doesn't say the hunger for what. Either you're hungry or you don't get it.

As three more people leave, I see Jan through their eyes. They've been listening to us for a month or so. We have been reasonable, respectful, and in a general sense, one of them. Jan's the opposite and more. He's brusque, cold, and clearly not one of them. His appearance is garish and confrontational. His face is thinner than it was when I first met him, as "Dr. Cox," and with his large hooked nose and burning eyes, he looks like a raptor. A raptor seeking prey.

Jan embodies the opposite of the qualities anyone would ascribe to a guru and teacher.

Attention darts around the room.

He persists in the same solemn mien, speaking with a certainty that's counter to the relativistic spirit of the times, and you can see by all the furrowed brows that those who remain are grappling with what he's saying, what he's not saying, the way all his contained energy simmers, and the way he ties apparently disparate thoughts into a bombastic whole.

The mind sees no limits because it is the limits.

Learn to think without using examples.

You can stop all thought for short periods of time.

No system can be aware of itself at its own level.

Fake it until you can make it.

You are not what you think.

If you knew where to find it, you wouldn't be here listening to me.

Everything causes everything else and will continue to do so.

The Work does not need you. The question is: how badly do you need The Work?

Well over half the people stay. They listen for all they're worth.

And about half of the remaining half wind up in the group, so the complexity and richness of the group expands exponentially. Yeah, the organism is growing.

Among the new members are some women I can't stop looking at and some near-genius recent graduates of Georgia Tech. Perry is a whiz at physics, lives in an old farmhouse in southern DeKalb County, and is framing houses. His girlfriend, Marlene, can reframe a room with her singing, plus she has an easy way with a hammer and works with him when she wants to. And let's face it, with legs like that, she could work at any job site in the country. Ted is six foot eight, moves like a giraffe, knows a lot about everything, but won't tell you much. Dustin and Dale starred on the wrestling team and write computer code before most of us know what the words mean.

And then there's Lon Flack.

Judith the artist brings her friend Tricia the artist, who brings her boyfriend, Lon Flack. Lon and Tricia make quite a couple. Tricia looks like Angie Dickinson, and Lon is Mr. America. They drive up to the Unity Temple in Lon's green Cadillac. Someone says the car is money green, and the name sticks. He was a football standout at Florida, invited for a tryout with the Dallas Cowboys. Lon and I hit it off, and he says he turned them down. Turned down the Cowboys? Lon says he knew he was good, but he wasn't good enough to dominate in the NFL. "If you're not a star in the NFL, you're just getting the shit kicked outta ya by huge sadists," Lon says. "What would I want to do that for?" He lets it be known that he's making piles of money in real estate. He's older than the rest of the new people. Well over thirty. Maybe about Jan's age. You wouldn't expect a guy like this to keep coming back for more. But he does.

So does Jan have charisma?

Don't know if I would put it that way. He certainly doesn't appeal to anyone looking for a soothing, wise, all-welcoming holy man. He scares the crap out of those people. But for some of us, he's like Miles Davis, twisting tunes inside your mind and your mind inside your tunes. His abrasive persona hovers like a growling sentry. You have to make some effort to get past the gate.

Some nights when Jan is talking, it seems he's barely in control. While standing still. No gyrations, but his eyes are glass planets. The energy spits out of him. Like a guy blowing his horn so hard you wonder if he'll come undone.

But he stays on key.

Jan never loses control, and the words always, impossibly, come full circle.

One night, the last thing he says is: "Where is a tree's brain?"

≈ ≈ ≈

"Where is a tree's brain!" Grandpa repeats.

I can't tell if he likes it or not.

He pauses, then continues, "That's a question I never pondered. I wish the rabbis would ask questions like that."

Whew. I'm really glad Grandpa likes it. Because I'm glad when he likes any of this stuff.

≈ ≈ ≈

"Where is a tree's brain?" instantly becomes another of my favorites. It reminds me of Jan's question "What's the first word in the dictionary?" Because "Where is a tree's brain?" elicits brand-new insight: *A tree's brain is the tree.* A tree has no separate brain. Just as *we are our brains.* We all identify lines of separation. But they do not really exist as we imagine. This is a plump thought.

I am feeling my newfound, um, *arboreality.*

Words can change the equations, quake your topography.

≈ ≈ ≈

Grandpa says, "I love Judaism. But sometimes I wish the rabbis would put the Torah down. It's always the frame of reference for everything. Well, I suppose that focus on the holy text is common to all established religions. But I do find it refreshing, by contrast, that these shenanigans you're engaged with seem to actually use life itself as a frame of reference. Life becomes a holy text, so to speak."

As if I am a tree, I repeat to Grandpa, "Everything is happening at once."

Because "Everything is happening at once" is another packet of words that bumps me up a level or two.

Then Grandpa surprises me with a question. "By the way, does Jan Cox have a job?"

I tell him what I know. "Well, it's kinda crazy. Nobody talks about it directly most of the time, because Jan pretty much follows his own rule and doesn't talk about himself. But stuff comes out at parties. The booze makes Jan warmer, funnier, looser—as long as he avoids the seesaw between sex and rage.

"He owned a record store for a time. He has an encyclopedic knowledge of American music. In addition to blues guitar, Jan plays a wild piano, like Jerry Lee Lewis. He played in honky-tonk bands for a while. Anyhow, I think he sold the record store. Then, believe it or not, during the year I was in Israel, he ran for governor of Georgia against Jimmy Carter. He wasn't doing it to win and knew he had no chance. He did it for his own reasons, so he wasn't beholden to anyone. He spoke his mind. Ran an unconventional race, to say the least. The press loved him because he was a candidate with a brain, plus he outdrank all the reporters at Manuel's Tavern. Carter came to like him, too, and Carter wrote the introduction to Jan's book, Magnus Machina. *Self-published. Carter came to regret the association. Later, Jan went to law school and passed the bar."*

Grandpa throws up his hands and says, "Oy vey."

≈ ≈ ≈

I read the tools chapter of *Carpentry* and go downtown to the supply house where all the union carpenters shop, on an industrial stretch of Courtland Street, and buy all the basics listed in the book.

My new leather apron overflows with shiny new tools. A tri-square. A framing square. A plumb bob. A chalk box. I value the way each tool is made and want to be worthy of each. A block plane. An awl. A framing hammer and a finish hammer. A cat's claw. The way a musician admires a new instrument. The leather smells like hay threshing in the soft hot Galilee breeze.

The shopping spree is expensive. About a week's wages at State Road Steel. So I have to make something of all this. But I hardly know what to do with these shiny sharp instruments or even how to hold them.

I study the fat, lavishly detailed and illustrated *Carpentry*.

In the old barn at the Holbrook place, where Madeleine and I are living in Alpharetta, I scavenge a pile of tongue-and-groove oak.

I meet with James from the group. Now that he's licensed, he's starting his own architecture firm. I tell him about the oak. He grew up building things. He understands the impulse. And he knows I'm doing it because I can't do it, and because we share an Aim, and because we have become friends. We meet at his drawing board. He says what do you like, what do you need?

Well, I don't have a dining room table.

James nods. A guy should have a dining table.

I tell him I like the golden rectangle.

I love the way he unfurls the roll of tracing paper, like he's spinning a rolling pin across the drafting table. With elegant, minimal flourishes of his mechanical pencil, he anchors the conversation.

On the tracing paper, a table appears, following the proportions of the golden mean, 1:1.618. It's almost four feet wide. That's one wide dining room table. James says you'll have trouble wrestling it through doorways and stairwells. You could make it shorter, keep the ratio, and it'll be easier to handle. But I like the length—almost six feet—and the shape is irresistible. And I can wrestle pretty well. James says well, okay then, you're using floorboards for the top. How about stair nosing for the rails? And butted pairs of stair nosing for legs, mitered into the rails . . . yes.

His hands are talking to the paper. The lines on the paper talk to my eyes. A table starts to take form. Amazing. That looks great.

I get to work, culling the oak first and using a fat plywood substrate as the template of right-angle rectitude. The living room of the old farmhouse becomes my shop. Madeleine tries to believe that a dining room table will emerge from all this mess. But you can't get to the bedroom without padding through sawdust.

I struggle almost daily with lumber that is not a table, not anything.

≈ ≈ ≈

The Tasks keep on coming.

"Subscribe to a magazine you would never normally choose, one that's outside your interests."

At the magazine rack in my favorite bookstore, it takes about eight seconds to find exactly what I don't want to find: *Fortune* magazine. The journal of Big Business. How corporate titans fight for the corporation, humanity be damned. The Fortune 500. The rich guys who manufacture Agent Orange and DDT. And shit, I promised myself that I would actually read the damn thing. I'm dreading it. But guess what? The magazine arrives, and to my amazement, it's interesting and intelligent. I get it. Business is about growth. You measure growth with money. And business is about solving problems and seizing opportunities. Plus, money is good to have. It's widely accepted. I wouldn't mind having more of it. Grandpa would heartily approve.

One week Jan says, "Everyone eat a hamburger."

Madeleine and I go eat a hamburger. She's been a vegetarian most of the time we've been together.

The next week he says, "Quit eating meat."

Jan never rescinds the rule to "quit eating meat." So we're all vegetarians.

Jan says you don't know what a puny cage you rut around in all the time until you pop out for even a moment. Look at actors, he says. They are not aspiring to do what you are attempting here in The Work, yet they routinely adopt new personas in the practice of their art. Yet you, all of you who say you want to do the unnecessary, remain trapped in the coop of your own personalities—while an escape to freedom is actually quite easy. But you hardly even try. Don't you find that interesting? Don't you find that disturbing?

He announces a Task. "This week, go somewhere, anywhere, out in ordinary life—a restaurant, city hall, the library, a car dealership, a plumbing supply house—or take a city bus ride and act like, say, an accountant from Brazil. Put on your best cheesy Upper Amazon accent—trust me: no one will know a good Upper Amazon accent from a crappy one—and blab about being on your way to an interview with the *Atlanta Journal*. Ask directions to the newspaper building, then start complaining about American beer."

Everyone's laughing.

He continues, "I'm just making this up as I go along, so you will make up whatever seems preposterous to you on the spur of the moment. Just go out there, and just completely become somebody else for a few minutes, somebody you would never believe yourself to be, while interacting in the most common of circumstances. Circumstances that would be common if someone else were doing it but preposterous to your ordinary self. Just do it, keep your eyes open, and see what you can see."

So while fighting waves of fear, I stroll into the Mercedes-Benz dealership on Pharr Road in Buckhead, the country-club-bish, old money side of town. The salesman welcomes me to the dealership and asks if he may help me.

"Ah," I announce in a sorta-French accent. "Peerhops, yes. I need beet of asseestahns."

I explain that I am a member of the Belgian royal family, here to study America so I may better serve my own country when I am called to do so. He nods and affirms that he, too, appreciates international relations.

"Peerhops you notice I dress as Americain," I say with a ha-ha-ha. "Thees ees fomilee . . . eh . . . how you say . . . fomilee koostom. We, when een America, look like Americain, yes?"

The salesman has never met anyone from the Belgian royal family before, and he is honored to have the opportunity now. He also wants to know if I might be interested in any particular model.

"Ah, of course, of course. I am quite fahmeel-yar weeth awl mo-del. I do prayfair zee cabriolet. How you say zees?"

He helps me out with "convertible."

"Yes, I am interested in zee *co-vair-tah-bluh*."

Actually, I am relieved that we are getting along. And I'm relieved that he can't tell I'm a complete fraud. I'm also surprised at how much fun it is to be addressed as the Duke of Belgium. He says we have a new 450SL on the lot. Why don't we take it for a spin?

"Speen," I say to him. "What ees 'take for speen?'"

He explains that this means drive the car.

Ah, yes, I comprehend now, but this will not be necessary, since of course I am quite familiar with zees car. You know, zee Autobahn. So very queek, yet so see-vilized, ha-ha.

The truth is I have never driven one and would definitely like to take the new 450 for a spin with the top down, but I'm not sure I can hold on as the Duke of Belgium for twenty more minutes because I'm about to explode right now from all the energy billowing through my entire body, the entire showroom, and the entire universe.

As I leave the Mercedes showroom the sky shines like porcelain, and the clouds—well, I just really like them.

A delirious happiness. From pretending to be the Duke of Belgium.

It's not about a joke at the expense of a salesman. It's about exposing the joke of your own limits—and how much energy from the universe resides untapped right there on the other side of "you." I get more out of a phony conversation with a car salesman than I do by talking to Jan. That's funny. More from a bogus conversation with a car salesman than from talking to the guy who knows enough to point me past the disappearing limits.

≈ ≈ ≈

The next week the Task is, "Adopt a tree. This is a solitary Task, so choose a tree you can visit on your own and get to know it privately. Revisit regularly. Learn from your tree."

Instantly I know my tree. It's a monster poplar growing near the creek deep in the Lullwater Preserve, a lush stand of old growth timber hidden in plain sight on the Emory University campus. The photo I took of it is hanging in Mom and Dad's foyer.

I haven't been to the tree in years, maybe not since I took the picture in college. But I know right where it is. I like that it's hard to get to. You have to cross the old mill creek on a fallen log.

So quiet in these woods. The din of the city melts away. Down the path. And there it is. The crown fans out, branches stretch for sun. Up close, the massive trunk, solid as a big building. It thrives on the rugged creekside slope in the topsoil made of its fallen ancestors.

As we humans grow in the humus of those who precede us. Everything keeps happening at once.

≈ ≈ ≈

The pile of oak in the living room becomes a tabletop, now turned facedown on the floor, and during the painstaking process of fashioning and attaching the rails and legs, the whole thing still fails to resemble a table. Step by careful step, weeks and weeks of this-is-never-going-to-be-a-table, until one day Byron comes out to the farmhouse to help me turn it over. It's heavy. We lift it off the floor, slowly rotate it, and gently ease the legs onto the floor. And, damn, there it is, a broad-beamed dining room table. James was right. This is one wide table. Can we squeeze it into the kitchen? We wrestle it sideways through the doorway, set it up in the farmhouse kitchen, and wow. It dominates. We pull up chairs and open bottles. It makes the beer taste better than beer. We hold block plane shavings up to the afternoon sun and trace the swirls of tree time.

The next week, as born-again vegetarians, Madeleine and I are enjoying platters of rice and beans and greens at our substantial amazing new dining table, and I say, "The table makes everything taste better."

She nods.

I ask, "But what's with the hamburger? Why would Jan tell everyone to go eat a hamburger if we're just going to—"

She says, "Makes sense to me. It's so we won't adopt the holier-than-thou attitude that usually comes with being a vegetarian. So you eat a hamburger. Big deal. It's not going to kill your cosmic potential."

Madeleine can be chilly and brusque, but I get what she means. In the language of Gurdjieff, it's called getting identified. Being identified is the sticky goo of consciousness. Being identified with not eating a hamburger eats up a lot more brain space than just eating a damn hamburger.

The table: I'm a carpenter now. I can use these tools.

≈ ≈ ≈

Madeleine and I decide to get married. We've been living together for four years. It's not the length of time that binds us, though. These myriad experiences bind, ranging from college graduation to awed moments at Poet's Corner in Westminster Abbey to Christmas with the Golfarellis to a sojourn on a cattle ranch in Israel. And now we are intimate partners on this rigorous, private path and nothing can stop us. So it seems natural and strong and right that we embrace the next step to solidify our common commitment to the goal: marriage.

When we tell Jan, he registers surprise and looks away for just an instant to gather himself, and this surprises me because I wonder what he might have to gather, but the blip lasts only a second and he quickly gives our marriage his blessing.

The hope and promise of conscious love are born again, and I hold the goal close and quiet.

Since The Work is the focal point of our lives, the wedding is not a big life-consuming deal as it is for many couples. We plan a small gathering in the back yard of her parents' home in Ft. Lauderdale, and we manage to finesse the awkwardness of Reverend Dad's daughter marrying into this Jewish family of mine.

≈ ≈ ≈

The whole region is booming. You don't need to read the want ads. You just drive around and find a job site.

You find somebody to shout at and shout WHO'S THE BOSS?

Then you find the guy that guy pointed at and shout NEED HELP?

And that guy shouts GOT TOOLS?

You shout YUP.

Then that guy shouts WHEN CAN YOU START?

And you shout HOW ABOUT NOW?

I hire on with Purcell Peeler. He says call me Peeler. He's got a laborer working for him. He sees my big leather belt full of tools and figures I'm a real carpenter. The house is framed, and he says why dontcha go hang these doors. I don't tell him I've never hung a door before. But I got a pretty good picture of how to do it from the book. So I get set up with my four-foot level, or plumb stick, as they call it out here, an awl, some shims, and am about to set the first screw when Peeler says, "Lemme in there." Maybe I'm not fast enough for Peeler. He pulls eightpenny framing nails out of his apron and just pounds the hinges into the jamb. You can't secure hinges with nails. Jesus, Peeler. The nails are going to work loose when you swing the door over time. Maybe I don't know that much about carpentry, but I know a scam. Peeler is a quack. While he's whaling away on the hinges, I grab my level, load up my tool belt, and get out of there, quick. I don't think he even saw me leave.

The next day I hire on with Colson Hendrix. He's got a real crew. They come in from Dawson County every morning. From Dawson to northern Fulton might be just twenty miles, but these are mountain men on the creeping edge of the metropolis. Colson is the opposite of Peeler. He commands respect because he knows what to do now and what to do next, with that rare combination of perfect posture and ease with his place in the world.

He puts me on soffit and cornice with Beuler. Not sure if that's a first name or last name. Beuler wears a cloth nail apron. All he's got on him is a finishing hammer and soffit nails. Sees my big leather apron and probably figures I gotta be a *real carpenter*. But damn. He drives nails straight up through the soffit plywood into the barge rafters twice as fast and twice as neatly as I can. Tap, tap, tap, and his nail is perfectly sunk. I'm a ditz next to Beuler. Working three times as hard, accomplishing half as much. Plus my arms are exhausted. But I keep doing it.

On payday Colson hands me my check and says you work real good, we want you to stay on the crew. But I can't pay you more than Beuler.

I say all right, that's fair.

I'm gonna come back and get as good as Beuler.

≈ ≈ ≈

Congruity. It all fits together. Everything feeds everything.

One night after a meeting, as I'm talking to Lon Flack about his latest moves in real estate, some of my Task-germinated *Fortune* magazine jargon enters the conversation. Payout, payback. Return on investment. Risk and reward. I am curious after reading *Fortune* and contemplating Grandpa Phil's career in business. I see Grandpa out there in St. Louis, where the carloads of pelts are his real estate. It's a high-stakes game. Except it's not a game at all. I'm asking Lon as if I'm asking Grandpa, "How can you tell when a market is overstimulated?" Lon can tell I'm not a businessman. Not pretending that I am. But he likes my curiosity.

He says I might have a job for you.

On Monday I'm visiting his office at Perimeter Center East. This is the new generation of office space, in what they call office parks. I have never been in an office park. Where's the park? Unless you mean office parking *lot*. Because asphalt acres surround these lonely shiny boxes.

Inside the boxes are lobbies too big for their own good. Like I'm supposed to say wow, heck of a lobby, Lon!

And windows that can't open? Who thought that was a good idea?

I feel like an emigrant from a moldy past, grumbling about new smells.

Lon explains bird-dogging, which is my job. I go find deals. That's when Lon buys something I find, something he can resell to investors.

He explains what he's looking for—acreage on some of the TVA lakes in middle Tennessee—how to find it, and how much money I'll make. It's multiples of what you get trying to keep up with Beuler banging nails.

Colson Hendrix wishes me well and shakes my hand while Beuler says with a grin, "Come back when ya learn yourself how to drive a nail, why dontcha?"

The next Monday I follow I-75 to Chattanooga, then up to Dunlap and get on Tennessee State Route 111, a skinny ancient lumpy two-lane built before bulldozers. It hugs the ripples of the land, so for a hundred miles you climb the crests and surf the troughs of a green sea in the grip of a Force 10 geologic gale. All the way to Sparta, and then down the road to Smithville, the village-sized county seat.

I sift through the tax maps in the county courthouse. The guy at the courthouse helps me locate properties on Center Hill Lake and shows me how to get the owners' names. I call them on the phone.

Somehow I figure out that success depends on the pacing of the conversation. You let them set the tempo.

"Hello, is that Mr. Russell?"

"Well, yeah, I s'pose it is."

"Hey, Mr. Russell."

I tell him my name.

"Uh-huh."

"Well, it looks like you got some back acres down there on Center Hill Lake."

And he says, "Yep, I reckon we got some lakefront down there."

And I say, "Yep, I thought you might."

And nobody says anything.

And after several beats, I say, "Well, I might want to ask you about the acres down there by the lake."

And he says, "Well, all right, then."

Which means you might oughta come on out here so's we can talk about them acres.

Turns out I'm really good at dealing with backwoods locals like F. D. Russell and his wife, Frances. They're from Grandpa's generation. But they've lived an opposite life. Born in these hills and hollers, been here the whole time. Vertical farming with a pair of mules.

F. D. and Frances spend the down payment on their inaccessible back acres for indoor plumbing.

1975

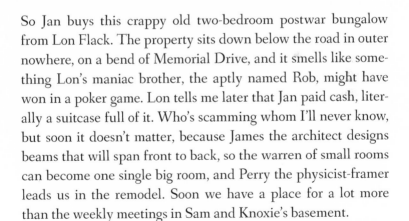

So Jan buys this crappy old two-bedroom postwar bungalow from Lon Flack. The property sits down below the road in outer nowhere, on a bend of Memorial Drive, and it smells like something Lon's maniac brother, the aptly named Rob, might have won in a poker game. Lon tells me later that Jan paid cash, literally a suitcase full of it. Who's scamming whom I'll never know, but soon it doesn't matter, because James the architect designs beams that will span front to back, so the warren of small rooms can become one single big room, and Perry the physicist-framer leads us in the remodel. Soon we have a place for a lot more than the weekly meetings in Sam and Knoxie's basement.

So from now on, when Jan is done talking, instead of some quiet conversation before everyone disperses, a snare drum appears on the stage we built in the huge main room. Jan dispatches a compelling staccato beat while others back him up on congas, bongos, claves, and a cowbell. The rest of the group, now more than forty of us, forms a circle, keeps the beat with clapping or jumping, and one at a time we leap into the center, whirling and gyrating. A tree's brain is its legs. Feels like flying sometimes. Euphoric.

Feet in all worlds.

After the dancing, cases of beer appear, and the weekly afterparty bangs with a tribal vibe.

Feet tapping in all worlds.

Jan introduces a set of yoga exercises—pointedly called Running the Numbers, not yoga—which are to be done every day, preferably in the morning. The sequence starts with a headstand. Good morning, upside-down world. The sequence proceeds to bend your spine. First concave. Then convex. Seven positions in all. Twenty minutes later, you're a different, looser, cooler, better you.

≈ ≈ ≈

A few months later, Jan selects only a few of us, one at a time, for "shutting down." The instructions are typed:

Pick a day in the middle of the week and arrange your schedule so you can willfully spend twenty-four hours alone in the house on Memorial, no contact with anyone, starting at 10:00 a.m. No food. Water only. No other stimuli or any connection with the ordinary world. Do not go outside. Do not bring any writing material or any reading material. Some books will be there if you are so inclined. Sleep as much as you want, but every hour you're awake, chase Dorka for twelve minutes at the top of every hour. Keep your eyes open, and see what you can see.

Chasing Dorka is one of Jan's very specific forms of meditation: in the classic Buddha sitting position, cross-legged, head and spine erect, and wrists on knees, you recite twelve pairs of syllables that sound Arabic, starting with *Ash-Raf.* The tempo is your heartbeat. On the first beat, you picture *Ash* on your left eyebrow; on the next heartbeat, *Raf* on your right eyebrow, and so on through the syllables, until you get to *Dorka,* at which point your head drops and your mind maintains nothing for as long as your mind can maintain nothing and then—whenever "then" is—you lift your head upright and start again from *Ash-Raf.* Through the cycles. For twelve minutes. At the top of every hour.

I get settled in on my weekday of shutting down. Looking around. This space is usually packed with people. Quiet and empty now. Not a natural place for solitude on a workday morning, and even though you want to like it and want to feel uplifted by monastic moments, you don't. It just feels weird, and nothing happens.

But if I had wanted "natural" places to be on a weekday morning, I never would have taken up with Jan in the first place.

No furniture in here. Sitting on the floor, looking around, up at the ceiling, where we installed the skylight. Looking down at the floor.

Shag carpeting. Why did Jan pick shag carpeting? Reminds me of Judith the artist saying, "His bad taste is really a challenge for me."

Then I picture Jan's black Cadillac Eldorado clad in shag carpeting, like a giant dreadlocked hog. As if it weren't cartoonish enough already, with its six-foot-long hood and plush white bucket seats designed for elephant butts.

I turn to the reading material.

A copy of *The Conference of the Birds,* a Sufi parable from Persia about how only a few of the flock of seekers succeed on their flight to Paradise.

And *The Way of a Pilgrim*, the Russian fable about a religious seeker who relinquished everything in order to focus on praying continuously and how devotion to this practice transformed his life.

And a copy of a book Jan made by hand. I remember seeing it when I attended those few meetings at the Miller Building, when I first joined the group. It's a menagerie of mimeographed pages, and the words "vanity press" pop into my head. I laugh out loud for a second, because this mess of pages would have benefited from a dose of vanity. But I thumb the pages and am fascinated. They're packed with mandalas and diagrams of hierarchies of intelligence and magazine collages and Jan's eccentric penmanship. And those upper-case *I*'s that he dots. I still hate a big *I* with a dot over it, and I'll hate it again after enlightenment, too. The dot sticks up above the whole line and looks stupid. Stupid, like arranging books by height instead of by subject.

But the handmade book, as I flip through it, broadcasts exuberance. The graphics and the free-form, happy mysticism of these pages predate Jan's heavy-handed rules and the solemn exclusivity of his whole presentation. No ordinary versus extraordinary in here. It's all about the big bang, raw energy, transcendent unity, and, yes, sheer exuberance. The pile of pages telegraphs some kind of original ecstasy he must have experienced in a seminal flash.

Exuberance. Maybe exuberance is one of the ancient Greek humors, the substances that comprise the human body. I'll call this humor the *exubatron*. It is the unidentified subatomic particle of higher consciousness.

I break out my against-the-rules pen and paper and write *exubatron*. I like the way it looks on the page, the way it feels in my veins.

Whoa—it's almost the top of the hour. *Chase Dorka for twelve minutes at the top of the hour.*

Assume the sitting position. Back straight and hands just so on my knees.

Yes. This is good.

Scrolling across my mind: *be still and everything changes*.

I'm nodding.

I break the rules again. Write it down.

And then, between beats of the Dorka chase, a perfectly pedestrian phrase rises on the seesaw of attention: *nothing is happening*.

Nothing is happening. Yes! Nothing is happening! Finally, nothing . . .

Nothing is happening: it's the opposite of *everything is happening at once*.

And they are both true.

This is only the second hour.

Time to inhale.

Plenty of time, too, for nothing. But nothing takes a lot of time, doesn't it? Who knew? Nothing is so time-consuming! Now I have no time for anything! A grin on my face. I feel my body laughing. And those words that fell out of my life-changing haircut reappear: nothing changes everything.

As far as I know, I never would have *shut down* if not for Jan.

≈ ≈ ≈

One particular Friday meeting night, following a long week in Tennessee, I carouse at the afterparty until around midnight, then I tell Madeleine I'm going home. Her car is at the party. She says see you in a little while.

It's about thirty miles from Memorial Drive to our dark and

quiet Alpharetta farmhouse. Way out past the metropolis.

Every time I return there: *Ahh.* Our bedroom, with windows on three sides, my side facing the pasture. Head on the pillow.

Trying to not wonder when my wife will get home.

The last glance at the clock, it's about quarter past one.

Soon I'm sleeping.

Then, don't know when, I'm not sleeping.

Sitting straight up in bed.

Where is she? She should be here by now. What time is it?

It's 3:23. The party has been over for a while. *She should be here by now.*

What if she got in a wreck?

Legs kick the bedsheet.

She didn't get in a wreck.

Did she?

My head is a full moon. Churning thoughts with teeth.

Words from A. R. Orage, who wrote about conscious love: jealousy is the bitterest of emotions because it is associated with the sweetest.

But fuck Orage. He sucked me into this stupid fantasy, *conscious love.* Conscious love my ass. What does he know, anyway?

What if she did get in a wreck? My legs, still fighting the bedsheet.

3:25.

She didn't get in a wreck. Did she?

On my feet. Looking out the window. At what? I don't know. Getting dressed. Going where? Don't know. Where is she? Pit in belly. Shoes on. Out the door. Ready to fight.

It's 3:27.

Fists tight. All balled up and ready.

But outside the farmhouse, nothing out here to fight . . . So quiet out here.

I clutch the quiet like it's a ribbon of salvation, and a switch flips for a blessed second. And another. And another. Holding on for another and another.

It's 3:30. God, this is slow. Wish I could leap a year.

Distant sting of tires on pavement. The switch flips back. I'm peering down the road like a carnivore stalking prey. Maybe that faint sound is Madeleine's MGB. All my attention locks on the road . . . Goddamn it, she should've been here hours ago. The rage rises like lava in my throat.

3:31.

The sound of the tires on the rough asphalt fades in and out of the curves and valleys. Sound carries for miles out here.

I wanna hear the crunch of tires on the gravel driveway so I can pounce on the car door and scream where have she and Jan—

There. I said it. Madeleine and Jan.

Never thought it before until the words fill the silence.

Madeleine and Jan.

I see her hand on his shoulder while they're *dancing*. Her hand cupping his shoulder. The two of them hump-dancing in the corner of the kitchen.

Now it makes sense. The way her voice sounds different sometimes when I call from Tennessee. Like somebody else is right there.

I see the two of them melting and twisting into a gruesome lumpy ham on a hot spit in a Hieronymus Bosch painting of hell.

The sound of that one car fades into the silence and disappears.

But the silence dilates with howls of the damned in the painting of hell, howls that only crazy people can hear, and I decide to teach her a lesson.

3:33.

Three fucking thirty-three in the goddamn morning. *She shoulda been here by now.*

Flying through the house. Now I know what I'm doing.

Out of my toolbox, I grab the oversize framing hammer. A grid on the hammer face, with a straight claw on the backside. Works like a crowbar for breaking things down. Ripping shit apart. Teaching things a lesson.

The handle is hickory, serious as steel. I really like this hammer. It beefs me up.

I'm calm now. Crazy calm.

I pull up face-to-face with Madeleine's favorite possession. The heirloom dresser she inherited from her grandmother's Middle Georgia mansion, 1920s.

The big hammer rises overhead, both fists wrap the hickory handle—yeah, I'm gonna teach this piece of furniture until it splinters, all over the floor. She'll learn a lot from these splinters.

Big hammer close to the ceiling, straight claw aimed down, ready to destroy.

Here's to Madeleine and Jan.

Fuck you.

And fuck you.

Ready?

Um.

No.

The hammer freezes up there.

I take a breath and heave into another hemisphere.

Can't do this.

The switch flips back.

Inhale.

Zen.

Earth.

Lower the framing hammer.

Open fists. Hammer falls.

Crash!

Scares me for an instant in this silent night. Hammer loud on the farmhouse floor. The room shakes, and the windows rattle.

I get the hell outta there.

Outside. *Ahh*. Phew.

The cool subterranean blue fields and deep charcoal sky.

It's 3:36.

Out here in velvet space.

Desperate to scream at Madeleine.

Desperate to be better than this.

Grasping at the rafts of my own experience. The moments of arrest.

Observe yourself. Split your attention.

Right now these acts of intelligence are way more than discretionary diversions for a restless spirit. Right now splitting the attention is all that separates me from furniture-smashing madness and the county slammer.

Here it is.

The choice.

I asked for it. I signed up for extra duty. Got more than I asked for. But that's what I wanted: more than I was asking for. But still, never imagined this. Because you can't imagine what you can't imagine.

Your choice. Pick a universe to inhabit. They're both right here. By the same pasture. Under the same sky. Inside the same head.

One breath at a time. One tightrope. Over a pit. One breath at a time.

Either participate in your own evolution—and take one conscious breath right now and now and now and now—or be hurled into hell.

Outside on the porch, I gather myself into the classic meditation position and focus on chasing Dorka. Heart pounding. Easy to find the beat. Over the left eyebrow, *Ash*. And then over the right, *Raf*. Over the left eyebrow, *Sith*, and over the right, *Kah*. Oh, that's nice. Working my way through the syllables.

Another world. Another world right here in Alpharetta. Right here in my head.

I peek at my watch again. It's 3:40.

Never mind the time.

Something else comes to mind. From the Torah.

Moses and the parting of the Red Sea. Instantly makes new sense, not as a parable but as a choice of consciousness. I'm inhabiting my brain in a new way. It's an exigency *right now*: splitting the Red Sea of attention. Pharaoh's army thunders one throb behind me. I gotta follow the parted waters, one heartbeat after another. So the jealous rage—Pharaoh's army—doesn't engulf and enslave me.

On the tightrope between the worlds. Beat by beat, breath by breath.

Your choice.

Apocalypse or rebirth.

I start to look at my watch but stop.

I focus on chasing Dorka instead. One syllable after another.

To my surprise, as I string these beats together, it's suddenly easy to make a rational plan.

Thinking calmly while being chased by Pharaoh's army. Teetering on the edge of an abyss. I can do this. The way Rich Kidd learns to maneuver in live fire.

First, acknowledge that I don't really have a choice. I can't turn into a monster and smash her stuff and break her face. So I have to do this other thing while the reflexive lesser self writhes and bellows: sit here, wannabe-Buddha-like, and sort this out.

What if she did get in a wreck? I don't really know for a fact that she didn't, so what it boils down to is that I have to wait for one of two sounds: either the telephone jangling with news of disaster or the distinctive exhaust notes of her old MGB laboring up the hill.

So I get up from my meditation posture on the porch and position my car so that when she approaches I can disappear out of the driveway with no headlights onto Old Roswell Road. Because I do not want to listen to any mumbled, booze-drenched explanations—or lies—while she has a freshly fucked glow on her face.

Something shifts during these early morning hours. Hours, hell. It hasn't been hours.

It's 3:57 now.

It's second by second. Each beat. Of this loud heart. Every moment a fulcrum on which large forces bear.

The pasture and the moonlight and the hush of the earth and this new sense of hey man, you wanna smash other people's stuff? Or are you better than that? Your choice. Nodding at the burnished silver grass. Because shit, yeah—I'm better than that.

The ordinary mind and the extraordinary mind are revealed as if for the first time.

Right this second, I like my middle-of-the-night front-row seat to the shenanigans of the ordinary mind writhing and a clear view down Old Roswell Road.

An irregular *plink-plink* of sounds rises from the night. A faint breeze rustles the treetops. A twig falls on the roof of the car, sounds really loud. A dog barks in the distance. Another dog answers.

Breathing makes a sound.

The whole thing is a miracle, really. Air flowing in and out of some holes in your head while you ease forward, through the parting waters of the Red Sea.

The switch stays flipped.

At 4:17 a.m., a different sound from far away. A car labors up the hills and coasts into valleys, the sound humming and fading and, yes, inching this way. It gets a little closer. What kind of car is it? I can't tell yet.

Then, in a flash, I hear the signature sound. The incongruously happy MGB exhaust notes. Here she comes.

Grab my wallet and keys and hurry out the door, crank up the car motor, and pull out of the driveway with no lights and disappear around the bend just as her lights in my rearview mirror turn into our driveway. Then I floor it.

Accelerating away from my lesser self. Like I'm a jet engine. Jets accelerate by dumping shit behind them. Vroom.

Free, at least for this moment.

Pain will surely follow, but right this second it's not worth a second thought.

≈ ≈ ≈

"So what did you do after you left the Jan Cox group that night?" Grandpa wants to know.

I don't say anything. Gathering some thoughts.

He says, "Your life was enmeshed in the whole thing. Even your job grew out of the experience. But you have shown yourself to be adaptable. This is a critical quality for success. So of course I am curious what you did next."

Adaptable. Maybe so. But not in the way he's assuming.

"Grandpa," I start, then sigh.

"Oh, no," he says. He smells where this is headed.

"Yes," I tell him. "The truth is I didn't even think about quitting."

"Oh, no," he says again. "The man takes up with your wife, and you still think he's a 'teacher'?"

Grandpa is exasperated. Like I've never seen him before. He doesn't want to hear it, any of it, because it's against everything he stands for, everything reasonable and manly. But he can't deny his true nature, his essential open-mindedness, so with resignation he says, "All right, then."

As in: So tell me.

I tell Grandpa the truth: I don't entirely know why I didn't quit that night.

I pull out a clean sheet of paper and a pen. "Let's see if I can get to the bottom of this. Or at least tease out a bit of sense . . ."

Amazingly, Grandpa's question is a question I've never really asked myself.

He's watching and doesn't rush me.

≈ ≈ ≈

A list forms on the page.

1. I'm addicted to these ideas and methods. An addict doesn't leave his dealer.

2. Madeleine and I were going to break up anyway. Part of me is glad she's gone. I'm excited by the unknown, happy to be free of her barnacles, and I don't miss her at all. Except when I miss her extremely.

3. The tribal bonds. This is my tribe. These are my people. Raw energy. Talent. Brains. Curiosity. A roomful of shiny-eyed laughter.

4. That night changed things. *Ordinary* and *extraordinary* are palpable in a new way; I feel them physically, coexisting in my body. But I have new sway over which prevails.

5. My alter ego, Rich Kidd in Green Berets, signed up for experiences that change him. When the experiences do change him or wound him, he doesn't just quit. He's in more than ever. Ready for the next mission.

6. The enlightenment I'm seeking—it still lies ahead on this path. I'm not gonna quit until I experience it for myself.

7. Ultimately this: *I don't totally know* why I stay. But the fact is I don't just stay. I'm in more than ever.

≈ ≈ ≈

The bottom falls away.

And everything happens at once.

Madeleine and I move out of the farmhouse in Alpharetta. We go our separate ways. She asks for alimony. I laugh at her. You want money for leaving me? Bitter laughter catches in my throat.

A recession hits the real estate market. Lon Flack's real estate investments in Tennessee become worthless. My job disappears. I was getting bored with it anyway.

Jan's right-hand man, Dwayne, and I become roommates. He seems really excited about it. I'm not. We find a place in a faux Tudor apartment complex ridiculously named Woodcroft. It's exactly the kind of place I would never live in. But Woodcroft is about a mile from the house on Memorial Drive, where the group meets, and what the hell.

Jan institutes a new practice called Quasa, or quiet time. On

Sunday evenings, the house is open. No talking allowed. On the shag carpeting, people stretch like panthers and sit like the Sphinx. I still hate the carpet, but I love being there. Every Sunday. I stay until everyone leaves, then linger alone for hours, and lock up when I lock up.

Not that we're full-time monastic. We've got way too much energy for 24-7 monastic.

Another round of new people joins the group. Sometimes I think the group is the magnetic force. But Jan says no. He is. If it weren't for him, we wouldn't be gathered.

One of the new people, Lily, invites everyone to her apartment on Saturday night. Everyone wants to go, especially because she's such an unlikely resident of Riverbend, Atlanta's notorious singles complex. She's highly intelligent, serious, and self-contained. What is she doing at Riverbend?

My first thought is, "She's brave to have us all here."

Turns out bravery would not be required. The evening clicks on charm and luck and a walk-in closet, and I click on all three.

A bunch of people from the group plus a few friends of friends all become new lifelong best friends for the evening and treat Lily's apartment as if it's their stepmother's. Some people run down the hallway to the pool. Jan shows up with Madeleine. It's no big deal anymore. Sometimes it seems as though it's always been this way. The party gets looser and wilder and louder. Jan especially likes it loud. The apartment throbs, and I get into a conversation with a friend of tall Ted's girlfriend.

She's Greek. She could have stepped out of a three-thousand-year-old bas-relief, with her copper skin and thick jet mane and shiny black eyes. She tells me her name, Eve, and I say, "You look biblical." We're standing very close. She doesn't move away. But she doesn't nod or smile. So I whisper, "More like Delilah than Samson."

She likes that, which is all the encouragement I need, and in no time I'm even more entertaining than my normally highly entertaining self.

So is she.

I like that she's doesn't crowd the conversation. It's got space. And she's smart. I like smart. Not that the conversation is going slowly. It might sound slow, but it's not. The pauses accent the badinage.

Soon we're talking about walking into walk-in closets, whereupon we agree to walk right into the walk-in closet in the middle of all the people in the middle of Lily's studio apartment. Everyone sees us disappear in there. In no time, we're on the floor, naked, pushing suitcases and boxes out of the way, finding and losing each other through Lily's hanging dresses and skirts and slacks, and Eve is on top of me, we're doing it, and she doesn't stop even when the door opens and closes and opens and closes and opens and closes and opens and closes. Every time the door opens, a strobe flash magnifies Eve's magnificent twisting body.

We emerge as heroes. Everyone is laughing and applauding, except Madeleine, who looks empty.

The next week Eve comes over to visit for an agreed-upon chess game.

From one extreme to the other. Seems normal to me. That's what this is all about, now that the bottom has disappeared and space is free.

But I can't concentrate on the chess pieces. I keep looking at her, and she beats me. Easily. And leaves. I never see her again.

But I don't think about her for long because of Melanie and Carol. They will see me whenever I want, and I feel strong and rich even though I'm damn near broke.

1976

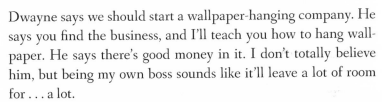

Dwayne says we should start a wallpaper-hanging company. He says you find the business, and I'll teach you how to hang wallpaper. He says there's good money in it. I don't totally believe him, but being my own boss sounds like it'll leave a lot of room for . . . a lot.

We name the company Paper Tiger, which is a great name for a dumb idea. Judith the artist designs these distinctive orange business cards, featuring a black-striped tiger coming at you from an orange field. We print them on the heavy card stock left over from our Task to bring more people into the group. I distribute them, in person, to interior designers in fancy showrooms all over town and tell them how good we are even though I don't know what I'm talking about. Sure we can hang the untrimmed prints from France, flock and foil, too, no problem, all our work is guaranteed, it says so on the business card, right here, and the phone starts ringing.

Dwayne neglects to mention how much he loves to tell somebody what to do all day long, so I have to listen to an infinite loop of statements like "Rotate the razor blade twelve degrees toward your spine." And I'm thinking fuck the goddamn razor blade while I rotate it a good thirty degrees away from my spine just to make him crazy.

He also neglects to mention that each roll of wallpaper is different, so you have to constantly adjust the paste, discuss how to adjust the paste, and discuss why the paste should be adjusted one way or the other, especially when you factor in the vagaries of the wall surface.

I learn two things. One is that Dwayne needs to shut up. The other is how much I hate wallpaper.

≈ ≈ ≈

Dwayne and I check messages when we get in from either working or not working to see what women or clients have called, in that order. On the answering machine one day, Jan says to both of us, "Meet me at Memorial at seven-thirty tonight."

At seven-thirty, his car is outside. Inside, Madeleine is with him, next to an ice chest packed with beer. They're having one. He tilts his head at the beer. We open one. And gulp. No one has spoken. That's okay. Jan denigrates conversation so much that we have become a group of people who pause silently for minutes at a time. You rarely see that—a long, comfortable silence among friends.

But we all know that Jan will be the one to break the silence. We sip and wait.

When he finally does speak, Jan's deep voice is intimate and tender, but what he says is jarring. "I am going to stop the group for the time being."

Stop the group? What does he mean? Make everyone in the group stand still for a month? Stop what? You can't plant something and simply stop it, can you? I mean, this group is organic and alive and it has a life force, and you don't just *stop it*, do you?

Jan looks at me and says, "Call everyone on the list and tell them there are no more meetings until further notice."

Looks at me? Am I the right-hand man now?

I nod back. Sure, I'll call the list. Around fifty people.

Whoa—my beer is gone. I grab another and pass some around.

≈ ≈ ≈

Day after day, when Dwayne and I get in from working or not working, we listen to Jan's messages on the answering machine. His inflections imply that each message is unique. But every day, he says the same thing: meet me at Memorial tonight. So every night, we gather at Memorial—Dwayne, Madeleine, and I —in these fascinating rambles with Jan.

Jan pours himself into speech, so what he says often goes down as a liquor that permeates cell walls and packs way more than information.

He says, "I don't know whether or not I will continue doing this."

He leaves it hanging there for absorption.

I had never wondered *why* he does all this with the group or what it might take to do it.

"It takes a physical toll," he says. "And I have choices in life. I don't have to do this."

Hmm. Jan is breaking his rule against self-talk.

But hmm. Fascinating. I had never expected to contemplate this arrangement, and in the long silence that follows my mind peers into the unknown and prowls around.

"But no matter what happens or what I do, I will not abandon the three of you."

Silence again.

Then laughter. Mine. Lots of it. I roll on the shag carpeting. Can't stop laughing. A phrase of Jan's tickles me like helium: *the upside-down nature of things.* Crazy. You would think, if you were thinking linearly, that if your woman takes up with a guy who's supposed to obey his own rules against taking up with somebody else's woman, you would possibly maybe kill one or both of them . . . happens every day . . . or at least you would feel like shit for five years and hate them both, but here I am having an *upside-down* blast of a time *falling up*—"falling up" is another Jan-ism for what happens when you let go and tumble into the abyss—while Jan is talking about himself, breaking his own rule against talking about yourself, which doubly proves the upside-down nature of things because the rule has value but breaking the rule right here right now this way is way better than the rule, which is one more example of the upside-down nature of things . . . maybe you pressurize a rule by following it so that it explodes when you break it, but then a third wave of laughter washes over me because I'm taking comfort in the words "I will never abandon you" from the guy for whom Madeleine abandoned me! And oh, yeah, speaking of upside down, last month I was a married junior real estate ace, and now I'm hanging wallpaper for the wives of real estate tycoons. With Dwayne. Wallpaper: it feels so good when you're not doing it. Not-hanging-wallpaper belongs on the Buddha's eightfold path.

Maybe I'll just not-hang-wallpaper all the way to enlightenment.

I open one eye. Madeleine and Dwayne are smiling at me because Jan is smiling. At me. Jan is drawn to certain kinds of laughter like flies to horse shit, as he puts it. He never asks for an explanation. He gets it, though; he gets the joke that elicits broken-bungee riptide laughter, and maybe that's one reason he's leading this group. If he is anymore.

Day after day, week upon week, the four of us convene at the house on Memorial. Dwayne and I become regulars at the neighborhood package store, buying Schlitz by the case. Jan and Madeleine are always already there, but despite this pattern, the evenings follow no format.

We talk about sailing and Redball Express.

Redball Express is a guy Jan knew. Years ago. This is not a straight-line story. It is an upside-down-nature-of-things story. Jan sparks a little when he talks about Redball, and Redball comes alive for me as the Dean Moriarty character in *On the Road*. You had to put this together from riddle-scraps of conversation: Redball imbued a situation with fizz and divinity and fear and possibility. Redball Express and Jan Cox kindled each other and smoked pot together in the back of a '55 Chevy, barreling around the canyon roads outside of Chattanooga. You could hear them howling, enflamed.

But Redball did not end up well. Not well at all. Just howling, at no moon.

As if Jan is saying . . . *follow in Redball's footsteps if you can, but choose a different destination . . . be careful with all this. You can have your blown-away moments and still careen off the rails, like the Redball Express.*

Jan's Redball monologues riff like scat singing. His eyes laugh with Redball memories, but the portents are solemn. Fall up into the abyss, but keep your bearings.

Jan sails into a conversation about sailing, not a subject familiar to Dwayne, Madeleine, or me. A day later I start reading *Sailing Alone Around the World* by Joshua Slocum and can't stop.

Slocum is the great-granddaddy of modern yachting. He set out alone in his gaff-rigged sloop in 1895. His book recounts this epic first solo circumnavigation of the globe. The next night, all we talk about is Joshua Slocum. Jan brings yachting magazines. Soon we're comparing sloops, ketches, and yawls. I buy a copy of *Sail Power: The Complete Guide to Sails and Sail Handling*. It's a technical manual, similar in scope to *Carpentry*, and I study it as though it were a textbook. We make jokes about getting a full belly on the genny—that would be a fully trimmed genoa sail—like we're old salts, even though the closest we've been to sailing is these books right here. But the four of us talk so seriously about a transatlantic voyage that one night I announce, "If we're going to take this trip, I just want everyone to understand that whatever negative feelings may linger about this new relationship between the two of you," meaning Jan and Madeleine, "will not matter to me at all."

Everyone stares at me.

Jan recovers more quickly than the others and responds, "You are amazing. You are truly amazing."

≈ ≈ ≈

While sprinting with a football, as the oncoming tackler closes in on the exact, inevitable point of impact, it is possible in the instant before that inevitable impact—with great body control—to clamp down and curl in and conserve your hurtling full-speed momentum just briefly enough so that while the tackler is entering the impact zone, you don't. You withdraw from inevitability for one camera flash. You conserve that crunch moment's worth of life force so that one moment later, you release the conserved energy and explode into pure space over the tackler tackling the ground, and you're free.

Sprinting. Dodging. Condensing mass and momentum down to a point outside time for no time at all, then letting the mass and momentum transform the contained energy.

This multifaceted endeavor with Jan, despite all the language he employs, remains at the core a physical process—and while the physicality of the experience includes the external and athletic, it also includes the internal and invisible process of shaking sleeping corners of the human experience awake. So the condensed moment of the stutter step in football, when your corporeality disappears for a nanosecond, connects with other, larger-scale dynamics of contraction and expansion.

This image of contraction and expansion (death and life) comes to me after Jan says, "Call everyone in the group. Tell them if they want to pursue this, then be here at Memorial at the usual time on Friday or don't bother to come back."

On Friday at 7:30, people fill the room. Everyone on the list shows up. Right on time. They can't wait. As if they're all drawn in tight, like a stutter step in football, bunched up and ready to pop.

Jan takes his place at the front of the room, and the conserved energy uncoils. Everyone is airborne for an instant, exuberant, eager to carry on. Sally forth. Break down the barricades. Jan has made his decision. He's all in. The train has left the station. We're tearing up the tracks.

≈ ≈ ≈

My old friend Byron and I meet for a beer. As high school kids from an insular Jewish social circle in Jacksonville, Florida, we share roots you can't explain and don't need to. Now we're riding waves of experience we'd never imagined.

Byron followed Jan's suggestion to get a job at the Ford plant in Atlanta. He worked on the line with burly working-class dudes, grew new muscles, and earned a fat union paycheck. Then he followed me in working as a bird dog for Lon Flack. Now he's serious about becoming a successful businessman.

I'm in the middle of a beer, in the middle of a sentence. Byron talks over me. He says, "You're quoting Jan all the time."

I freeze. He's right. Damn. Damn it. Shit.

Byron and I still have some competitive high school guy nonsense between us, but at the heart of it all, solid friendship binds. No one else could have said it so bluntly. *Quoting Jan all the time.* Shit. I didn't want to be like this. I never wanted to be a lifer in any group. My vow that night before starting The Work again, the vow in the mirror, a shiny black pupil holding my gaze.

I nod and pull myself together. I look at Byron. "Thanks for telling me."

He nods.

A few days later, James the architect and his wife, Judith the artist, come to visit my sad digs at the Woodcroft apartments, where I'm roommates with Dwayne. From living on the farm in Alpharetta with Madeleine to this? They mention personality and essence, as if to say—look at yourself, what have you become, from an environment that enriches you and your wife . . . to this? But they swallow their words, and Dwayne is there, and Dwayne annoys them, as he annoys just about everyone, and suddenly they have to leave, but they can't hide their sadness.

I want to talk to Grandpa.

≈ ≈ ≈

Grandpa says he probably spent more of his lifetime uprooted than rooted.

He doesn't seem upset about this, at least not now. Not anymore.

"You know, I never had roots in Augostowa. The soil there was inert. I couldn't gain any purchase there. And later, when I worked for my brother-in-law, I was always just marking time for an exit. My life was not really a life at all. My roots were in the future. But the future is sand. Just like the past."

He interrupts himself with a sigh.

"My roots were in necessity."

He smiles a bit and says, "My roots were in desire."

Then he shifts his focus and says, "Everything comes from somewhere."

His hand rises to stop me from speaking. Not that I have a reply.

I wait and think about what he says. Everything comes from somewhere. Hmm. Jan makes a point of saying, "All this comes from me."

Grandpa's hand relaxes again, and he says, "I think they call it hunter's eye. I've talked with trappers in Montana about stalking game in the woods . . ."

And I'm thinking, Grandpa talking to trappers in Montana in the 1920s! This feisty little Jewish immigrant from a Polish shtetl is chatting it up with grizzled old mountain men from the Wild West!

"... and they would not have said it like this, but here's what they told me. By dint of paying global attention to shadow and motion, and by listening for the crunch of hoof on earth, the hunters experience something. Their vision is enhanced, and even while aiming to kill, they enter something larger than the human realm. I suspect that your not-staring exercise distills some of that experience."

Wow. Even though Grandpa and I don't hunt, what he says has the ring of truth.

I never would have associated not-staring with hunting. Hunting seems the antithesis of anything evolutionary. But maybe this "hunter's eye" is the core experience from which not-staring has been distilled over the centuries in those secret schools that Gurdjieff talked about.

But Jan never frames it that way. He says, "All this comes from me and me alone."

Well, I don't know about Jan's grandiose claim, but I am grateful to see it all through new eyes, so to speak, thanks to Grandpa.

≈ ≈ ≈

I do love the way Grandpa revisits the not-staring practice.

Hunter's eye.

Time is a function of impressions.

This is true. The more impressions you pump into a unit of time, the longer it lasts.

The not-staring exercise is a physical practice with ramifications.

It generates new thought.

Breathing is the one autonomic system you can instantly modify with your attention. But if you forget about it, it just carries on without your help. This is a perfect metaphor for the difference between the ordinary level of consciousness and the extraordinary.

Jan would say, "I could make a whole school out of any one of these ideas."

Meaning he could establish a group, a Work group, and focus on one—just one—single practice of this endless spool of practices he unwinds. And this spool keeps revolving and intertwining your mind, your body, and your essence in new combinations.

Just as these impression-generating Tasks slow time down, so, too, the concentration of far-fetched experiences speeds time up in a different sense.

You can *live through* faster.

Meaning that some of the pain that is ordinarily mollified by time heals faster now, because you are *living through* the time-experience continuum faster.

So after six weeks or so of practically hating each other—after Madeleine left me for Jan—she and I grow weary of being enemies and become new best friends, the way two guys follow a bar fight by sobbing, "I love you, man." From now on, we pretty much tell each other everything.

1977

At least I quit quoting Jan all the time. But that doesn't really mean I'm any less immersed in it all. Jan says to me, will you build a running track around the house on Memorial Drive? Of course I will. None of us ever says no to such questions. And I do get involved in it, calling track coaches and gravel suppliers. Plans develop. A dump truck unloads a mountain of gravel in the driveway. I lay out the oval with stakes and chalk lines, and we build the track. It's really cool and track-like, even though it looks a little silly tightly looping the small house, and you have to run twenty-seven tiny laps to go a mile.

After the track is in place, Jan gathers a group of us, points to the blank wall on the back of the house and says to a group of us, "Let's build a steam room."

What? A steam room? On the back of this crappy postwar bungalow? Who would ever think of such a thing? Plus I have no idea how to build a steam room. But Ronnie the Lockheed engineer designs a cheap, ingenious solution using toilet-tank parts to maintain water levels in the reservoir and a water-heater element to generate steam. Everyone gets involved in the carpentry on the back of the house, starting with pouring footings in the Georgia clay to support the wall for the new room. The steam room. After a bunch of weekends and evenings, the room is done, and the specialty steam-room paint is dry. Ronnie ceremoniously flips the switch. Soon the reservoir burbles and the room drips heat. We all take celebratory turns in our private sweat cube.

From another point past the limits of imagination, Jan institutes a new regimen: on meeting days, do not eat all day long. Arrive early enough to run around the track for twenty minutes, then shower and sit in the steam room. Naked. Everyone. In the steam room. Naked.

He announces this as if it's common practice for fifty men and women to sit around naked together and sweat.

We take turns. Four or five at a time. All the surfaces are white. The steam is thick. We sit on a bench. The wet bodies seem to float in the hazy space. We look at each other. Almost everyone in the group is in great shape; their health shines, their bodies are beautiful and exotic, and most of the women are drool-worthy.

The preposterous and forbidden become a natural, mostly asexual joy that nests into Jan's tree of surprises.

≈ ≈ ≈

Surprise would be Jan's stock-in-trade. At least part of it. The surprises range from crude to clever. Better than clever.

Inspired, sometimes. Not that I always like them, the way you don't appreciate a face full of ice in a snowdrift. Or the way Rich Kidd does not appreciate every little thing about sacrificing for his nation. But we do sacrifice in our respective wars. We invest a lot of now for a beam of forever.

One of Jan's surprises could be an unabashedly voluptuous compliment—always shocking at first because so many of his surprises are negative, such as the rule to never drop anything, never break a glass, never sink a bent nail when we work on the house, and never express hostility of any kind; and also because of the way Jan pours himself whole into speech . . . the intention alone hooks you . . . and so the impact doubles, as it does on the night he finds out that computer whizzes Dustin and Dale had excelled as nationally ranked collegiate wrestlers for Georgia Tech. He applauds them up and down all over.

Surprise studs Jan's weekly talks, too, when he holds forth for about an hour. One night he says, "Some of you people who keep the greatest distance from me personally get the most out of all this."

The statement beams like light segmented by a prism. He validates the people who don't want to be around him, who are afraid of him, and who don't trust him. As if he is saying that even though you people out there on the outer ring don't spend time with me, I see you. I see what you are doing. At the same time, he tells people like me, who are around him all the time and treated as if we are on some kind of higher level, that proximity and apparent favoritism mean absolutely nothing.

On the other hand, Jan does hold me close, and shows me some of the handwritten exchanges he's had with people who won't get within twelve feet of him. I am struck by the intelligence and wit and insight, and it jars me.

These are the kinds of curveballs I pay for—not just with

the weekly dues but also by embracing this endeavor as my life's work.

But the crude surprises are really crude, and it's impossible to tell if Jan delivers them on purpose or if he just loses control and then buries the transgressions under bluster and a veneer of fresh resolve. It's confounding.

I missed one of the extreme episodes. Byron told me about it the next day.

I left the party shortly after midnight because everyone decided to drive up to Tim and Phyllis's cabin on Lake Allatoona, the ugliest lake in Georgia, and I didn't want to go. By the time they got there it was probably after 2:00 a.m., and they just kept drinking through the night.

Around 5:00 a.m. they all go out to see the sky get light, and Jan starts making out with Tim's doe-eyed wife, Phyllis, right in front of everybody, and then one thing leads to another until Phyllis has unzipped Jan's pants and is stroking Jan's erect dick right in front of everyone, including Phyllis's husband, Tim.

Was Jan going all rogue and outrageous just to shock people? Test people? See who would attack him or quit? Or did he just lose control of his dick? What the hell?

"So what happened next? Did she give him a blow job?" I ask.

Byron says, "Everyone was looking and trying not to look, and then Jan suddenly pulled up his pants, walked to his car without saying anything, the way he leaves meetings, and drove away."

If Byron hadn't told me, I never would have known. No one ever said a word about it. But everyone who was there remembers it. And now so do I.

≈ ≈ ≈

For reasons unrelated to Jan's dick, James the architect and Judith the artist, along with Lon Flack and his girlfriend, Patricia the artist, all send Jan notes thanking him and explaining why they are not coming back to the group.

They have participated in a ceremony in downtown Atlanta with a guy named Adnan, from the Sufi tradition in Syria. The ceremony transported them to the kind of exceptional state Jan points toward; toward which all these methods and surprises lead; to a state way beyond the ordinary; to a clear, soaring state of mind and spirit untainted by circular thinking and emotional sludge.

Adnan transported them there in this ceremony.

The ceremony that drew them away from Jan wove together meditation, subtle rhythms, and controlled movements. The power of it all seemed to spring from . . . well, Adnan himself.

Jan responds immediately in a way that surprises me. On the phone, he says, "Call everyone and tell them we have an emergency meeting tonight. Everyone has to be there." And he hangs up. Click. He does that. I can't say it's comforting. But neither is he.

We all gather.

He announces that James, Judith, Lon, and Patricia have quit the group. He doesn't care that they quit the group. Anyone can leave at any time, and people do. All the time. And he never asks why.

Yet in this one particular case, Jan does care why they left.

Jan is very blunt: "Don't get seduced by an Adnan. Yes, there are Adnans who unwittingly have the ability to transport you to another state. I say 'unwittingly' not in the sense that they don't know they have the ability—yes, they do know—but it is something they don't understand. Oh, they understand that people will benefit from it and pay money for it, but they do not understand it in the context of what it means to be *more conscious.* Their ability is accidental. It is not something they cultivated through effort and understanding. It is analogous to being very tall. Yes, being tall is exceptional, tall people know they are tall, but that does not mean tallness is the result of consciousness or intention. And yes, catalyzing a transcendent experience in others is exceptional, but that does not mean it is conscious."

This is the only time Jan forbids an outside experience, aside from his rules about no recreational drugs and no casual sex between group members.

Jan goes on to say, "If you want to continue here, you cannot do both. You are either doing this or looking for shortcuts that ultimately go nowhere."

Hmm. Jan is unusually ruffled about this Adnan business.

Hmm. I am not opposed to shortcuts. You are shortcutting ahead of yourself. Maybe I wouldn't mind a bit of Adnan short-cutting action. In a way, isn't this entire process in The Work a series of shortcuts? Evolution itself can be seen as following shortcuts on the path, a way of quickening and leap-frogging and lurching toward vitality, a more robust life.

Is the growth process supposed to adhere to some order? The name of Gurdjieff's group in London comes to mind: the Institute for the Harmonious Development of Man. Is Jan proscribing guys like Adnan because such guys, and such experiences, would actually short-circuit a masterful harmonious development that Jan is orchestrating? I do believe, on the strength of my experience, that Jan's labyrinth, his almost infinitely faceted path of unimaginable facets, actually zigzags to illumination. But how would a temporary springboard to the extraordinary harm these efforts?

Is Jan merely corralling his followers for fear of losing our attention and the benefits he expects from his leadership?

These critical, discomforting questions—when, rarely, I do

pose them—always bounce me back to one of the two rules he emphasizes the most: do not get involved with me personally. Which I take to mean don't second-guess him. Either do this on his terms or go away. So I try to bury the questions. But they linger.

≈ ≈ ≈

The do-not-get-involved-with-me-personally rule does benefit everyone who takes The Work seriously.

Jan says, "It's not about me. If you get tangled up with whether I ought to be a certain way, then you're off track. You are not here to worry whether I'm up to your standards—or anyone else's, for that matter. What you are here for is to do something extraordinary your own damn self, and if all your damn self wants to do is to argue with me in some way, well, you can do that without being here, without being part of this. You can root around in your habitual, ordinary mind and pick me apart until the end of time. But if you really need to get down to the business of pulling up some old roots and growing some new ones, then you see it's a full-time job, and you don't have time to worry about my shortcomings."

≈ ≈ ≈

Grandpa says, "When I left my brother-in-law's employment and started my own business, this was quite something for me. To have come this far. But I was just setting out on my own. Just beginning. I opened a bank account. But the bank president was a swindler, and a significant portion of my money disappeared. The banker wound up in jail, but that didn't do me any good. Fortunately, some of my money was elsewhere, and I was able to remain solvent."

I start to seethe on Grandpa's behalf and want to re-kill the long-dead banker. But Grandpa continues, with equanimity, in another direction.

"During this time, I felt the inspiration of love directed at a young pretty maiden."

I forget the evil banker and nod at Grandpa's young romance while hiding my amazement that even though the language of business has remained fairly stable over ten or twenty decades, the language of courtship, romance, and sex has changed completely. The dictionary calls his use of the word "maiden" obsolete.

"She was the daughter of the grocer on Ludlow Street. I would shop there often for one or two items at a time, just so that I might chance to see her again. I was daydreaming about her wherever I went. But I hardly think she knew anything about it. Not giving any expression to my feelings, I suffered the consequences."

Suddenly I feel paternal toward him. It's as if he never really had a father. A father should be a ladder that the son may climb, a ladder that will facilitate the son's ascent to manhood. Sounds like something Grandpa might say. But Grandpa didn't have that.

Then he says, "I didn't know what to say to her. But I knew how to conduct myself in business, and the money, when it came, helped me to establish myself in other ways."

"The struggle," *I say to him.* "To make a life. Away from Augostowa."

And he nods and says, "You can't do everything you want in a lifetime. The money helped me grow roots in the New World. Roots for the first time in my life."

≈ ≈ ≈

Grandpa ogled the grocer's daughter for several years but never could muster the nerve to initiate a conversation. Then he met Grandma and married her.

My situation is different.

Jan braids his rules one way, his behavior another. These braids twist together like cobras.

One of the bedrock rules that never changes—up there with "don't get involved with me personally" and "express no hostility"—is "no casual sex between group members." Not that we all always abide by it. But the rule, for what it's worth, is a rule.

And Jan vividly establishes in a talk one night the absolute importance of treating your spouse, lover, or significant other with the utmost care, respect, and devotion. Your viability in The Work depends on how you treat this one person. As if your whole life depends on it. This one person is your fulcrum of the extraordinary. Jan extols this level of devotion as a key to a kingdom. He turns lyrical, rhapsodic. The other person's welfare is your welfare; the other person's joy is your joy; the other person's potential in The Work is your potential in The Work. All without using the word "love," he pours solemn love into the room. He ends the talk without a Task, because the Task is obvious, and we are uplifted by it. As if a medieval troubadour has sweetened the roomful of us. Maybe a troubadour like Adnan.

Another night Jan talks about the way an awakened man or woman experiences life.

He is careful to talk about this in the third person, never identifying himself as that "awakened man," even though he implies, and everyone infers, that he is that man. Of course. That's why we're here.

And then he says, "The closest an ordinary person comes to awakening is the moment of orgasm."

I call this a sterling statement. Bright as polished silver.

Sex as a trampoline to altered states.

Hell, yeah, I'm all in on that there sterling statement.

My old friend Weston, from college, comes to mind. When he joined the Hare Krishnas, he accepted that they were forbidden to have sex other than for the purpose of procreation because the Hare Krishnas believe sexual pleasure is mere illusion that shrouds the godhead. That may be an extreme view, but myriad religions and cultures paint this central, sensual, unifying, mystical gift in various shades of sin.

Jan busts all these fidgety notions in one sterling statement.

Instead of sin, sex!

Sex can be a stepping stone on the path. Or a trampoline on which to bounce higher.

Jan says sexual attraction permeates everything. Even grains of sand on the beach. They are attracted to other grains of sand. It's everywhere, this urge to mingle and merge and liquefy.

Jan condones sex. If you want it, you should have it, with gusto.

When engaged in the sex act, he says, devote all your attention to the sex organs.

And Jan is a generation ahead of the rest of the culture in defending homosexuality. He doesn't make a big deal out of it. He simply says if that's what you're attracted to, that's what you should do. It is of no concern to anyone else.

I love that he treats sex as just one of many realms of human intercourse, so speak, in which we might wander and wonder.

My own thoughts come over time.

Women have a place. Men have a thing. The place and the thing belong together. This is a splendid arrangement.

Why, then, I wonder, do we suffer worldwide taboos against sex? From what common fear or urge do disparate cultures generate these proscriptions? Maybe the mind mistrusts sex because sex befuddles the mind: the mind doesn't want to let go, and orgasmic moments go way past the mind even as the mind frets that such worlds hover out there beyond it. So the mind makes up rules to control what it can't control, this compelling erotic tide.

Sex is the process that funnels primal life forces into new life forms. It is mystical how this happens. No matter how much we know about the science of it, sex remains mystical. Physical mystical phantasm.

Decentralize my central nervous system.

One night at a party, we all get to talking about art, and Picasso's name comes up. Jan says, "He must have known something, considering all the women he had."

Jan uses the term "know something" in the esoteric sense: knowing beyond the obvious and ordinary.

So seduction and special knowledge feed each other? I eagerly accept this happy hypothesis as truth. Yes. If seduction and orgasm can speed me to enlightenment, well, I'm available. I want to volunteer for special experiences.

At parties, the more he drinks, the more Jan talks up the joys of conquest. Everyone laughs. And as a DJ with delightfully wild, eclectic musical tastes, Jan will generally play "Why Don't We Get Drunk [and Screw]" by Jimmy Buffett at least once at every gathering.

Jan does ooze a kind of bad-boy sexuality, crazily woven with his sharp, contrarian, brilliant bombast.

Beak nose. Heavy on his feet. Air of raw energy, danger. Unpredictability. Focused attention. Steady, cabling eyes. And his hands, great-looking masculine hands with golden mean proportions.

No matter how drunk he gets, Jan always abides by his rule to never trip, stumble, or break anything. He can be sloshing around his own feet, but he'll never trip on the stairs or drop a glass. He lumbers along. With a heavy, Jackie Gleason grace.

This heavy physical grace plays best on the dance floor.

Jan's whole body, like it always does when he dances, drills down to the bass line under the bass line.

Jan zeroes in on computer whiz and acclaimed wrestler Dustin's new girlfriend at a party. She's never been here before, in this completely windowless, completely carpeted room, disco ball wheeling on the ceiling. Six-foot loudspeakers, one in each corner, shake space. Dustin's girlfriend has a great ass and legs; she looks like Jennifer Aniston, and in about nine minutes, Jan goes all wrapped reptile on her.

He dances with her the same way he danced with Madeleine in our old farmhouse kitchen in Alpharetta.

The party goes on, but nobody knows what he's trying to prove. She just showed up here! How about a little courtesy extended to Dustin and his girlfriend? What the hell is he doing? Everyone wishes he would quit. Everyone gets squirmy. But Jan keeps dancing with her. Or at her. He's dancing at her. I wonder why she doesn't walk away. She obviously hates it. Doesn't she?

Yes. She hates it. She and Dustin are soon living together, but she never again shows up at a group party. She never sees Jan again, because she doesn't want to. Ever.

He's not always like that. Sometimes he's appropriate. But his appropriate comportment is rare enough that it's equally jarring.

Grandpa. I can't explain to Grandpa that this is my sexual milieu. Where devotion is extolled but desire rules.

≈ ≈ ≈

Tom Amear works for Jim Davie at Jim's high-end landscaping company, Plant Aficionados. They're installing a gazebo over a slate patio. A rafter gives way, and Tom Amear's feet whoosh sideways, fifteen feet up in the air. Tom is from Libya.

No one knows how he wound up in America, but through Jim he joined the group with Jan and all of us, and despite a vast language barrier—Jan's redneck locutions and endless run-on sentences bamboozle more than a few home-grown citizens—Tom seems to keep up with everything. But not right now. Tom is falling through the air. The first part of Tom to smack the slate patio is his head. Tom sprawls in the slowly widening blob of his own blood. The ambulance rushes him away, and the ER doctors say it's bad. The next day the ICU doctors say it's worse. They say his brain is swollen, and he's going to die.

Jan calls an emergency meeting and says get me a piece of his bloody shirt. Jan sizzles when he says we are going to devote every ounce of our attention to Tom Amear.

"Put the pedestal in the center of the room. Tom's shirt goes on top. Everyone form a circle . . ."

The drums and the dancing soar. Feet snap the floor on the beat. Time stops. Locomotive energy. Holy energy. Transformative. We are lifting Tom—and ourselves.

The doctors declare it a miracle. Defies medical science. Tom walks out of the hospital, and the only evidence of his certain-death brain trauma is the droopy left side of his face. But his permanent I'm-so-glad-to-be-alive smile lights up the right side of his face and practically renders the disfigurement invisible.

Life forces flow where life is.

≈ ≈ ≈

Grandpa pops up and says, "I propose a drink. We should have a nip together."

"What's the occasion?" Maybe he wants to toast Tom Amear's miracle.

"The occasion is," he says, "that we should have a drink."

I could drink to that.

He says, "Peppermint schnapps."

"I don't drink schnapps." Hoping he'll pick something else.

"You do now," he says with a smile.

Well, schnapps—crap. I did bring that bottle back after my Great Uncle's funeral. A lot of it was left because nobody drinks schnapps anymore.

"The good glasses," he says.

I know exactly the ones. I would drink anything out of them with Grandpa. Schnapps, well, sure. Even a nip of creosote, probably. It would be a privilege. He left them to Mom. She's already passed them along to me. They're so precious I hardly ever use them. Grandma Rose chose them for the top shelf of the breakfront that now graces my dining room. A set of glasses, each with a heavy cylindrical crystal stem that fills your palm. Liqueur glasses that are masculine on the bottom for grip, act as ballast for the booze, and feminine on top for your lips. The flaring rims of each glass, each one a different jewel tone. These glasses, and the gold-rimmed china filling the breakfront along with them, said "Promised Land" to Grandpa and Grandma.

At Seder in Daytona Beach as a kid—when you were supposed to be looking at the Haggadah—you could hardly divert your eyes from the jewel-bright shot glasses, the gold-rimmed wineglasses, and the gold-rimmed plates.

Grandpa Phil gets the emerald glass to match his eyes. I get the sapphire to match mine.

Both full now, schnapps to the brim.

We clink.

He throws his down.

I lift mine. A bit of the oily liquor leaks onto my fingers. But not much. Most of it fills my mouth. Whoa. Peppermint whirlpool blast. Hot and starry. I swallow, but it all goes up instead of down, and my scalp bristles. Everything is blurry and brilliant.

"I like schnapps, Grandpa."

Grandpa rises from his chair, assumes his full height, and keeps right on rising. He's inhaling, and he's not exhaling. His torso keeps expanding. His arms telescope outward, and his mouth opens.

A mighty liquid sound startles air and flesh. Sound as clear and weighty as these sacramental glasses. Grandpa is singing opera. The hair on my neck stands up. I don't know the song. It doesn't matter. It's not a song. It's bigger than a song. The air is made of mirrors. His face is a lamp. The last note stretches out and away.

Without asking, I pour another round. This time we sip, bit by bit.

"I saw Caruso at the Metropolitan Opera when it was on Broadway and Thirty-Ninth . . . I could have seats anywhere in the loge, but I wanted to sit in the orchestra. In the center of the sound."

"You went there on your wedding night."

"How did you know that?"

"Mom told us. She told us as children. More than once. The way she said it, I knew it was important. But it wasn't until much later that I understood what it meant. People usually do something else on their wedding nights. You really, really love opera."

He nods.

Opera. The large tones roll, thrillingly.

Then he sits.

I tell him, "Well, none of us inherited your pipes. And I don't know why, really, but I've never even been to an opera. It's inexcusable, now that I think about it. But you are not going to believe who exposed me to it."

He wants to know.

Jan Cox.

"During parties, at the house on Memorial Drive, Jan is always the DJ, and his musical tastes run everywhere. One night he was on a roll. We'd all been drinking for hours, and he played one thing after another. All of it music from genres and sub-genres I'd never heard before. Over-the-top wild Las Vegas show tunes by Louis Prima. Then boisterous, irreverent country music by the Geezinslaw Brothers. Then he spun a record that stopped everything. Pavarotti. I guess he's my generation's Caruso. Pavarotti stopped everything. Transcendent."

Grandpa likes this. "Your Jan Cox is a man of many conflicts. But the opera reflects well on any man."

≈ ≈ ≈

At Jan's direction, we do public presentations from time to time, following the model of what we did when distributing the orange flyers. Each time, we organize into smaller groups, so everyone gets involved. We speak to whomever shows up about the truth of our own experience and understanding. And people always do show up to hear what we have to say, and at least half of them disappear as soon as Jan meets with them. But every time, some people stay, so the group keeps growing even as people leave. New people with new brains and new talents show up in their places.

New people like Emerson Cato. In many ways, he's a lot like the people at the core of the group: quick-fire brains, not too full of himself, and dissatisfied, reaching, scratching. And, like a lot of the people in the group, Emerson has developed his standout talent. He's a nationally recognized master of the viola. With his chin on the instrument and his fingers just so, Emerson's bow and wrist and strings and attention and posture all mesh as perfectly as you wish your life would.

But Emerson is also fundamentally different from the rest of us, because almost everyone else in the group can reasonably try just about any sport. Emerson can hardly fake walking. Without the viola, he has no center of gravity, so you give him beverages in a plastic cup and a wide berth when he takes a drink.

So it's surprising that Jan invites Emerson Cato onto Sam's speedboat up at Lake Lanier, about fifty miles north of Atlanta. He's the only klutz on the boat and new to the group on top of that. But I'm glad he's there. I like Emerson: his brain and his knowledge and his self-effacing manner. And I always idealize new people in the group, all intelligent and curious and serious and scared and eager.

Early June, with springtime still zinging through the hills and across the water. The forecast sounded grim—must be why we have most of the serpentine lake to ourselves—but a perfect day emerges, with dry air and happy skies. Sam opens her up on straightaways and then slices into a nameless cove on impulse. Everyone's got a beer and a smile, and for all of the seriousness of The Work, Jan always lathers his lectures with irreverence and imbues these weekend outings with lots of silliness, so most of the time these excursions seem like a beach movie.

The cove narrows. Sam kills the motor. The instant silence startles. Birdcalls echo in the close woods. Water splashes when our wake slaps the stern. I could have lingered there in the small channel between converging hillsides all afternoon. But Jan gets bored and itchy, Sam gets the message, and in no time we're back on the main bay of the big lake, speeding.

Sam throws the boat into figure eights. Jan loves the action and is egging Sam on, to pitch the boat into tighter and tighter circles, so Sam whips the boat hard into an arc until port is all freeboard up in the air and starboard burrows into the lake. Half of us soar ten feet above the lake. Half of us curl away from abrasive water walls. We're all screaming.

Sam lifts the throttle, and we belly flop on our own wake. The hull heaves in the churning.

Everyone on the boat laughing. "Play it again, Sam!"

The speedboat accelerates. Everyone starts chanting and counting the seconds, beginning when Sam cuts from the straightaway and ending with a cheer when the hull surfs its own waves.

Jan slugs another mouthful of beer and stops laughing. His face narrows to a single point. So everyone else stops laughing, too. Jan doesn't say anything. He catches Sam's attention with a head feint, then drags a finger across his neck. Sam cuts the motor.

The motor dies. We rise a few feet when the rooster-tail wave lifts the stern. So abruptly quiet out here. And the lake— the lake seems to triple in size, and it changes from a blurry freeform speedway to a sheet of wrinkled satin.

Jan looks Emerson Cato right in the eye and says, "Jump in the lake."

Everyone gets real silent.

Emerson's eyes are cooking.

Jan doesn't blink.

Nobody breathes.

Emerson Cato's voice shakes when he answers, "I can't swim."

Everyone's hoping Jan will lighten up. Jan, with ice water for blood, attracts the opposite type—people with warm tribal impulses. It's anything but a democracy, though. Jan always throws it in every newbie's face: "This isn't for everyone. If you're not all the way in, you're out. I'll throw you out. If you don't need to do this, then by all means don't waste my time."

"Jump in the lake," Jan repeats.

Emerson looks at the people on the boat. My eyes meet his. I want to tell him it will be okay. I hope it will be. I wish I could jump in the lake for him. I never met anyone who can't swim.

Emerson hauls up from the seat, faces the lake, and sorta crawls with chubby knees onto the gunwale, squeezing with both hands as if the gunwale might save him, and from a crouch he takes a shaky step and enters the air.

Arms flailing before they hit the water. Emerson's hairy concert-hall skin clashes with the slick black lake. A dull thud and a sloppy splash. I hope he knows enough to hold his breath. He's in now, submerged, fighting his way through a cloud of bubbles.

The lake has never been so huge.

Emerson's head bobs to the surface. He's gasping, panicky. Loud. Eyes roll around their sockets. Like pinballs knocked away from the flippers and out of the game.

Everyone locked in on the thrashing.

All bodies cocked at Emerson. Each and all, we want to save a gasping brother. But nobody wants to cross the defiance line with Jan.

Unclaimed hatred, ropy air.

He didn't have to take it this far.

Impossible to know how long Emerson thrashes about in the dark lake. Seconds? A minute? I don't know.

Finally Jan says to no one in particular, "Help him outta there."

I wrap up one of Emerson's forearms, someone else grabs the other, and we hoist him back on deck as if his pudgy body is weightless.

Emerson is relieved. Shocked. The way you are after surviving, unscathed, a certain-death moment. Exhilarated. Thrilled, too, the way an awkward kid in middle school would be after sinking a pair of free throws.

Jan is thrilled and throws an arm around Emerson, whispers, "You did it."

Jan is always openly elated at anyone's breakthrough, although the leaps are usually private moments, not the public consequences of Jan's outrageousness. But whatever the circumstances, Jan thrills like a kid at Christmas whenever anybody springs to a new level, a new discovery. He loves it like he loves liquor.

Jan engages Emerson in a long, private conversation all the way back to the dock.

But Emerson doesn't say much. I can't really read him. Something else is going on in there.

We never see Emerson again.

And Jan never speaks his name.

Jan calls it *where your foot is nailed to the floor*. The critical weakness. He zeroes in on it. The primary seam in your personality. He doesn't hammer everyone. But when he does, everything cracks.

≈ ≈ ≈

Jan simply calls one exercise Walking.

One night, instead of a regular meeting, in which he always holds forth for about an hour before the drumming and dancing that follow his talks, he simply announces, "We're going to do Walking." He directs everyone into a big oval that fills the room.

He doesn't explain what this is about.

This is about everyone in the room *doing this exactly*.

Everything based on the left foot. Left foot first. Because this endeavor, the sum of everything we do here, is the Left-Hand Way. About once a year, Jan frames our endeavor that way. He never defines it.

Start with palms on chest, left hand on top, chin on clavicle.

On specific footfalls the arms unfold just so and your head rises hydraulically, so that eight beats later all arms are outstretched, palms out and open, necks cranked up, and all eyes skyward. From the open position, the contraction ensues like sunset so that eight beats later you're back at the folded-in position, chin on clavicle again and palms folded on chest, and on the next beat the unfolding ensues. Like sunrise. Everyone in unison.

Beat by beat.

Loop by loop.

Expanding.

Contracting.

The only sound: your breath, and feet on the carpet. Everyone in lockstep.

Soon everyone is inhaling and exhaling, breathing together.

Soon it seems the walls are breathing, too.

Unity upon unity.

In the same room where we always meet, the same people, but now the room and the people are transformed. Harmonious parts of a whole. I love them, these people, every one of them, even the ones I don't like.

The walls are gone.

Mindfulness, meet mindlessness.

We do this only once.

Once changes things.

≈ ≈ ≈

Jan insists that nobody ever sustains the effort enough, even though people in the group are making progress. He keeps adding rules. Rules way subtler than the Ten Commandments. Rules like little widgets to capture and supercharge energy spilled unwittingly in the discharge of habit. The way a turbocharger on fast cars captures energy lost to the exhaust system in order to enrich each explosion of the spark plug. More speed from the same motor.

"Never say good-bye." He's never said good-bye since we started meetings at Sam and Knoxie's house. He just gets up, doesn't look at anyone, and walks out the door. So that's what everyone else starts doing.

He says, "Be the first to say hello."

He doesn't really explain these rules. He leaves it you to discover the potential benefits. And the list keeps growing.

Get at least an hour of exercise every day.

Don't say "I" for any duration you choose; the longer the better.

Talk less.

Don't identify yourself.

Don't yawn.

Be of continual good cheer.

Rejoice in new sights.

Become an ever-hotter outlet for life.

Pursue anything in which you have no interest.

Don't return anger for anger.

If you must talk to yourself about problems, use a fictitious persona and voice.

Rules won't transform your world all by themselves. But they do multiply the possibilities. As though you're a deck of cards. Shuffling the deck so you're dealt new hands to play in new ways.

≈ ≈ ≈

I quit hanging wallpaper because wallpaper is bullshit. It all erupts one day when Dwayne tutors me on stuff he's already tutored me to death on while the homeowner listens as if Dwayne is the God of Wallpaper. All I wanna do is get outta there. We thought we'd be done right after lunch, but now it's dinnertime, the whole family is watching us, and we still have five more goddamn strips to hang in this miserable kitchen. So Dwayne the Shakespearean wallpaper lecturer steps theatrically off the ladder and plants his right leg square in the bucket full of dirty, pasty water that we use for rinsing the sponges. The water floods out of the bucket and across the kitchen floor. Dwayne's foot gets stuck in the bucket, so the bucket clops around the room with him. His attempted escape sloshes more water onto the floor. It's really funny, but it's not funny enough to warrant my hysterical meltdown. I can't stop howling. I try to reel it in, but I can't. I am deliriously, uncontrollably, inappropriately happy, as if this is the best thing that ever happened to me. I glance at the homeowner, an earnest accountant-bureaucrat type. He's looking at me with more shock than he showed when Dwayne sloshed dirty water all over the floor in the first place, while Dwayne's now-liberated soaked right shoe squirts pale liquid and squeaks like a kitten toy as he drips around the kitchen wondering how to clean up the mess.

The peals of my own laughter are liberating—completely: they liberate me from the curse of wallpaper. I know I'll never hang another strip again and will be free forever.

Dwayne and I part as friends. He says he'll miss me, but I doubt it, and sure enough, soon he finds someone else in the group to micromanage.

I celebrate my freedom for days, until I figure out that I have to find a job.

≈ ≈ ≈

To my surprise, I get hired as a waiter at perhaps the coolest restaurant ever on the Atlanta scene. I've cooked at different places, ever since summers in college, but I've never been a waiter. That's the main reason I'm trying it, plus I need a job.

The place is called the Hassan Container. Middle Eastern food is still a novelty in Atlanta, but to serve exquisite exotic platters in luxe caravan-style rooms hung with heirloom textiles and tapestries—this beguiles. Tables are full every night.

But I am even more surprised when I go in for training, expecting a brusque session in clipped English with Akram Hassan himself, the Palestinian owner. Instead the manager, Cara, introduces herself and hands me a menu to study. But how can anyone study the menu when she's in the room? A movie star is explaining the baba ghanoush. "And make sure not to confuse it with the baba au rhum. That's a dessert. It's happened—dessert for an appetizer. People eat it anyway," she says with a laugh. "Who doesn't like dessert first?" As if Ava Gardner is standing three feet away, the same dark hair, a face that holds light, and the strong, fluid posture of a ballerina. But this Ava Gardner is laughing along with me, charming, disarming, and alive, so even though the other waiters say Cara and Akram Hassan are in some kind of relationship, I can't wait to get to work every day and grab every possible moment to perpetuate these intensifying conversations with Cara while concealing the extreme effort required to appear nonchalant.

She's from Woodbine, the tiny seat of Camden County, in southeast Georgia, about fifty miles from Jacksonville, Florida, where I went to high school.

"Ever hear of Crooked River State Park?" I ask her.

She practically owns the place. They used to put their boats in at Fancy Bluff Creek, right by the park.

"Mr. Benjamin used to take our Boy Scout troop camping there almost every month."

We agree—we probably almost met there in our previous lives as teenagers.

Now we are both twenty-eight. Born a month apart, in neighboring counties as far apart as Baptist and Jewish.

One evening in the third week, during a lull in the dining room, Cara and I happen to pause by the largest, most spectacular tapestry in the restaurant. I run my fingers over the silk. The pattern swirls up and out of the corners, like it's alive and trying to tell us something important.

"I think it's trying to tell us something important," I say. She just looks at me. I lift a corner of the tapestry and ask quietly, "Ever seen the back?"

Clusters of threads poke up like tiny corals, imitating the full-spectrum event on the front. Maybe the back is more amazing than the front.

No, she never had seen it before. The back. Her fingers trace tidy tiny knots.

Then I say, "You wanna play tennis next week?"

As if expecting the question, she says yes, she does. We agree on a time.

All I say is, "That's great. See you on Tuesday." And I hurry off, refilling waters to hide my excitement, afraid of saying something stupid to ruin it.

My life funnels into Tuesday.

On Tuesday at 7:00 p.m., she answers the door.

Classical music is playing on the stereo. She lives alone in a small, neat house. She motions to the plush green sofa. It's not a movie star's digs, but it feels like home and it smells clean. The windows are open. We sit on the sofa.

"The windows are open," I tell her. "When I'm elected president, I'm gonna make everyone open their windows."

"Well, then, I guess I'll have to vote for you."

"I do not take your vote for granted," I tell her while wondering what the boundaries are here and wondering about the nature of her relationship with Mr. Hassan—she refers to him that way, "Mr. Hassan." Not exactly a term of endearment. He's older than we are. He's gone half of every week, teaching art at the University of Tennessee in Knoxville. One of the waiters who's been there forever says, "Akram thinks he's Picasso." Well, whoever he thinks he is, I hope he's in Knoxville tonight.

"When you put your boat in at Crooked River, where did you go?"

"Cumberland Island. We went out to Cumberland."

"Cumberland? When it was just a wild place?" Cumberland had recently been designated a national seashore.

She laughs and says, "We used to sneak up on the wild horses. And we went into the old mansion before it burned."

Dungeness, the old Carnegie mansion. As close as we'll come to a mythical castle in the Deep South. I never rummaged around in anything legendary when I was a kid.

"There were clothes hanging in the closets," she says.

Cumberland is still a kind of Shangri-la, where you can stroll naked from the open, shifting dunes into the insular, shady live-oak groves, because you can.

Cumberland through childhood eyes. It's enough to make you want to have sex with someone.

She doesn't ask about my racket. I don't ask about hers. We don't mention tennis.

But the talk comes easy. We are laughing and talking and not worrying about what will or will not happen. I haven't touched her.

Around 8:30, a knock on the door.

Oh, shit. Is it Mr. Hassan?

I freeze. Cara opens the door. Whew. It's Julie from the restaurant. She's the sous chef. She just dropped by. With a six-pack of beer. She should be surprised to see me here. But she isn't. Did Cara tell her I was coming by?

But who cares, because we're all three in the small kitchen enjoying Julie's beer. I'm leaning against the countertop at one end of the room. Cara is right in front of me. We're both facing Julie, by the refrigerator, and we're talking about work, the way coworkers do, and the conversation dovetails to art, which is easy because the restaurant itself is a kind of art piece, and I make the ridiculous comment that Robert Smithson's startling *Spiral Jetty* could put the "ass" back in Picasso. Maybe this seems extra funny because of Mr. Hassan's fixation with Picasso, but whatever the reason, they are both laughing. I can't take my eyes off Cara's back. Her back is laughing. As she is laughing, I put my hand on her—just firmly enough. I don't want to remove it. She doesn't pull away. She leans into me ever so slightly. My hand lingers and wanders. I can't hear anything else Julie says. I try to laugh along when they laugh. Strong girl muscles in the small of her back. It could take all night to explore this area, to inhale it. I wish Julie would leave. And leave the beer.

Then Julie says, "Well, I better get going . . ."

Neither of us begs her to stay.

I don't even know if she leaves the beer.

The door closes, and . . .

We're all wrapped lip to lip, belly to belly, hip to hip, arms round and round.

Clothes fall to the floor.

Naked on the green sofa, her skin, can't stop grabbing palmfuls, and we're doing it for a second, and we stop, and then we can't stop.

We sleep. We are one. We wake up, and we do it again. We fuck like masters. We are spent. We are rich. We sleep.

≈ ≈ ≈

We sleep until a knock on the door, middle of the night. We scare awake. She motions me to the dining room. My car is plainly visible in the driveway. Unmistakable. A giant red-and-white 1960 Chevy Impala, the swoopy-finned one that used to sit in Ronnie and Rachel's driveway. It's mine now.

Mr. Hassan is at the door. He has seen the Impala.

Muffled voices, his and hers, all bunched up, can't hear what they're saying, but what they're saying isn't good.

He slams the door. Cara and I sit still and silent. His car roars away.

But I am feeling amazing and don't want to feel unamazing and she doesn't want me to stay now after bad words that steal bliss, so we kiss good night but she hardly kisses me back, and I tell her I'll see her soon, which I have to.

Early autumn air, spectacular. Windows down, badass 283 V-8 climbing uphills like they're downhills. I'm unified with night and feel safe and grand in the shadow of the whole earth. The lush enveloping feminine urban forest is all I see on rolling, winding streets. The city is velvet.

It doesn't go away the next day. I love everybody.

≈ ≈ ≈

These awakened moments link and collect and laminate as a new sense of the world, a new platform for expansion. That's how we know what Jan is pointing toward, always pushing, cajoling, challenging, confounding, surprising, inventing new switchbacks to ascend . . . we know what he is talking about and reaching toward because we inflate and bristle and thrill in these moments that unlock all moments.

These awakened moments you remember. Where is this finer consciousness the rest of the time?

This path embraces all experience, Jan's many rules notwithstanding. But the rules aren't based on shame and guilt. They are signposts and reminders and barbs and needles and riddles to poke you awake, to keep your eyes moving, your mind clear, and your body eager for action.

Never think the same thing twice.

Take up a new sport.

Never let your thumb touch your index finger.

Cherish your hobbies.

"I am taking away your suffering card."

Why do you want to know more if you won't do what you already know?

$I + \text{Not-}I = \text{Everything}.$

≈ ≈ ≈

I never go back to the Hassan Container again. But I call Cara.

I keep calling. She doesn't answer. One day she answers. She sounds remote, listless, a stranger to the unified world we celebrated just the week before last.

But I am married to our aboriginal moments.

She says call back tomorrow. Tell me when, I'll call.

So I do call at the appointed time. She says wait a minute. She puts Mr. Hassan on the phone. He says, "We don't want to talk to you anymore. You need to stop calling here."

≈ ≈ ≈

We don't want to talk to you pounds through the line. Can't breathe. A little sick.

The shock you feel at the sudden loss of a loved one. Cords severed.

Thoughts tumble automatically. Of course that's why she didn't call back. Should've known. Still feeling sick. She picked *that* over *this*. She picked some kind of masochistic tangle with "Mr. Hassan" instead of . . . this . . . with me? It's awful. That's why she never called back. Shoulda known. It's awful. She picked *that* over *this?* I feel sick.

I find my breath. And catch it. And everything changes, easily. Because something fundamental has changed since I outran Pharaoh's army that night at the farmhouse in Alpharetta. My center of gravity has shifted, and I don't even think about smashing her furniture with my monster framing hammer.

I can do this. I will suffer briefly, acutely, for some compressed block of time. Yes, I can do this. This is not a rule or a plan. Simply a recognition of how I'll get through.

Like Rich Kidd in a nasty battle, I have taken some shrapnel, and it will hurt, this lump of experience, but I have been through this before, and it will not diminish my sacrifice for the cause.

An immigrant businessman loses his ass on a carload of pelts. He doesn't abandon his quest for wealth. He goes back to St. Louis the following spring and makes his best move for the coming season.

You quit identifying yourself, and these body blows don't seem so personal.

≈ ≈ ≈

Jan decides to move into the house on Memorial Drive. To live there. He didn't ask anyone's opinion. Not that he would—partly because in The Work, opinions have no value, as they are mere automatic outcroppings of ordinary consciousness that grow on your mind the way hairs grow in your nose. All of a sudden there they are, and if one is plucked, here comes another; and even if opinions were exalted, Jan wouldn't ask for mine because Jan doesn't ask questions unless they are actually requests, such as, "What would you people think of building an addition onto the house?"

This is not a question.

Evenings and weekends assume the spirit of a barn raising. We set up lights and work past darkness on this oddly isolated near-acre of land that sits down below a bend on Memorial Drive. If Jan ever does ask my opinion on the matter, I'll tell him this is a really dumb place to build a house. It's a dumb place to live, on a six-lane road with traffic noise and no place to walk.

Sure, it's a grind to work during the day and then work again into the night, but the effort produces energy and the energy spawns joy and everyone benefits.

"Everyone" includes Jan, of course, who benefits by acquiring a new domicile. You could call it, after his suspension of all group activities last year, his marriage to The Work. Or, since Jan does not seem to be the marrying kind, you could say that he and The Work are moving in together.

Except he does let it be known to a few of us that he is leaving his wife. Yes, he is married and has been married the whole time, including his time with Madeleine, and has two sons. We try to hide our surprise. He confides this personal information as if we knew it all along. But it's impossible to imagine him in any common circumstance, especially a regular marriage, and it's impossible to imagine teenage boys calling him Dad. The easiest way to deal with headachy matters like this is to obey the rule "Don't get involved with me personally in any way."

So not long after we convert the crappy postwar bungalow into our meeting house and add a steam room and a running track, we add to the original boring box a tall triangle containing a bedroom, kitchen, bathroom, and an office space in the top of the triangle, complete with shelves where Jan arranges books by height.

When the place is finished and Jan moves in, a vague sort of postpartum depression settles over the group. Even though we are glad to have our evenings and weekends back, we miss the molecular buzz stirred by the jazz of hammers syncopating and saws singing in the night.

But Jan recoils at a lull as much as a politician recoils at spending time with his family, so stasis is only a fleeting condition in our tribe—like a blink between rapid eye movements.

Jan announces, "We have to find a new meeting place."

Even though the main room in the original bungalow remains the same, Jan no longer wants us meeting in what is now his house.

A few of us find an old mansion on South Ponce de Leon Avenue in the Druid Hills neighborhood, near Emory, and with Jan's approval—because the main room is large enough for meetings and because seven of us want to split the rent and live in the rambling rooms—we sign the lease and move in.

The old mansion comes with an odd provenance. It was built as a honeymoon cottage for Lucy Candler, the sister of Asa Candler, Jr., at whose mansion I worked with dry drunks in service of the national interest.

And one more junction of time and real estate is uncorked two blocks up Ponce de Leon, where the Hare Krishnas have established an ashram in a pair of old mansions. On impulse one afternoon while walking by the compound I ask a devotee in the front yard, "Is Weston around?" I wonder about my let's-go-seeking-in-India friend from college. The ponytailed devotee calls Weston by an unpronounceable name and ushers me into my old friend's office. It's been seven years since we were planning our epic journey to find truth, joy, and wisdom.

Weston, in robes, lights up when he sees me. He wants his underlings to invent activities to keep the new devotees busy. It's a disorganized, casual conversation. "Well, then, let them sweep floors again if that's all we got right now." Weston is disarmingly open about his leadership position in the path he has chosen. And he is disarmingly curious about the path I have chosen.

"So what are you up to?" he asks.

He asks again. "No, really. What are you doing?"

He knows I'm doing something. We recognize each other as if we are trekkers on parallel ridges.

But I slink behind the we-don't-talk-about-it walls that Jan has constructed—they are not my walls—and I fail to rise to Weston's honest, caring curiosity.

1978

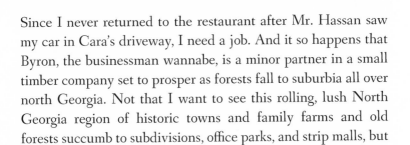

Since I never returned to the restaurant after Mr. Hassan saw my car in Cara's driveway, I need a job. And it so happens that Byron, the businessman wannabe, is a minor partner in a small timber company set to prosper as forests fall to suburbia all over north Georgia. Not that I want to see this rolling, lush North Georgia region of historic towns and family farms and old forests succumb to subdivisions, office parks, and strip malls, but it is happening, and if this business model puts some veneer logs to their highest and best use, well, I'm all for it.

Weirdly, the office of Oakman Timber Company is on Lenox Road, directly across the street from the Hassan Container. From the ninth-floor windows, the restaurant is plainly visible, standing alone in the Lenox Square parking lot. Cara's car and Mr. Hassan's are parked side by side. But just like the neighboring counties where Cara and I grew up, these buildings are worlds apart. I didn't run into her at Crooked

River State Park when we were teenagers, and I won't run into her now.

Byron and the other owners spend half a day coaching me on my job, which is a lot like bird-dogging for Lon Flack, except I never leave the office. It's all on the phone. I learn how to casually pepper my inquiries with terms like "sight index" and "board feet on the stump" and "wolfie," which means low-quality timber with lots of small limbs.

Then I pick up the phone, and with aerial photos in front of me, I start chatting with landowners about their timber and what it might be worth, and to everyone's surprise, I am ridiculously good at it.

New clients come on board. I'm keeping Byron busy scouting properties all over the region. The money starts rolling in. Byron and I meet at the Lullwater, our watering hole in Emory Village, to celebrate. I keep looking at the new waitress. God, is she cute. Like a young Melanie Griffith, only better. But it's her easy laugh that catches me. She tells us her name. Kate. I'm going to remember the name. Kate.

But after a couple of beers, I get engrossed in the conversation with Byron when we talk about how much money we're gonna make in the timber business and the idea that we should do something amazing with it, something we would never think of doing, even something Jan would never think of, and we wonder what in the hell that would be.

We decide to go to Asia. We're going traveling. We are going to Asia. And we are serious. We'll get to San Francisco and let the cheapest flight across the Pacific determine our destination.

This is exciting. And funny, because it was right here in Emory Village, at Jagger's bar, that Byron suggested I go to Europe eight years ago.

This is also a way to stop thinking about Cara.

≈ ≈ ≈

But what really stops me from thinking about Cara, after I apply all the master-of-attention exercises from Jan's compendium again and again and over and over, is Kate.

The next time I speak to her is back at the Lullwater Tavern one night after a meeting. I'm there with Madeleine.

I look around but don't see Kate.

Madeleine and I sit in the corner. We lean into the conversation. We nurse our drinks. Probably looks like we're on a date. But we're not. We're leaning in because she's practically whispering . . . about her troubles with Jan, now that they've been living together awhile. Whispering, I guess, because we're not supposed to think about him, let alone talk about him, so this is extremely against the rules, and maybe whispering will protect us from whatever, but who cares, because she's telling me stuff way more riveting than Jan's rules.

Madeleine is upset because Jan tells her to go to her room when he has other women from the group over to the house for sex.

This is not a one-time event.

This happens a lot.

This is all tangled up.

First I bought into Jan's edict "Don't get involved with me personally" so completely that I really haven't really gotten involved with him personally, at least not enough to worry about his sex life, but yeah, I should know better than anyone, Jan really does fuck around.

Another of Jan's big rules circles my brain, like an aerial banner flying around at the beach. "No casual sex between group members." What, no casual sex, all of you, just save it for me? Then another banner loops around with one of Jan's refrains: "An ordinary man demands it of others. The extraordinary man demands it of himself." So we have two sets of rules here. A bunch for us. None for him? This is hardly extraordinary. This is quite an arrangement. Live with one of the women in the group and make her wait outside while he fucks the others?

Well, wait a second. Here I am getting all tangled up in this. For one thing, his sex life really is none of my business. And look—quite a few of the women in the group are simply gorgeous, and alive and smart and funny and who in his right mind wouldn't want to merge with all that intelligence and mystery? And, yes, I've had my opportunities. And took them. And it made me a very happy American. I am eternally grateful. So why am I getting judgmental about Jan's adventures? Well, when you're so arrogant that you make your significant other go to her room and wait while you fuck her so-called friends, then it changes the equation. And it stinks. So it's not about being judgmental. It's about a bad smell stinking up good work. A stinking, leaky, overstuffed ego: is that the culmination of all this effort to extraordinarily transcend the ego?

And then the irony. She was the one fucking around with him when she was with me. And now she wants me to help her, as if I could, when he's fucking around on her? Is she a fraction as aware of the pain she inflicted as she is of the pain she's suffering?

One of Madeleine's finest qualities is the gracious tempo of her conversation. Silence is as welcome as speech. I don't say anything for several minutes while digesting all this knotted-up fuckedupedness.

Finally I say, "Look, I get it. And I'm sorry. It's a mess. I'm sorry." Maybe I'll say more later.

I look around the room to escape this miserable muddle of Jan and Madeleine, and whoa. Kate in the corner, just standing there, elbow on the counter, hips tilted, smiling just a little. She must've been in the kitchen when we came in.

"I'll be right back," I tell Madeleine.

I need to stand up. I gotta shake it off, like I got a brain full of fleas from somebody's dirty-rat life. I need to move. And I have a destination.

≈ ≈ ≈

The Lullwater Tavern is surprisingly empty tonight, and nobody is between Kate and me, so she sees me approaching but stays all cool and doesn't shift her posture or her smile. The first words I say to her are "Can we go out sometime soon?"

The first word she says to me, after a long pause, is "Why?"

After a long pause of my own, I tell her that's a good question—but I have a good answer. "We will have a really good time, the best we've had in minutes."

She laughs a little and we talk a little and she gives me her phone number.

I call her the next day.

We're getting together on Friday.

On Friday, in the first minute of our date, I ask whether she minds if we go measure something. It's a commercial space that "this friend of mine" has asked me to look at because he's going to open a law school.

That friend would be Jan. He passed the bar—miraculously, he says, since he didn't study and didn't care but made a multiplicity of lucky gut instinct multiple choices—and emerged with the badge but had no intention of practicing law. So now here comes his latest idea, a law school as a moneymaker. Or so he says. It's not something I have any interest in. But I like to measure empty spaces.

Especially with Kate. Kate and I are going to measure the rooms.

She likes strolling across the giant empty echoing offices with one end of a hundred-foot tape. We have a great time with the measuring tape. She has never measured a building before going to a movie.

Then I tell her I'm going to Asia soon. So I have to catch up on my hippie Americana. "Do you mind if we see *The Last Waltz*, a documentary about the Band's final concert?"

She doesn't mind at all. I'm in love. She's smart, she's funny and silly and beautiful, and she's read a lot books I haven't read and talks about Shakespeare and what she might do in theater.

We sleep together that night, and the next night, and the night after that and all the nights after that, and it is all perfectly easy and pure and natural and perfect.

Kate is why I quit thinking about Cara.

≈ ≈ ≈

I'm reluctant to go into all this with Grandpa Phil. All this plea-sure and experience he was denied.

So I say to him, "Jan's shenanigans notwithstanding, he's holding up his end of the bargain. He said it, plain as day—if you want a hero or a god, go somewhere else. You won't find gods or heroes here. But if you want to kick yourself up to something else entirely, something you can barely imagine from your little perch, well, jump right in and hang around as long as you're getting something."

The people in the group radiate health, and everyone laughs a lot. People bloom.

The process evolves, just as we do.

It's not The Work anymore. He never calls it The Work and doesn't talk about Gurdjieff anymore. Never mentions him or Ouspensky.

Jan keeps changing the name of the group and what we do.

For a while, it's the DeKalb Chess Club. Later, the Koray Adventure. Anachron. This Thing. New Intelligence.

He also writes a book entitled The Death of Gurdjieff in the Foothills of Georgia. *Which is ironic in view of the fact that he never talks about Gurdjieff anymore.*

I never read it. As much as I'm all in, I get enough of Jan's words. But other people around the country do read it. An entire intact group from Oregon opens a correspondence with Jan.

Not sure if Grandpa is even listening.

I say to him, "The rabbi could be so boring."

I'm going to say more, but Grandpa interrupts.

He says, "You're all crazy. All my progeny are crazy. But at least you're doing something with your crazy instead of just being crazy. I only hope you will get somewhere with all this nonsense. Oy."

≈ ≈ ≈

A couple of days before Byron and I leave for San Francisco to book a discount charter flight to Asia, Jan and I get together, just the two of us. He shows me a necklace, a thin silver chain hung with an intricate silver serpent. Finely detailed, ready to spring. Looks like it came straight from medieval Japan. An amulet, a reminder. Fierce as the path we travel. A reminder to do what you know, so you may learn more. He doesn't say that. He says nothing. Just hangs it around my neck and leaves. Surprisingly tender gesture. Another surprise. Right when you don't expect it. A force-of-life serpent guarding my throat.

I wonder if Jan will miss me. I laugh. He'd never admit to missing anyone.

But I don't really care. This is exciting. Going out there to rev the motors that drove us to all this in the first place, without Jan's scaffolding for support and direction.

But the day before we're scheduled to leave, Byron rushes to the hospital, doubling over with severe stomach pains. What the hell is this? He can't get sick now. We're already three days into a leave of absence from Oakman Timber, and we're both braced for tearful girlfriend good-byes.

Damn: acute appendicitis. He's recovering from the appendectomy. When I enter the hospital room, before I get a word in, he announces, "We're going. I can fly next week. Maybe I'll sneak out sooner." He tries to laugh but can't and grimaces instead. His belly is wrapped in bandages, and he can hardly move. But he insists. He's all in. We're doing this.

Well, okay, then. If he's that feisty about it, this will work. We can do this. We're going.

We'll meet in San Francisco in nine days. He'll fly. I'll drive.

≈ ≈ ≈

From an auto drive-away company, just like the one that supplied Sal Paradise and Dean Moriarty with a Cadillac in *On the Road*, I ask if there are any cars going to San Francisco.

Nope, the guy says. Closest we got is one you can deliver to Seattle. It's a new Cadillac. Suddenly I want to go to Seattle. Only one thing wrong with the car, he says. Someone stole the radio.

"Three thousand miles without a radio?" I say to the guy.

"Yup. But the seats are real nice."

Yup, the seats *are* nice. Extremely. Plush, puffy, velvety foam-rubber engulfments. On these seats, I'm halfway between floating and sinking as this two-ton barge rolls north from Atlanta.

I didn't say yes to a radio-less car because of the seat, though. I said yes partly because of the urge to go. The arrangements have been made, the job is on hold, and Kate and I have already cried good-bye.

And partly because of this Jan-induced predilection to opt for what I would never automatically choose. As he would say, "This is not about turning you into a mad band of masochists. Never do anything to harm yourself. Rather, this is about creating reminders, in the form of surprises and discomforts, to redirect your attention where it will serve your Aim."

Three thousand miles without a radio? Yes, sure, I answer before thinking. Thinking would have led to *no*. But thinking just wants to perpetuate thinking.

Less than an hour out of Atlanta, at the edge of Lake Allatoona, I glance at the odometer. Thirty-one miles. Only 2,969 miles to go. Shit. How am I gonna do this? How am I gonna sit here and get there?

Shit. I'll have to listen to my own bullshit for 2,969 more miles. It's not the miles, really. It's the space. The brainspace. An empty brainspace, as if I am spit from the rain forest into the Sahara. Shit. Nothing out here except sunshine and infinity and clarity. Makes sense why everyone's so busy all the time. It's easier to be frantic than it is to inch across a thousand miles of banging brain.

I-75 crosses over Lake Allatoona. I look sideways across the muddy, yucky, yellowish lake where Phyllis stroked Jan's dick at dawn, everyone watching while trying not to.

This is funny. It's lot funnier now than it was on the night, or morning, it happened in real time. If such a thing exists. Real time. It should be reel time. Not that this is a movie. It's a reel.

Is it still mile 31? A lot is packing into mile 31. Probably because it's a prime number. I prefer my numbers prime.

Two thousand nine hundred and sixty-nine miles is a big divot of the space-time continuum in which to trap your own bullshit as it bubbles to the surface for observation. Plus some of the bullshit isn't bullshit. You can mine some gold while panning for bullshit.

Turns out this car is a perfect petri dish for the propagation of bullshit. Utter comfort in cushy seats in a nearly new plush-mobile without a care in the world—a girlfriend I love who loves me back, a job waiting for me, and a relentlessly fascinating cult to fuel to my fire. What's not to love?

Yeah, that lasts about ten or a hundred seconds, if attention lasts ten or a hundred seconds. Then bullshit rushes in like Bay of Fundy tides.

How come I'm not rich? I should be rich. Then I could buy this Cadillac, put a goddamn radio in it, and drive to Asia. I oughta be rich enough to hire a barge to float this hog across the watery parts. Wish I were six foot eight. Then I'd be one of those amazing unheard-of Jewish NBA players who meditates and makes a billion dollars a minute. Fifty-eight miles to Chattanooga. God, I'm still in Georgia? I haven't even been gone two hours? Sure, I wish this car had a radio. Am I an idiot? Why did I say yes? Christ, I'll never get there. How am I gonna get to Seattle alone? Without a radio? I could sing. I know, like, what—

twelve or twenty songs, including my Bob Dylan repertoire *and* "The Star-Spangled Banner"? I snort out loud. Twelve songs won't even get me to Chatsworth. That's not even halfway to Chattanooga from here. Shit. I'll sing anyway. Fuck it. I'll sing really loud.

Whoa!

What kinda bullshit is that? Where does this shit come from?

It's Zork!

Zork shows up for a while in Jan's weekly talks to the group. A short while, actually, because the subject matter and the ideas and Tasks always change. But each is useful, and here I am driving to Seattle with him. Zork.

Zork is everyone's individual "I" combined. It manifests as the voice in your head. So when your internal conversation says, "I wanna be in the NBA," it's not really "I." It's just . . . Zork. Zork is noise emanating from the machinations of ordinary consciousness, all random, repetitive, and vapid but delivered with such urgency! Such annoyance!

Characterizing it all as Zork depersonalizes, and deflates, the onrush of "I want . . ." It's not "I." It's not "you." It's the noise of the bio-mind factory.

This chair is good. This chair is plush. On this chair, in this comfort, at this speed, with all due appreciation to the seven-liter V-8 motor, I say out loud, "Wait a minute. I have a choice here."

The windshield is one screen. The rasp of Zork is the other.

I may enjoy this wide window on the whirled world.

Or I'll be a zombie for Zork.

Like the choice I faced on the porch that night in Alpharetta, only without the exigency of whether or not Madeleine was fucking Jan. This time, it's purely for the reward of the efforts.

My own Seattle-or-bust Zen koan rises like a mirage beguiling a crazed desert pilgrim: "Can I endure my own mind farting for three thousand miles?"

I count my breaths. At the wheel. Rolling speeding. Mile marker thirty-five. The wind is my radio. The sky is my god. These seats are my steed as I speed west. For days.

Day three. I am getting somewhere. Somebody is the bull and somebody is the matador and somebody is driving this Coupe de Ville without a radio on the ribbon of US 2, now spooling across northwestern North Dakota, in these burnished hills, untraveled, untrammeled. Holding the steering wheel with both hands, like a flag clutching the pole.

Divine.

Long, long breaths in long, long minutes. I drink it in, Zork-free mile by Zork-free mile, a free-for-all. Here's hoping I never get there, because here I am.

≈ ≈ ≈

In San Francisco, we provincials are stunned at the cityscape built on igneous poems.

"You feel okay?" I ask Byron.

"I feel great," he says.

I smell a lie. The belly bandage shows through his shirt.

"How was your ride?" he asks.

"Amazing," I tell him. "Just not long enough."

He thinks I'm kidding.

We peruse the *San Francisco Bay Guardian*, looking for flights.

Byron wants to know why I'm wearing a necklace. He doesn't call it a necklace. "That thing around your neck."

"Well . . ." I stall. I get uncomfortable with the way Jan picks a few of us as special. Even as he bashes notions of "special," he reinforces it. But it's all out in the open. We've both bought the program, Byron and I. And Jan pulls it off because somehow he makes everyone feel special. Jan's the one who suggested that Byron get a job on the line at Ford. Byron never imagined such a thing. He loved it, and it was life-changing. And when Byron quit the Ford job, Jan nudged him to take up running. Byron is not, by nature, a runner. He is now. Even though he doesn't fly off his feet, the way natural-born runners do, he loves it. Outrun your nature, people!

"Jan gave it to me."

Byron cradles it in his fingers, close, as tenderly as Jan did when he hung it. He nods. "Nice," he says.

We find a flight. Two seats on a charter flight to Singapore, with a change of planes in Manila. Three days from now, in the evening. We book it.

On the morning of the third day, Byron says, "We have a problem."

"Man," I say with a laugh, "we don't have *problems*. We have *solutions!*"

He pulls up his shirt.

The incision is red. Oozing. The drippage is brown.

He speaks first. "It's infected," he says.

"This is a problem," I tell him.

"Not a solution."

He's worried. So am I.

"This is not good," I tell him.

"I've been ignoring it," he says, "so it'll go away."

I nod. And state the obvious, which is not always obvious when you're staring at pus. "Well, we either stay or we go."

He nods.

"What do you want to do?" I ask him. "You got more say-so here than I do."

"I wanna go." Byron says he wants to go.

"You want to go to Singapore with an infection?"

"Yeah. I want to go."

"You gotta get this taken care of first."

He doesn't want to. He doesn't want to go to a doctor who will tell him not to go, because he wants to go.

We talk our way through this. We know this infection needs medical attention. We might be provincial, but we're not rubes.

But damn, we want to get on that plane.

We have desire on our side. We decide that desire has medicinal properties. Not as crazy as it sounds. We talk through this. We saw what happened to Tom Amear. We were there. We were part of it. We bent our attention to the miracle. Desire has thermal, physical properties. Desire can change minds and behavior, and if it can do that, it can scorch some pesky microbes.

Byron and I do not take this lightly. We are making a commitment. We have never done this before. Are we crazy? Well, um, yes, at least a little. A little laughter. We hafta be a little crazy to take off for Asia for as long as the money lasts. Sane people have jobs and work in offices and save for retirement. The laughter feels good, but we are not really laughing. His health depends on our focus and desire.

We are going to get on the plane.

We are already doing this.

We are devoting our attention, laser-like, to cure the incision. All our random thoughts will unify, the way disparate photons unite in a common wave, capable of more in unison than what could be achieved by an equal number of waves or particles acting independently.

We are going to seal the incision. We are not smiling. Neither are we frowning. We are concentrating. We can do this. We envision the wound healing. We say a few words about the wound healing. We close our eyes and see the future: the wound is mending. Our attention unifies like laser light.

The afternoon ticks by as slowly as flat miles on the Great Plains. But just as driving can become meditative, just as the journey becomes the destination, so does our focus on this healing mission become purposeful, and we percolate. At the airport, none of the annoyances registers because we are very busy mending the incision. On the plane, we settle into our seats, make eye contact, and nod.

We are doing this.

The plane lifts off. The coastline fades fast. We speed backwards through time zones. Everything is a metaphor. Lasers, time, flying, healing, mending, attention. We eat when they bring food, which is most of the time, but even as we chew we are unified in our efforts to heal this deal. Even as we relax and fall in and out of sleep, *we keep doing this.*

We look at our watches, but they don't mean anything because we don't know what time zone we're in, and what happens to time when we cross the international date line? And at what time, ha-ha, does that happen? But even as we sit and slump and eat and sleep and laugh at what time it is, we are really doing only *this, this one thing*, and we feel good about it even though we don't say anything directly about it. We fall asleep again.

We are awakened by an announcement from the cockpit. "Good morning from the crew!" The captain sounds ridiculously chipper. The horizon is indigo, the sky black. "Local time is five a.m.," he says, as if this is fantastic news.

Local time? Byron and I look at each other. Local? What's

local out here? All you can see is Pacific infinity. Nothing local in sight.

We start laughing and can't stop.

Byron lifts his shirt.

His belly is dry.

The wound is clean.

Attention is physical.

The laughter caramelizes to joy.

≈ ≈ ≈

"Attention is physical?" Grandpa repeats. "Is that something Jan Cox told you?

"No. Jan never said that. That came to me—"

"Interesting," he says. "Attention is physical?"

"It came to me physically, the idea did. It came to me the first time when we were doing the Walking exercise. Everyone in unison, arms opening and closing in sync with each step of each left foot, filling the room, saturating space, and we were all breathing in unison, and we were lifted, each of us, to serious, purposeful, beat-by-beat bliss.

"I felt it physically, and the words came: 'Attention is physical.'"

Grandpa looks like he's scrutinizing a bundle of pelts. He isn't buying just yet. But he's still listening.

"Backed up, I guess, by my reading in science. Jan says, 'If you need a hobby, take up physics. Or biology. Take up a science.' So I read all the science news I can, and if something doesn't make sense, all these Georgia Tech graduates in the group can make sense of it, and so over time I get it that transactions in the brain have mass, and energy flies around like crazy, so even at the abstract level, so to speak, attention is physical."

Grandpa is listening.

"But the physical information came first. When we did Walking. And then the experience with Tom Amear. And now this with Byron."

Grandpa says, "I never experienced such miracles of attention."

"Grandpa, your whole life was a kind of miracle. From the Dark Ages to modernity in one giant, incomprehensible leap. Isn't that a miracle?"

His eyes soften.

"Wrought by attention, Grandpa."

≈ ≈ ≈

The plane lands in Singapore. The sun is shining. But we can't figure out what day it is. How many hours ago did we cross the international date line? We have to figure out what time zone we were in when we crossed it. Never mind—that's too complicated. We'll figure it out later. Or never. We got too much other stuff to figure out now. So we try to figure it out, piece by bumbled piece. The money. The ride to town. A place to stay. We see a sign. The Ah Chew Hotel. Perfect. But do they have Kleenex? We get a room. Look for food. We don't know what anything is and order it. It tastes amazing. Ouch! Our mouths are on fire! But we can't stop eating it and complaining about it, involuntarily crying cayenne tears. Welcome to Asia, gringos! Feast and weep!

≈ ≈ ≈

Up the lightly traveled, undeveloped eastern coast of

Malaysia, at a village restaurant, a rat runs across a guy's bare foot, and the guy doesn't care.

We stay next to the jungle in shelters on stilts, right by the shore of the South China Sea. The shelters sit above the backyard of a guy almost as old as Grandpa. He rides his bicycle and smiles a lot. Somehow, we communicate. He points to the jungle. He pantomimes war. He gestures and points and shows us how he disappeared in there. We figure it out. During World War II, he disappeared into the jungle and subsisted and waited until the coast was clear. And then he came back to the coast, clear as light. He is happy to be here. And so are we. The breeze tosses the palms.

On the island of Ko Samui, in the Gulf of Thailand, in its last years as a tropical paradise, we stay for days in lean-tos on the beach. I stroll alone way down the seaside path to a perfect turquoise cove and sit on a rock. On the far bend of the path, at the curve of the cove, three figures appear silhouetted against the tropical brightness. I look away, at diamonds glittering on the water. Then look again. They are approaching.

Three women. They keep getting closer. They are coming right at me on this path. Here they are. I stand to greet them. "Sawat-dee!" It's all the Thai I know. The language barrier is insurmountable. But the smiles all around are big and eloquent.

They point at the sun, straight overhead, touch the face of the watch one of them is wearing, and spin a finger around once. We are communicating. I nod. They point into the jungle and skywrite a house. They are inviting me to meet them right here tomorrow at noon and spend the night with their family in the jungle.

Byron asks, "How do you know somebody means 'right here at noon tomorrow' when you can't understand a word they're saying?"

I don't know how I know. But I know. The next day at noon,

there they are. I follow them away from the beach into the jungle. The path curves, we stroll, easy batik shadows soften the tropical sun.

The matriarch and extended clan welcome me. She directs sons and daughters to take me into a palm grove. I break all the safety rules, leave my backpack in the house, and follow them. One of the sons climbs a palm tree barefoot, then descends with a green coconut the size of a basketball. Cuts it open. The flesh, velvety and melting, fixes me in happy silence. I want more. In the language of the coconut, I'm fluent.

≈ ≈ ≈

Grandpa says, "Money is a language. But English is easier to learn. First you learn a few words, words for objects, and you point with your hands, so your hands fill in for the verbs. Then you learn some verbs. Then it snowballs." He laughs. "'Snowballs' is a great word," he says. "English is full of words like that."

I'm glad he likes the English language.

His smile fades, and he says, "The coins changing hands when I was a child. I was riveted by the coins changing hands. The coins had life. More life than the rest of Augostowa. The coins had the power. Hands would open and close quick and tight around them. The coins riveted me. The money look on grown-ups' faces. Waxed and cold with straight lips. The men listened to the money more than their wives or the rabbi or anything. The coins had more power than people did.

"The language of money you learn differently if you work seven days and manage to save a dime. That dime means something. It represents something. Money may be an abstraction, but it is more connected to physical objects, and time, than words are."

Money a more powerful language than words? I never thought of it that way before.

≈ ≈ ≈

This archipelago of tongue-tying moments—beginning with my quiet consequential solo ride to Seattle and continuing in new form as lasers sealing Byron's belly—perpetuate all through Thailand and Sri Lanka. It all speaks with new fluency. London. And Atlanta. So green and lush it appears from the air. I'm home.

Kate and I can't wait to crush each other.

We crush beyond anything we imagined.

"Keep on crushin'" is our new slogan. Better than the R. Crumb original.

Kate and I catch our breath. It takes a few days or a week—who knows? I tell her, "Because we're on the international date line. You never know what day it is. But you don't care because you're so happy to be there."

She says, "You're a fun date."

I tell her, "You're a fun international line."

She says, "You're stupid."

"You win," I tell her.

"Okay, I'll win you."

"Stupid and all?"

"Yup. Stupid and all."

1979

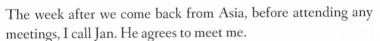

The week after we come back from Asia, before attending any meetings, I call Jan. He agrees to meet me.

We have a warm greeting. We sit down and order a beer even though neither of us wants one.

After about a minute of small talk, which is more than either of us normally tolerates, he asks, "Well?" As if to ask why I called this meeting.

I look at him and don't feel in any hurry to answer. His tone and manner surprise me. The truth is that I don't have an agenda for this meeting. It's just that I feel on fire and don't want the flames snuffed by any return to normalcy. Any better ally against normalcy than Jan Cox?

"Well," I say, "it was amazing. I just wanted to say hello before getting into the swing of things."

I can't read him, but something is off. Does he think—or fear—I'm announcing my exit? Or is he, for once, bounced from his familiar I-know-everythingness because he has never spent four months of his life rolling through sunburned Buddhist alleyways and paths by the sea and the whirligig that is Bangkok. He doesn't know how to ask the first question about it. Why doesn't he ask questions? Hmm.

≈ ≈ ≈

The power is conserved. This new life I'm living—I'm really living it all through and up and out and down and around.

I call Kate the Great Fox of the West, always in caps, on the refrigerator and in conversation.

The job at Oakman, faint hum in the background though it is, is easy, and who cares if they're all crazy?

And the work, the real Work, churns like a locomotive laying its own tracks in transit.

And instead of moving back into the old Candler mansion on Ponce de Leon, where the group meets, I settle into a small one-person cottage on a creek a few miles away on Shady Valley Drive. Shady Valley—the name is apt. The oaks tower overhead and shade me from the hubbub of living with people in the group all the time.

≈ ≈ ≈

Late in glorious autumn, one afternoon when I happen to be home, the phone rings.

I pick it up. "Hello?"

Hum of silence on the line. "Hello," she drawls.

Cara. It's Cara. Oh, no. Oh, yes. A spear of sick excitement. It's inevitable now, after eight seconds of conversation. We're going to see each other. We are going to do it again. But I don't want to. Wish you hadn't called. Do not want to do this. It is not good. But I am saying, "Why don't you come over here right now?"

≈ ≈ ≈

It gets worse. I'm staying home more, alone, leaving Kate alone at her place a few blocks away, in case the phone might ring at midnight or one or two, when the restaurant closes up, and she might come over for a few hours.

I'm lying more and more and spending more nights at my little house.

Kate and I knew we would be living together by now. But we are not, and she doesn't understand why.

I am sick about this, but I latch on to Jan's edict "Fake it until you make it." That is to say, become what you want to become so that you become it.

So faking it becomes real enough . . . everything seems wonderful, inside and out, even as it's not wonderful at all.

This goes on for months.

I feel dirty.

I love one.

I am addicted to the other.

I am inadvertently mirroring the disconnect between Jan's

speech and Jan's actions: desire trumps devotion, despite language to the contrary.

He seems okay with it.

I am not, but try to be.

≈ ≈ ≈

It all blows up in the early spring.

Cara shows up in the middle of the night, drinking, and sometimes she smells.

Then she always comes over drunk. I don't even like the sex anymore. I tell her this is no good. Cara doesn't argue. We quit. I am relieved.

I haven't seen Kate in almost two weeks. Now I can't wait, now that I've finally figured it out. But it's been a long time. And now she has figured it out.

Kate figures it out.

I confess.

Then we have sex.

Then she tells me she has met someone.

Then we have sex.

Then she says I can't see you anymore. I'm with him now.

Then we have sex.

She gets up to leave. To leave for good. I don't want her to go.

I say, wait—we made love three times today, and . . . . we don't love each other?

She says maybe we do, but this is good-bye, and she's done, she leaves, and it's over.

Three times. Her way of saying "I love you, but you fucked it up, damn you, and I can't get over it. I'm marrying him."

Does that make it burn any less?

No.

More.

≈ ≈ ≈

So it all burns up. Everything blows up and goes to hell. I'm standing in the wreckage. Shell-shocked. It's all my fault. This implosion is all mine. Shit. All the lies of which this shattered edifice was built falling from head to heart and landing hard. I am disgusted.

At least I'm clear on whom to blame.

The pain bellows. It weighs more than I do.

≈ ≈ ≈

"Grandpa, we were insulated from money when we were growing up. We never saw people cherish the coins, as you did. Mom could never find the money in her purse, but it was always in there. Money was always as mixed up as her pocketbook. One day we couldn't have something that cost a dollar, and the next day we got something we didn't care about for ten dollars. Plus we had a layer of protection. You. You were there in the background, so we never thought about falling out of comfort. We were insulated. We couldn't feel the coins, as you did. We never

learned the language of money, as you did. Not that we were rich, but . . . we had everything we wanted, and it wasn't enough."

Grandpa chews on this. He has never heard such a thing.

He repeats the words one at a time.

Everything we wanted. Wasn't enough.

"I just happened, by circumstance of birth, to skip over the money part. So I never became fluent in the language of money, the way you did."

"But you were just a child," he says.

I start talking faster than I'm thinking. "You ever hear of Rimbaud?"

I don't wait for an answer.

"Arthur Rimbaud. The French poet. He practically single-handedly invented modern poetry in the 1870s, and he quit writing before he turned twenty! So who's to say all youthful fancy is fantasy? Einstein worked out the theory of relativity when he was twenty-six. Because he had been thinking of practically nothing else for his entire youth. I'm not saying I'm Einstein or Rimbaud, but for every one of those geniuses there are a million kids who do take their personal riddles seriously. As seriously as a businessman takes money."

Grandpa is considering this.

Then I blurt out, "The young discount the passion of the elderly, and the elderly discount the gravity of youth."

After a long pause Grandpa Phil nods and says, "I know about the hole at the center."

1980

Starting over, chastised, with everything.

I return to carpentry. Four of us from the group form Heart-wood & Sons, a contracting and construction company. Even though we all treat the business as secondary to The Work, we do take the jobs seriously and start earning a reputation. We have skills. Impeccable integrity. We're smart, young, full of energy, talented, devoted to quality, and we also have an eye for design and form. We get better at bidding, which is really hard to do on a remodel, and the workmanship is, well, at a very high level. And the business grows.

Perry, the physicist-framer, meets this guy Ken McDonald, who has a pointy silver goatee and looks like an Alpine watch-maker. Without any prompting from us, Ken takes a paternal interest in Heartwood and practically gives us an entire carpentry shop on Ponce de Leon, across from the giant Sears, Roebuck building. For a very nominal monthly sum, we suddenly have it all: a shop with a table saw, radial arm saw, drill press, planer, band saw, routers, hand tools, plus giant work tables with vises, lumber racks, and a little office with a drawing table.

So now, with the shop, we're making furniture and custom built-ins.

Everything happens at once all over again.

I hit it off with Daphne, a good-looking woman who happens to be the heiress to a major captain-of-industry fortune. We start spending time together, but after a little fling, we become just friends. She visits the shop. She meets the guys. She's impressed with the spirit of the enterprise, the talent and the brains. And for reasons none of us fully comprehends, it has something to do with a fortune-teller she trusts, and against the desperate entreaties of her family—maybe this is her act of rebellion—she decides to bankroll our first spec house, on a vacant lot in an urban pioneer neighborhood called Virginia-Highland. She puts up the entire sum, in cash.

We obsess over the design of the spec house. We make a list of criteria. Less than two thousand square feet. Every room with double exposures. Save the two large trees. Three bedrooms, two and a half baths. And a sense of space. It has to feel bigger than it is. When you factor in the size limit, save-the-trees, and double exposures everywhere, it seems impossible. How can we make the house do all that?

We have design meetings. Nothing we come up with is good enough.

It seems impossible.

How can we do this? But everything is all lined up, all over again. Our efforts in The Work seem to mesh with our work.

So at the same time we're trying to solve the design riddle, Jan issues a Task: "Do something creative once an hour, on the hour, for five minutes." For two weeks.

Seems impossible.

How do you do that?

It's not something you can turn on and off like a spigot, is it?

Well, it's good we're self-employed. Because whenever the big hand hits twelve, we're all breaking out our little journals. And it turns out that—guess what?— creativity *is* something you can turn on.

Empty pages begin to fill with five-minute sketches of what I'd never noticed before, such as what I see in a spoon: funhouse reflections of the tree in the window or the underside of my sandwich.

Or new thoughts will clang at the top of the hour. I love them. Such as:

Growth is blasphemy that works.

Everything is either a hallway or an ocean.

If you pleasantly surprise life, life will pleasantly surprise you.

Synonym for "dictionary": the book of doors.

Happiness is not the object of the process but a precondition for the process.

Let's go east by my moral compass until we pass the sunrise.

If you can get out of the house, you can do anything.

One afternoon at the top of the hour, out of nowhere, I start writing *Autobiography of a Mule*:

Sometimes I just stand still. It's not like I want to stand still. I just don't care. And if I don't care, I can't move. You wouldn't believe what goes on in your mind. All in short sentences. Part of the time. They beat on your butt. It feels like the sound of distant yodeling. The farmer is going crazy. You want to laugh out loud. More than you want to move.

This turns into a one-page piece that I read to the group after a meeting. It cracks everybody up.

And one night after work, at the top of the hour, after we've been wrestling with it since who knows when, the spec house comes to me whole.

It's a two-story house centered around the core of foyer and staircase. I'm sketching as fast as I can. Off the core are three peninsulas, one being the sunken living room between the trees we have to save; another being the dining room facing the backyard, with triple exposures; and the third being the kitchen and breakfast room. The bedrooms upstairs align over the three peninsulas. Later, when I draw it out to scale, it comes to 1,857 square feet.

The Heartwood partners say yes, that's it, you did it, and that's exactly the house we build.

Daphne's father, a large-scale developer, comes to see the completed house he told his daughter to shun and compliments us: it's the best spec house he's ever seen.

We raise the price.

It sells. Full price.

We pay Daphne back and have a pile of beer money left over.

≈ ≈ ≈

Grandpa's eyebrows rise. Profits must be put to better use than buying beer.

I shouldn't have said that, even kidding a little. You don't talk about money that way around Grandpa, the way you don't crack crime jokes to victims of crime.

He says, "Somebody has to die first. But I hope nobody dies first yet."

I don't say anything. Not sure what he means. What's he talking about?

"Passages," he says. "Everything is a passage. But the scales of the passages change, to be sure . . . the scale changes moment by moment."

Huh? I can't tell if he's talking to me or himself.

Then he says, "Sand. Thirst. Water. Sunshine. Mountains. Time. Blood. Gravity. Darkness."

As if he's assaying the elements of life on earth. Doesn't matter that I don't get the context. Feels like I'm privy to nuggets of disembodied wisdom.

He's nodding, looking far away, and continues. "Grain and grapes. Water from middle earth. Caves where our people hid. A place that collapses time."

I shiver. In recognition?

He leaves it at that.

He likes the shiver. He likes the spec house. He likes the good work and the success. He wants me to save money.

≈ ≈ ≈

I run into a knockout named Cynthia at Sevananda, the food co-op in Little Five Points. Same place I met her around four years ago. Everyone in Atlanta has a crush on her. Somehow, four years ago, I talked her into going out with me. But it was only once, reluctantly, because she was in love with an architect. Haven't seen her since.

She looks even better now. It's her self-possession that gets me, though. She's lighter and more alive, and the magnet she contains pulls even more than before. I'm surprised she remembers me. Yes, she'd like to get together. She'd like that a lot.

So would I.

Four days later, at my little one-person cottage by a creek off Shady Valley, I carry her upstairs to bed.

Two days later, high summer in the South, I ride my bike across town to her cool apartment near Piedmont Park. I arrive unannounced all sun-spun and sweaty, and she pulls me into the dark bedroom, throws me on the bed, and undresses me.

By the next week, we're seeing each other all the time. Her face intent like a Vermeer as she designs silk fabrics, makes the patterns, and sews the garments for private clients. I like to watch.

So does she. She comes to the job site sometimes and watches us work for a little while.

Cynthia makes me forget Kate. She has a great laugh. She's knock-you-off-your-presumptions smart and a gourmet cook. She loves the beach. And she loves the letters I send through the mail and usually keep secret if I arrive before they do. I can't always tell if she loves the words. And then she says, "Keep writing."

I want to tell her what I'm up to all the time, the time I spend with Jan and the group. I want to tell her before she asks, because it could be a problem. But one of the rules is Do Not Talk about This Activity. I don't mind breaking the rule. But the rule, startling and difficult at first, can become the lazy way out.

1981

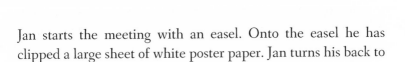

Jan starts the meeting with an easel. Onto the easel he has clipped a large sheet of white poster paper. Jan turns his back to us and draws a long horizontal line.

He turns around, faces us with his chest-first military mien, extends his index finger as though it were a stick, and stabs it on the line.

"The horizontal line," he says, "represents the line of consciousness of ordinary humanity."

Jan turns his back. In the middle of the horizontal line, he draws a vertical line. It barely projects above the horizontal line.

Jan sticks his finger on the wee bit above the line.

"That little bit," he says, turning to face us. "That's what we're talking about here. The little bit above the line. The little bit of new above the ordinary line of consciousness."

He points back to the horizontal line. "The line rotates in time. You have to see the line rotating beyond this flat drawing. You have to see it in three dimensions, inching its way up."

Huh? I'm thinking he could have drawn it as a giant wheel. I could draw it. At least, I can see it in my mind's eye. What he has drawn as a line is a really a vast wheel, always rotating up.

"Picture a giant wheel rotating upward," he says.

I nod. I get it. Jan always plugs in when somebody gets it. He acknowledges me with a sharp affirmative glance while continuing to hold forth.

"Each new generation of humanity is the medium through which consciousness evolves. That's what our efforts here are about. Seeing ahead. Seeing up the line of consciousness. Experiencing the future before everyone else does, when it won't be the future anymore."

Jan turns to the paper. He draws a circle around the intersection of the horizontal and vertical lines.

The circle represents one human consciousness.

The horizontal line—ordinary consciousness—flows right through each mind.

Each new generation automatically rises above the line, just a little.

You can rise above the line by conscious effort. That's what *extra-ordinary* is. It is literally a bit above the ordinary. Again: it is the slightly higher level to which each succeeding generation rises, and the extraordinary get there first. Then the rising generation follows. It is new at first. The new becomes ordinary all over again, because the horizontal line, which is really a wheel, has rotated up a notch. The extraordinary remains above the line no matter how high the line climbs. It's up there *in the future.*

Jan continues. "You can see this over time, as civilization progresses. To cite a gross example, consider that slavery was, only a few generations ago, accepted by most modern civilizations. Now it is reprehensible. You can see that the horizontal line has indeed lifted. But this upward trend is harder to see in the present."

He stifles a laugh, the way he does with his own private jokes. "Harder to see? Hell, it's practically blasphemy to declare that things are getting better! And that's the way it's supposed to be at the ordinary level—always serious as hell, everyone riveted on the bad news of the day. That's what makes the day so damn serious and urgent and all-consuming. The ordinary are not supposed to see up the line of consciousness, because they're needed right here right now."

He places his finger on the horizontal line in the drawing and says, "Right there, where everything is going straight to hell, that's where human energy is ordinarily spent. But I am telling you that everything is not going to hell. It is all evolving, and what you see as impending doom is merely the friction and bumps and starts and ups and downs of unruly growth. Evolution does not go in a straight line. You can see it in the turbulence of a flowing river, but you cannot ordinarily see it in life itself. You cannot see it, that is, until you peek above the horizontal line, and when you do—by God, there it is."

Then he adds, "By the way, the same is true for an individual. You get above the line and break new ground, but it's only extraordinary while you're doing it. As soon as you stop to revel in it, or think you have it, it fades to ordinariness, and you have to work your way up there all over again."

≈ ≈ ≈

Jan revisits this map week after week, with new twists, new takes, new snapshots of how to break above the horizontal line, how to go where this map points.

He says, "Neurologists insist you can't feel your own brain, but that's not the whole story. Maybe you can't, but you can when you get above the line. You can feel the stimulation in your own brain, physically."

Instantly, I know this is true because I feel it while he is talking about it.

I also felt it in fifth grade.

One mystical moment at Point Elementary School in New Hartford, New York, informs my life. After a four-hour morning of complete immersion in everything Mr. Loomis, our teacher, was talking about, and after a triumphant grasp of long division *and* the Missouri Compromise, we're in the lunch line, and I am hungry enough to eat a mountain, and I wonder—how can I be this hungry? *I was just sitting there.* And right then, I could feel my own brain bristling. The hunger came from my brain.

But while I knew this on a cellular level and never forgot it, I also never formulated the statement *You can feel your own brain.* But as soon as Jan says it, the words come alive, and the sensation is palpable. With his simple statement, Jan elevates the subliminal to the liminal. Yes, you can feel your own brain. You can actually feel your attention catalyzing, as if the tip of your brain is the crown of a tree generating new growth while taproots plumb the depths. *A tree's brain is the tree.*

All this sinks in. It is not just an idea. Not really an idea at all. Jan calls it a map. And like a map, it's real only when you go there.

≈ ≈ ≈

A few weeks in, it hits me. This is Jan's big philosophical, religious breakthrough, even though he never makes that particular claim for this diagram and all that it represents. (He seems to think everything he says is a big breakthrough.) But this map of the horizontal line of consciousness really is a leap in thought: the expansion we seek resides in the future, not in the past.

The religions point backwards in time to the original unsullied pure shining truth that must be revivified. "We are waiting for the Messiah," they say, which is really waiting for the return of the beginning, and you can't get there from here, and if you could, you wouldn't really want to because it's all used up. The same is true in tribes. Look at the way we in America canonize the Founding Fathers, sanctify their texts, and parse them as if they're gospel. It was pretty much the same with Gurdjieff, too. He worshipped the world of ancient knowledge and lamented its loss.

Jan Cox, by contrast, flips that world view on its head, and it turns all religion upside down. The way to salvation, so to speak, is not to yearn for a dead guy in a dead reality but to manifest the future now.

"The same is true," Jan repeats, "for what we do here. Only in the moment of accessing the future is anything really new. It's new only once. As soon as we access the future, it quickly becomes the past. And so it will be with everything I say and do here. It is new only once, and then a new future will come along, eat it up, and all this will be dust and bones. Something new will replace it all."

He stands back and looks at his drawing. He laughs to himself and says, "This is the map that eats itself alive."

That's when Jan renames our activity the Future/Now Federation.

≈ ≈ ≈

In late October, Cynthia and I spend a week in a two-room cabin on Hunting Island, South Carolina, an undeveloped barrier island between Charleston and Savannah. Beach-combing is our best sport. We play on the same team against nobody and win resoundingly every time. Purple-and-white shells are our victory medals.

And we bring my typewriter. "Keep writing," she says every day. She loves to see the white pages fill with prose. Every day. We want to stay forever.

In November we visit her grandmother, who gave her a mint 1956 Mercedes 180 sedan, which is not the reason Cynthia loves her but is the reason I do.

In December, she asks me, "What is the group you're in? What's it about? What is it that you're so devoted to three, four nights a week?"

This is a fair question. I've been dreading it for months. The unstated part of the question telegraphs clearly: *I have been respectful of whatever this activity of yours may be, but if we are*

*going to really, really be together, I need to know what you're
up to.*

Can't bluff my way out of the question with Cynthia, the
way I have with others. She's too smart, too cool, and I love her
too much.

But how to explain the essence of all this extraordinary
experience since I met "Dr. Cox" more than ten years ago?

I wind up with a puny-ass answer. I tell her the essence of it
is the kind of self-observation Jan adopted from Gurdjieff. My
answer lasts about two minutes, and while it's true enough, it's a
very feeble answer to a very honest question. I should have said
more. I could have shared any number of the amazements. I
could have told her about my life-changing haircut that hooked
me in the beginning. The door is open, and when the door is
open you should sprint for daylight. The yearning that drives
me to reach out and beyond for new experience and new states
of being could link with Cynthia's quest for perfection in silk
and the way she revels in the wind-driven re-formation of sands
and tides. But in this moment, when the door opens for all the
right reasons, I am inexplicably unable to connect these urges
and merge. So the gap that I fail to reach across becomes a gulf
that I cannot.

Maybe this is why most people in the group wind up in relationships with others in the group—simply because it's difficult
to explain.

In January, she dumps me. Reluctantly. But not reluctantly
enough. And she never says it this way, but it seems clear: I had
my chance to really, really answer. And I didn't. We could have
chewed on a cosmic lump of venison together, but it was my
place to set the feast, and I didn't do it.

≈ ≈ ≈

"*The future now. I do think well of this idea,*" Grandpa says. "*But I didn't need to know about your sex life.*"

All I'm thinking is—*Oy vey, Grandpa, I'm sorry. Oy. This is awful.*

But why? What's with the cringing? Shouldn't sex be an open subject between grandfather and grandson? Only because of it are we connected. And because sex is one of life's great glories, shouldn't we be able to share the joy? But maybe the problem is that we can't talk about it because he worked his ass off for forty years and I haven't, so why am I the one getting laid all the time—with shiksas, yet—and he's not?

Grandpa says, "*You can do only so much in a lifetime.*"

Now he knows what I'm thinking?

What does he mean by that?

Before I have time to think about it, he says, "*Never mind all that. We can talk about sex later.*"

I'm relieved. And hoping "later" is never.

But Grandpa is already on to something else. He says, "*The 'Future Now' is definitely one of the better ideas from all this you're so involved with . . . the way you put it—that salvation is to be found in the future, not the past. Yes. And I also find favor with your observation that expressing the unknown, even if it is known at some level, is of high value.*"

"*Of high value.*" I like Grandpa's old-fashioned phrases. Even if it takes me a moment to realize what he's referring to. The value in expressing what's known pre-verbally, such as the ability to feel your own brain. The ability to render subliminal knowledge in words confers new power on that knowledge. Feels like the Future/Now in process, a kind of engine that converts potential to kinesis. And I didn't know that until Grandpa said it the way he did.

1982

Jan says, "For the next three weeks, we are to focus exclusively on a new Task. Write a play."

He tosses it off—as if we are playwrights and this is what we do, as carpenters frame roofs. But we are not playwrights. The whole room freezes.

He continues. It's not just any piece of theatrical whimsy he's demanding. "Write a play about what you understand about what we are doing here. This must be a serious effort. It doesn't matter if it's a one-act play or a hundred acts. Write the truth about this effort, this Aim. The play must represent what you understand about what we are doing here. All other group activities are suspended. I strongly suggest each of you shut down, go somewhere, and hole up. Cut yourself off from ordinary life, and do this. Do the extraordinary."

He says it with enough menace in his voice to stir the ever-present threat. Nobody wants to be thrown out. It's the opposite of almost any other group, in which dues-paying members are coddled so they will keep paying dues. In Jan's group, members worry about membership. Royce the artist had recently been thrown out because he never could come through with the painting Jan requested.

Nobody wants to turn in a play so crappy you're thrown out.

And besides, that is a damn good question Jan is hurling at us. How do I portray what this is about? And oh, yeah: what *is* this—no bullshit—about? What in the hell is all this really about?

≈ ≈ ≈

Despite the excellence of the fundamental question—*What the hell is this really about?*—nobody in the group is enjoying the Task at all because none of us can see how to pound an answer into a theater piece. Not that anyone has a satisfying answer to work from anyway.

The customary buzz of projects subsides. We all isolate ourselves on the weekends to write the ultimate philosophical drama, and during the week everyone is uncharacteristically withdrawn, like hermits at a bus station. Some people are downright nervous. Some more than others, of course.

Wade in particular reminds me of Emerson Cato when Jan barked, "Jump in the lake." Instead of "I can't swim," Wade's tight face is saying, "I can't write a play." Terror, meet impossibility.

During my own playwright weekend, I applaud Jan's Task. It's a kind of genius, really, or call it the fusion of perceptiveness + imagination + desire. It's a perfectly thrown boomerang rotating in a broad arc on the edges of my brain. So I sit there staring at blank pages without characters or a plot or a single damn idea and applaud. And at the same time, exasperated that I am not on fire with the Task, as good as it is—oh, what the hell —I start writing a scene featuring an *Encyclopedia Britannica* salesman in ancient Greece who sells a set to guy who had contributed to volume 13 but had never seen the whole. Eventually the salesman becomes a contributor, and the contributor becomes a salesman. Maybe it could have been good, but it isn't. Jan won't throw me out for it, but I am not bumped up and expanded by it the way I should have been. My answer doesn't rise to the question, and my perfunctory effort feels like failure.

Three and a half weeks later, after the plays have been turned in, Jan starts the meeting. But instead of standing at his podium, he's sitting, relaxed, and instead of addressing us in his usual truth-or-die lecture mode, he is talking as if he were chipper, warm, and avuncular.

He says, "On Thursday night"—which is the day the plays were due, so everyone tenses up, even as General Cox is suddenly Uncle Jan—"I got a knock on the door."

He pauses. "It was Wade," he says.

He pauses again. This is shocking enough. Nobody knocks on Jan's door unannounced. It doesn't matter that we built the house. Nobody has to tell you: it's simply not done. You don't just drive out there and drop in.

Jan starts over and repeats, "I got a knock on the door, and it was Wade." And Jan is radiantly happy about it. "And I am here to tell you that I am finally being paid back." Jan is beaming. "Somebody finally got it."

Jan glows as if he and Wade had sex. Not that I think they did. But they obviously shared something that none of the rest of us has shared with him—except possibly the women who have sex with him, which, come to think of it, would be damn near half the group.

But this is different.

"I am finally getting paid back," he repeats with uncharacteristic happiness, as if we should share the joy, too, and applaud all his efforts as well as our own, which he does not acknowledge. Jan and Wade laugh heartily while everyone else fake-laughs nervously.

With a smile that I've never seen on him, Jan says, "He included me as a walk-on in the last act of his play."

Jan and Wade publicly indulge their private joy again.

He directs Wade to read his heat-of-the-moment words, hand-delivered last Thursday.

Wade sits down next to Jan, chuckling.

This alone is shocking. Wade doesn't chuckle. Wade is an extreme Presbyterian, an extreme Boy Scout, and his favorite words are "appropriate" and "mindful." The Queen of England chuckles quicker than Wade would. But this, apparently, is the new enlightened Wade, who is in fact sitting too close to Jan and chuckling. This is all shocking. To see somebody blossom this way. Morning glory.

And annoying. The whole thing is annoying. The way Jan and Wade feel so special. Well, aren't they so special!

The play that Wade reads doesn't sound like a play to me. I can't tell if it has actors. Or a stage. Or a time and place. Whatever it is, Wade finds great joy in the words, and Jan is still smiling, which is the longest he's ever smiled without any booze since probably 1952.

Wade keeps reading, and soon I don't care if his play or not-really-a-play has characters or a stage or a time or a place. It gets interesting. Great dialogue. A guy in a place, a place he wants to get out of, and then—*bam!*—brain matter splatters all over the walls. It's the guy's own brain matter decorating the walls, except the walls aren't there anymore, and I can see Wade writing his way out of the dead end of his terror and his failure to write a play, and it all comes together like cold air meeting hot air to make a tornado out of Wade's formerly compartmental-ized brain, which is how brain matter splatters all over the walls, which disappear so completely that even after the guy in the place-that-is-not-a-place went to sleep, he woke up the next morning and IT was still there. The walls were gone. And Wade was unconstrained the whole next day and realized that his play is not a play at all, and the complete joy of seeing the entire cosmic tomato of life in a new way culminated in a deci-sion that was not a decision at all. It was a simple certainty. Knock on Jan's door. Which is how the play plays out. Gives a whole new meaning to "live theater."

The room is quiet, transfixed, amazed, disturbed. Jan implies that we should be grateful for this wonderful break-through. But we do not thank the cosmic tomato or any atom in it. Everyone is trying to comprehend that the enlightenment thing that was supposed to happen to each of us apparently just happened—except it happened to someone else.

Sure, I wish it were my enlightenment, not his. But I'm not gonna get all stuck in it and afraid, like everyone else in the room. They seem afraid to talk to Wade because now he knows everything. I'm gonna find a way to connect with him.

So after the meeting I get a bead on all this by connecting with all the naked blown symphonic top-of-the-spine-blooming experiences I have ever had in this kaleidoscope with Jan—and even before Jan, all the way back to the fifth grade and way before that—and I walk up to Wade when nobody knows what to say.

I lean in and tell him, "Thanks for nothing."

And the two of us, we can't stop laughing. It's the first time I'm really belly-laughing with Wade, and it feels great.

≈ ≈ ≈

The group changes after Wade's big-deal breakthrough, which ripples and propagates and permeates the tribe. The inner outer reaches of joy find new faces to illuminate. Episodes of *it* come and go and stay and go. The accumulation of light does not obey math or logic or other boring stuff. The light bounces around, and we are mirrors shining and reflecting and redirecting.

It reminds me, in a stretch across dimensions, of Roger Bannister breaking the four-minute mile. Physiologists had determined that it was impossible for a human being to run a mile in less than four minutes. Then Roger Bannister did it. They asked him about his training methods. He said he didn't mind taking a day off, but only if he felt great. On sick days, he ran his ass off. And after he broke the barrier, so did many other elite runners.

Wade smiles a lot more now.

But he's still Wade, the serious, born-to-be-a-do-gooder, earnest and reliable. He's all Wade all the time, but with a special new cosmic friend who makes him more okay with the fact that he is who he is even though he still has to plan when to be spontaneous.

And Jan is still Jan, but he's happier, even if the word "happy" doesn't really fit him. He's still a fire-eating sex-maniac booze hound brimming with insight packed in acid, but he's a little happier now.

On any given Saturday morning after a late-night party, Jan is likely to have one of us call around and ask who wants to go to the beach.

"Jan says we're leaving in an hour."

Ten or twelve of us in a few cars zip across Georgia on I-16, and by Saturday afternoon our city-bound toes wiggle into Tybee Island sand dunes just the other side of downtown Savannah. Golden hour lights up a beer, and that's not all. Enlightenment winds blow like the Roaring Forties, everyone laughs the day away, and Jan doesn't scare any landlubbers into deep water.

Yet Jan remains true to outrageous form when he's more than likely, after a mere couple of hours at the shore, to stand up, point toward Atlanta, and lead the motorcade back to the house on Memorial Drive for whatever's left of the night.

The thing that was supposed to happen is happening. We are in the middle of it. Tentacles without a skeleton. People in Oregon who have been reading Jan's self-published book, *The Death of Gurdjieff in the Foothills of Georgia*, now want to "work with him." He flies to the West Coast. Soon he flies there every week. Soon a group from Los Angeles contacts him, and soon after that, Miami. Then New York.

≈ ≈ ≈

And Cara calls. Out of the blue. Every goddamn thing happening at once. Jesus. I was done thinking about her, even after Cynthia dumped me, which is the time a guy would think about such a woman he had known in such a way, but I did not think about her until I picked up the phone and heard the voice.

She says one syllable. My name as a question in that lilt of hers. "Jon?"

Within, I don't know, ten words or eight or eleven or seventeen, I am saying into the phone, "Why don't I come up there, then?"

She waits two long beats and says, "That would be nice."

She lives in North Carolina now.

Like an electric circuit—when someone flips the switch, as she did, she called me, she flipped it—it's on. All I can think of during the five-hour drive is Cara. She replaces Zork, who is still there, no matter how many dollops of enlightenment or dizzy desire you savor. Five hours of this.

In the afternoon, when I get there, she's the original Cara, the pure south Georgia incarnation of Ava Gardner with her own brains and presence, and we don't get within three feet of each other.

Her small house, in the hills past Chapel Hill, smells clean. The windows are open. We walk in the meadows out there and into the woods and fields and back and forth. I love the tall grasses where you can fall down and hide and still see the sky when nobody can see you seeing it. Except she stands there seeing me see it. I get up. We keep walking. Dusk now, dusk colors. We still haven't touched each other. She leans up against a tree. I unbutton her jeans. They fall off, with a little help. She undoes mine. We fall down, crush the tall grasses, and grab and lick and drool and fuck right there at the dusky edge of the woods.

In the morning, we have a short conversation.

"You wanna live together?"

She waits a few beats, the way she does, and says, "Yes."

In the next breath I ask, "In Atlanta?"

And in that same breath, same moment, she says, "Yes."

≈ ≈ ≈

Back in Atlanta, it'll be a month before Cara arrives.

Is this a good idea?

I had quit thinking about her. Now we're going to live together. Is this a good idea? But her voice and her surrender wash away cerebral sifting. Questions evaporate in the heat. We talk on the phone every day, counting the days, laughing.

Echoes from Wade's breakthrough keep bouncing around the universe of the group. Instead of fading to nothing, though, as echoes do, these energy waves amplify as various people in the group, quiet ones and noisy ones both, "get it."

The hum in the room kicks up an octave. The pitch of Jan's hurling ideas and Tasks modulates yet again, like a chord change from minor to major. When we dance to the drums after the meeting, the beat urges us on, and gravity backs off.

The interest from other cities increases. Jan keeps flying to Eugene, Oregon, to meet with a group led by Ron Ramos. They treat *The Death of Gurdjieff in the Foothills of Georgia* as a holy text, which means they don't take holiness too seriously, because Jan in print is almost as crude and profane and outrageous as Jan in person. Plus funny, irreverent, startling, and challenging. The "real" Gurdjieff people denounce the book as blasphemy, which makes the roomful of us laugh all night, and Jan flaunts their umbrage the way the Joint Chiefs of Staff sport their fancy ribbons.

≈ ≈ ≈

In the middle of the waiting-for-Cara month, I harbor an urge to *shut down* for two days. No food, nothing but water, no talking, no nothing. A complete withdrawal. On Friday, I tell Cara, "I'll talk to you on Sunday night." She's fine with it. She doesn't make me explain. I love this. I don't want to explain an urge. Or urges. Maybe it's about making sure we should live together. Maybe it's about these enlightenment waves, catching them and riding them. Maybe it's about wanting one thing to happen at a time instead of everything at once. Maybe it's about the polar vortex versus El Niño. Maybe it's about nothing. An urge doesn't have to be *about* anything.

On Friday afternoon, the door shuts. *Click*—and I'm all in with all alone. An infinity of forty-eight or fifty hours opens up like the beach and blue beyond when you cross the last dune. For a second, I remember the first time shutting down, at the house on Memorial. The shag carpet comes to mind, and I laugh at it. The strangeness of being in the meeting house alone on a weekday morning. I laugh at the strangeness. This time is different, and I laugh at the difference.

People imagine spiritual practices as difficult, serious, and otherworldly. This makes me laugh. Laughing is not serious, and saturation in the here and now is not otherworldly in the least. It's as this-worldly as you can get. But the thing is that this world is not separate from other worlds. This world is a portal to the others, and this is exquisite and subtle and obvious and funny and no big deal all at the same time. "Both are the same," I whisper. And, conversely, "The same are both."

The laughing is on the inside now. Not laughing at all on the outside. It's a cellular thing. A picture of Jan flashes across my mind, a time when he smacks a home run while holding forth on a meeting night. The energy peels off him and riffles through the room, but you can't see it on him. He's laughing in his mitochondria.

The seconds and the hours and the minutes float like a single blimp, because time is just one fat blimpety-blimp—this just in—and I am flying above the clouds, which are my regular mind.

Practically every thought I have is funny.

I am having a nice weekend. This is funny.

If you're standing exactly at the North Pole, all directions are due south. This is funny because it's obviously true but not obvious.

Where do these thoughts come from? They come from the body. This is true and new.

The thoughts stretch apart in time, like edge islands horizon-bound on a thought-free sea.

This voyage continues, easy, betraying all the prior efforts that made it effortless, across this thought-free mind-sea clear into Sunday morning, when the great ship of me runs aground on a reef.

The reef is not about Cara. I have hardly thought about her. This is good.

The reef is a phone call from my nephews, Ken and Eric. They are teenagers. I love them. That is not the problem. The problem is that they are going to have a layover in the Atlanta airport. They want me there. That's the problem.

Ordinarily I would be in the car and on the way to see them without hesitation, eager to grab a precious hour or two with these golden bucks.

But I'm not done surfing this here silent, astounding, beaming being-scape . . . immersed in a clarified pristine tropical lush place without form . . . and now rudely confronted with the drudgery of common thinking: should I go to the airport or not? The snake-tangle of thinking about stuff feels like a traffic jam. I want to see my nephews. But right here right now everything is perfect. And who wants to abandon perfection?

What am I going to do?

Reminds me, again, fleetingly, of the night on the porch in Alpharetta, when the choice between ordinary and extraordinary was as divided as the Red Sea.

This choice is hardly as dire as whether or not I ought to destroy Madeleine's heirloom furniture. I laugh out loud at how weighty this ultimately innocuous decision has become. But still, I have to decide, and still, I am caught between two worlds.

Okay, already.

Apparently my body has "decided." I am going to see my nephews. I know this because I am now getting dressed and packing wallet and car keys and locking the door and starting the car, all without having really decided a thing.

In the car, rolling. Wow, it's gorgeous out here, emerging from my lair onto sleek Sunday avenues splashed with light and shadow even as I fret about the other airport problem. Stems from the Sunday night when Cynthia was picking me up from a flight back to Atlanta.

It so happened that the one particular Sunday night of my return to the Atlanta airport was the exact night the new airport opened. When I left town that Friday, it was the same old quaint small-town southern airport where you can see clear from one end to the other when you walk outside. But when I got back, it had transmogrified into this complicated trapezoidal city with *underground trains*. What the hell? What have they done? If this is the Future/Now, I quit.

And it's covered in brown tile. Brown is the color of 1978. They think it's trendy in 1982? Trendy my ass. Whenever you pick the "now" color four years late, you're gonna hate it in a week. I already hate it.

This is funny. I am laughing out loud on the way to the airport because this is so stupid. Here I am, flying down the highway getting eaten alive by my loathing for the Atlanta airport. I mean, a guy could work up a lather over ad valorem taxes or the guy who stole his parking space or his girlfriend or both, but an *airport*?

This is funny. Laughing at your lesser, fussy self. I love driving to the airport. I should do this more often.

At the airport, when we find each other, I love Ken and Eric and we are happy together and I like the cold trapezoid brown-tiled goddamn airport. The boys are laughing and lit up and so am I and the airport shines. What a happy place.

And all lines disappear. The line separating shutting down from hanging out. Good taste from bad. Ordinary from extraordinary. Here and now, now and then, mind and body, this world and the others. The lines disappear like spaghetti when it's so delicious you consume them all and all you want is more.

≈ ≈ ≈

When Cara moves in, I haven't told her about Jan and the group. This is ridiculous. How can this be? I am the articulate one in the group, the one who explains what others can't express about this contemporary path to enlightenment, and I almost always man up and come through with a palatable, digestible explanation of the inexplicable. And now that my clear-eyed, sun-loving Cara is moving in with me, I cannot muster a reasonable statement of what in the hell I am up to in pursuit of the ineffable.

I just hope it's not too weird, disappearing to go to meetings all the time to do whatever for whatever. She knows it's something. I mumble that much, and she lets it be, so this makes me love her more.

Relying on magical thinking, I simply hope this problem just takes care of itself.

Amazingly, it does.

In the third week we are together, she shows me a newspaper ad for a group called the Future/Now Federation. She thinks it's interesting. She's gonna go. I nod and tell her, yes, it is interesting. Very interesting. That's the thing I'm involved in.

Cara shows up at meetings. She wants more.

We don't say it out loud, but this is remarkable. That she finds it on her own and grabs it and bites it and wants more.

So this wild, blind, sexually impelled "decision" to live with Cara turns out to be inspired. Though you can't really call it a decision if no mentation is included. If rationale had been employed, this never would have happened. Here's the woman who put Akram on the phone to tell me *We don't want you calling here*, and here's the woman who cost me Kate and showed up drunk in the middle of the night, night after night, until I got sick of the whole mess.

She fits easily with this new force and flow in her life.

At meetings, I gaze at her rapt face: an impossible convergence of internal and external worlds, to see her sitting here.

The word "awakened" comes to mind. Well, yes, awakened in the sense of union beyond the rational. Because here she is now, alive as light.

Click.

She has quit drinking. She laughs a lot. We play tennis. We plant a garden.

≈ ≈ ≈

A few weeks after Cara starts going to meetings, Jan asks me if I'd like to join him on his weekly visit with the group in Eugene, Oregon. I tell him yes, let's go, even though I don't feel right about leaving Cara so soon, but I can't say no to a trip with Jan to meet this new group out West, partly because of some vague fear that if I say no, then I won't be invited again, and partly because of wanderlust in the bones. I've never been to Eugene, and I want to go everywhere.

Traveling with Jan. I've done this once before. Back when he needed books to fill the shelves of the library at the law school he started, Jan asked me to go with him to pick up free books at the Library of Congress. Yes, that Library of Congress. Free books? To fill up a kinda-sorta law school library? These are junk books, I'm saying to myself. Reminds me of his books arranged by height. I know he reads—he has a fertile, facile ease with broad bands of knowledge—but he treats books as furniture you can look at but can't sit on, as if their very mass proves his pedigree. Junk books for a law school library? This is stupid. So I say to Jan, "Yeah, that sounds great. Let's go."

We fly to Washington and go straight to Senator Sam Nunn's office. Jan expects to see the senator. The receptionist gives us a big, hokey Georgia welcome, as if she's amazed that we came all the way from the piney woods to our nation's capital. Then she shows us to a seat. Jan hates to wait. I wonder if he'll last three minutes. He does. But he does not last six.

All we do the rest of the day is load up free books that the Library of Congress—which keeps all the books ever printed—does not want. As soon as the library closes, Jan wants to rush to the airport instead of drinking all night in Georgetown and blabbing about important things like where to buy beachfront property, how to chase women, the miracle of internal combustion, and how it is that reality is a fad.

So traveling with Jan is not necessarily fun. But this trip to Oregon has to be different. No shoveling books into boxes. These are real people, a whole self-assembled group that discovered Jan.

Well, not exactly self-assembled. The group has a leader, Ron Ramos, who is the anti-Jan in every way. Barrel-chested, pudgy Jan lumbers into a room with giant footfalls and audaciously announces, "I'm never wrong," while Ron crosses a room inaudibly and invisibly, his small frame on springy legs and soft feet. Ron would be the first to tell you he knows nothing. He's a background kind of guy, yet everyone flocks to him in a quiet way. I certainly do. I really like the guy. Jan puts people on edge. Ron puts people at ease. Ron runs a garage. He and some of the guys work on cars. "It keeps me honest," Ron says with a glint in his eye, certifying his utter inability to cheat anyone ever. I can't help comparing Ron's Honest Auto with Jan's Columbia Southern School of Law and its shelves of detritus from the Library of Congress.

But it's not as simple as concluding "auto shop, good / law school, bad." Everything with Jan is faceted, complex, cross-pollinated, and often at cross-purposes. Everything from a law school to a trip to Oregon.

So while Jan transparently faked the law school library, the core of the enterprise emanated from his profound respect and admiration for the law itself. He extolled this unified, abstract realm as a durable intellectual construct accrued over centuries across multiple cultures that served society and humanity. In meetings, he periodically revisited the law as a model of human endeavor. And just as he encouraged everyone in the group to study cosmology and astronomy, he similarly encouraged anyone to study the law as a tightly interconnected discipline. And some in the group took the challenge seriously. They benefited not only by passing the bar, but also by melding mind and experience in new levels of understanding.

Maybe Ron Ramos will open his Honest Auto in Atlanta so people in the group can become master mechanics. Maybe a joint enterprise will evolve: Columbia Southern Law School and Body Shop. Not that Jan would be partners with anybody. But the signage is fun to imagine.

≈ ≈ ≈

Jan and I share a room at the same mom-and-pop motel where Jan's been staying on all his visits here. It's decent and clean enough, but most important, it satisfies Jan's cheapskate requirements. I would have preferred separate rooms, but Jan doesn't offer, and I don't ask. So we hole up together and meet with the group on each of the two nights we're there. Our days are free. On the second afternoon, Jan and I ride borrowed bikes around Eugene. I keep pedaling away from him because my legs can't go as slowly as his. He keeps joking about how hard the seat is, but the jokes aren't funny, and it's obvious that he's just complaining. For the first time ever, I say to myself that Jan is a pain in the ass and a downer and I'd have ten times the fun riding around alone.

We get back to the room after no exercise and seeing nothing. Now we have hours before the evening meeting, so we're free to goof off. I open a book, settle into the chair to read. Jan stretches out on his bed, pulls down his pants, and displays his erect penis. What the hell? He is not making eye contact, because he is concentrating on his dick, staring at it for all he's worth. *What the hell?* Does he expect me to do something with his dick? I don't want to know what he wants. I have no interest in the thing he is holding. I can't get out the door fast enough—feels splendid to be free of him—and jump on the bike.

Flying uphill on the bike, riding hard and fast, like my legs come unshackled for the first time. I'm pedaling away from Jan and his dick as fast as I can, whatever works, and what works right now is flattening this steep gradient with rough raw energy and a feeding frenzy of impressions. Ahh, gorging on this cool happy hilly green college town, delicious, and even more delicious because I escaped whatever the hell that was in the room, and yes, everything is infinitely better in these sweaty sunny blazes without Jan and dick crowding my sight lines and brain space.

It works, whatever "it" is—the furious exercise, the glee of freedom, the speed, soaking up a new place. By the time I get back to the room, Jan has gotten himself dressed, and I don't have to think about "it" any more, because it's time to go meet the people who want to pursue higher consciousness.

I never go on another trip with Jan, and I never want to.

≈ ≈ ≈

After the meeting that night, I am again drawn to Ron Ramos. As I approach, Ron is talking with one of the Eugene guys and says with gusto, "I never knew that before!" *I never knew that before.* Such a simple statement, and Ron enjoys saying it. I enjoy hearing it. And I can't help comparing *I never knew that before* with *I'm never wrong.*

But Jan is on his game. His talks fly around the nervous system and the reality beyond the charade of language, and then he jokes about the fact that you use words to make jokes about the charade.

And then he says, "Why be a Möbius strip in a Klein bottle world?"

In terms of the ancient Greeks, Jan is fire, Ron is water, and Jan eats Ron alive—or boils him away—and most of the people from Eugene, Oregon, leave Ron and move to Atlanta, Georgia, to be in this group with Jan Cox. And I am the right-hand man.

≈ ≈ ≈

Grandpa says, "I'm not sure I'm keeping up with all this."

Well, Grandpa, neither am I. Maybe life itself could just shut up and shut down for a weekend so everyone might ooze around for a day.

"But if I get the gist of it," Grandpa says, "you and your people are drawn to a realm of finer choices, choices of attention, and you make the most of the lashings and the bracings of this Jan character to get there."

Whoa, Grandpa! Keeping up? I'd say you're tuned all the way in, putting it like that.

The lashings and the bracings? Grandpa's antiquated language can sound so edgy.

Grandpa talks over me and says, "I know lashings and bracings by my ascent from utter poverty to utter wealth."

He's nodding. Not smiling.

"And the wealth brought choices. Not that I could avail myself of all of them, for reasons I could never really comprehend. Maybe the loss of my youth extracted enduring tolls. But I did indulge a taste for schnapps and a love of opera, yet I also felt the need to be charitable, as I felt life had been toward me, so I sent money to my relatives in the newly founded state of Israel. And I supported your grandmother in her work for good causes."

Grandpa tells me about the interfaith dialogue Grandma arranged for the Daytona Beach Temple Sisterhood in 1953. Grandma insisted on including, among the panel of nine clergymen of various faiths, an African Methodist Episcopal priest —in the depths of the Jim Crow era.

Grandma invited Reverend Horace Mabry over the objections of the president of the sisterhood, who wouldn't let Reverend Mabry sit with the panel. He sat in the audience. Next to Grandma.

At a certain point in the discussion, the audience was invited to comment. Reverend Mabry rose first and spoke with a level of *erudition, flair, and wisdom beyond the level of the rest of the discussion.*

Grandpa nods and smiles.

He sees me smile, too. He sees me being proud of Grandma Rose.

Grandpa says, "So what kind of community service do you perform?"

≈ ≈ ≈

We don't perform any community service. Jan talks about it once. He says that as we accept new responsibility for our own consciousness, we must also embrace new responsibility for life itself to find new outlets for growth.

He often references "the Life of Life"—those capital *L*s are his—as if life is a higher force, with its own agenda-vectors and its own struggles. I love the idea.

So when he talks about helping Life find new outlets for its own growth, I'm ready to jump. But he never again brings it up in that way.

Later Jan presents this endeavor as "help for the healthy." He says that this might not seem to be a radical idea: help for the healthy.

He interrupts himself, as he often does—this time at the word "radical." The first definition of the word, he says, has nothing to do with the way it's used in the news or popular culture, where it's construed as meaning "revolutionary." The first definition of "radical" relates to the fundamental nature of whatever it describes: arising, *radiating*, from the root source—that's what radical is.

I have never heard any of it put this way—either this primary definition of the word "radical" or Jan's presentation of this endeavor as "help for the healthy." All other "help" functions in society, including religion and social services, generally attend to those who are lacking or damaged in some way: the poor, the spiritually troubled, the infirm, the addicted, the lost souls. Speaking irreverently, you could exaggerate and say that psychiatry serves the crazy, psychology serves the nutty, and social work serves the dysfunctional.

But the healthy want to grow and evolve, too. In fact, isn't one facet of robust health pure desire?

And the phrase "help for the healthy" implies that you have to be essentially healthy and functional to belong to the group, to get anything out of The Work; health is a prerequisite for undertaking the unnecessary, just as embarking on a pilgrimage demands fundamental strength.

Jan does proffer another kind of service all the time, in myriad forms: he urges us to embrace what we're not. Is this community service? Well, it doesn't fit Grandpa's idea of the term. But arguably it is a form of service. Certainly it is for the community of people he has attracted—this group of people who reach beyond. Beyond everything. People who flourish by creative assaults.

I + Not-I = Everything. It's not some theoretical formula or an abstract equation. It is our life's work. And it crystallizes a core truth of our odyssey: if you really want to become more than you are, then you must become what you are not.

≈ ≈ ≈

One night before a meeting, Jan asks me to gather Ted, Perry,

Dustin, Dale, Richard, and Wade. We assemble in Jan's private pre-meeting room, and he says, "I got a Task for you people. Study astrophysics. Each of you individually and all of you collectively. Simply get together and study astrophysics. Study it until you get it," he says. "And be ready." Ready for what? He never says.

Study until you get it? Astrophysics? What do I know? Nothing. Sounds impossible. Oh, yeah, that's why we're doing this. But who would think of *astrophysics?*

Everyone else in this Task group has a solid math and science background. Nearly all are graduates of Georgia Tech, and two of them have master's degrees. I'm definitely the ignoramus of the corps. I buy some books and a notebook to help me cram, just as I did in college, and pester these scientists with fundamental questions about matter and energy, gravity and electromagnetism. Soon we're talking about neutron stars and gravitational energy.

Facts gather and cluster, and questions form. The earth receives one one-billionth of the sun's energy. The sun converts five million metric tons of itself into energy every second. A star is a ball of gas that produces light. The atoms in room-temperature air fly around at two hundred miles per hour. Gravity doesn't really exist. Rather, what we call gravity is the geometry of curved space. From our viewpoint on earth, gravity warps space and slows time. The four forces in the universe are the strong force, the weak force, gravity, and electromagnetism. Huh? How can gravity be one of the universal forces if it doesn't exist? And if gravity is nothing more than a warp in the space-time continuum, where does gravitational energy come from? What's on the other side of the universe? What was there before the big bang? Are you really telling me that all these genius physicists fill a blackboard with numbers and Greek runes and all it means is that first there was nothing and then there was everything? Huh? Is that what you get from the infinite complexity of the cosmos? Is the universe a singularity? What force holds the electron away from the nucleus? What would happen to a photon theoretically trapped midway between two black holes?

We organize the facts, and we organize the questions, and one of the Georgia Tech alums calls a favorite physics professor at Tech, Dr. David Finklestein, a lovable brainiac, who meets us for lunch at the Stein Club, the old hippie bar on Peachtree in Midtown. Dr. Finklestein brings two graduate students with him. Ten of us gather at a long table in the second room. Feels a bit stilted, but Dr. Finklestein is gracious and asks what's on our minds.

Richard, who happens to be sitting next to Dr. Finklestein, goes first. Dr. Finklestein absorbs the question and the questioner, nods, and looks to the next person. And so each of us from Jan's group takes a turn.

Dr. Finklestein follows his own tempo after the last one and carefully says, "The questions you are asking are at the very forefront of what we're studying in astrophysics. Therefore I do not have simple answers to your questions, because there aren't any. However, I am happy to entertain the questions, as they entertain me. But first I have a question for you. Where do these questions come from? What kind of group are you in?"

We who do not talk about ourselves squirm and answer that we are just friends who are interested in physics. And the universe.

He isn't buying it. "Well, then, what kind of group are you associated with?"

Oh, no group at all. We aren't associated with any group.

He knows we're lying, and I feel like a creep because here is Dr. Finklestein ready to share his life's work with us, and he's saying okay, but first, what is your life's work? What drives you?

That's essentially what he's asking. I get it, and now I want to tell him, but I have already lied by saying that we are not in a group, and I can't expose that lie or the bigger lie we are all living, which boils down to believing we are so special that we're on a higher plane than everyone else so we don't have to engage with them, even a distinguished physicist who, for the love of sharing hard-won knowledge, takes the time to answer our questions. Shit. I'm such a creep. We're all creeps.

≈ ≈ ≈

Jan skips a Task for the week, at least in terms of a precise recipe for action or thought. Instead, without using the word "Task," he ends the meeting with a description of what he calls the bridge points in the spine. "These bridge points are gaps you can spring across to further your efforts here. You should discover these. Utilize these bridge points."

He rotates his body. We see his back. He points at his sacrum and pauses. "Here," he says.

Then he points at his neck, the cervical vertebrae, and pauses. "And here."

He continues. "The bridge points in the spine. I'm not going to tell you what they are or what to do with them, but I will tell you that they are essential to your progress here."

Nobody knows what he's talking about. But he has certainly got me going. Hell, yeah, I want to know what these bridge points are. Essential to your efforts here? Well, damn it, what the hell are they?

This enigma sticks like a dart in my brain, and it hogs attention just as some of Jan's other questions have: "What's the first word in the dictionary?" "Where is a tree's brain?" But the riddle of the bridge points is different. You can't figure it out the same way. It's about energy flowing up your spine, so you have to feel it to know it. You have to feel it the way you can feel your own brain when you're more alive than you usually are. And the answer, if there is one simple answer, doesn't come quickly or clearly.

It so happens that three days later I'm at the beach, on a pristine stretch of the old wild Florida between Summer Haven and Hammock, on the coast below St. Augustine. And I'm all alone, running barefoot in the surf, a favorite among what I call the primordial hobbies—engagements with the world requiring hardly any stuff or money. Drawing, for example. All you need is a pencil and a sheet of paper. And running on the beach—you don't even need shoes. You don't wear a watch. You're not measuring time or distance, and the only bodies in sight are large: the sky, the sea, and the beach. And a few small: shore birds singing and gathering, ghost crabs sprinting sideways.

Off and running. Feels so good, this simple motion. Toes grabbing thimbles of sand. Springing down the coast. Maybe I'll prance to Miami.

Nobody else out here. The riddle—bridge points in the spine?—hovers, but the water and the water music and all this happy sloppy motion shroud the question.

Thinnest wave remnants retreat across the sand. In the glittery liquid sheets, my feet broadcast bright cymbal accents to the roar of the surf. When the wave trails are ankle-deep, you can curl your toes up at impact to generate a private orb of salty rain dousing your body from the bottom up. Catch a splash with your lips, savor the brine. Running in a personal rain cloud in the sun at the beach. And then plunge flat-footed into those dark ovals of purple water beachcombers call runouts . . . in two feet of water, footfalls thud. Could be the kettle-drum feature of the beach opera.

As the beach flattens, the pace picks up, and with no effort I'm practically sprinting, and the quick light snap of feet on wet sand sounds like tiny taps on the hi-hat.

With no warning or thought or event to cause it, my head tilts back, and I'm laughing out loud. The sound of my own laughter dovetails with the rest of this unscored opera, and riding the tail of this unexpected out-loud laugh—I get it whole all at once: the bridge points in the spine. The bridge point in your neck is laughter. And instantly, I get the other one: the bridge point in your lumbar region is sex.

Bridge points in the spine: sex and laughter.

I get it whole and wholly and holy and say it again out loud, and it seems so obvious. Sex and laughter, bridge points in the spine. It's where you leap levels. Sex and laughter.

The following week, back in Atlanta at the next group meeting, I hand Jan a written account of these aha moments that spawned huge one-word answers to his delicious riddle.

He feasts on my written words. His face illuminates. He laughs out loud. He starts the meeting with a simple sentence while pointing at me. "He got it." Jan is beaming. He hands me back my pages and gestures for me to read them to the group.

≈ ≈ ≈

Cara gets pregnant. We weren't planning it. Not everything in life is planned. What kind of life is that? We didn't plan to have sex all the time, including that night on the footbridge in the little Lenox Road park with the brook and tennis courts because we couldn't wait to get home in ten minutes.

What are we going to do? Are we having a kid?

Jan never says don't have children, but he does say that children distract a person from the Aim. He says it's hard enough to do this without children. So he says without saying it that if you're serious about this, you probably shouldn't have kids.

But Cara and I each come to our private conversation with yes. The conversation is short, almost as short as that morning-after conversation in North Carolina when we "decided" to live together. We didn't decide anything. We were magnets clicking. The same nonverbal, nonintellectual, deep-rooted sensibility speaks a simple yes, and this is happening. We are going to have a child together.

At the next meeting, before the meeting, in Jan's private office, where I always go to see what's happening and what he needs, I tell him before he finds out some other way—you can't hide a baby growing in a movie-star body. And I tell him in private for another reason as well: if it's not against the rules, it's against the unwritten rules, especially for one of the inner circle of the inner circle.

Jan looks up from his papers. He's reading notes from people in the group and replying to each. With his deep frown, you can't tell where this conversation will go, up or down. I see him seeing me. I see him seeing that I'm doing this. This is a big deal, because guys like me, close to him, are not supposed to do this, and I see us, the two of us, eyeball-to-eyeball in the driveway of the Alpharetta farmhouse, and his brain is spinning fast the way it does, and he gets that this is happening, and he gives it his blessing.

≈ ≈ ≈

At a party after the meeting one night, a bunch of us wind up talking about how we got out of the Vietnam War. Byron's story is the most boring. He had a high lottery number and never had to worry about getting drafted. Perry got a teaching deferment and spent a year teaching physics to kids who hated him. Ted got out because he's too tall, six foot eight. If you're over six foot six, they leave you alone.

My story is more complicated—being in Israel and receiving a letter from the Selective Service, ordering me to their office on Walton Street in Jacksonville. I reply, from Israel, declaring as a conscientious objector to war and using "Dr. Cox" as one of my references.

Jan interrupts, takes the story from there, and says that he wrote the most amazing letter. He declares, "*My* letter to the Selective Service did it. Got you out of the war." He grins proudly.

This is a crowd-pleaser at the party and without a doubt the best how-I-got-out-of-the-war story of the night.

For all I know, it's true that Jan's letter worked—even though I never received any such statement from the draft board. But I never got called to fight in the war, either.

In this way, usually at parties, while everyone is drinking, and with Jan's tacit approval, we break the rule against self-talk. On these occasions, with an unspoken agreement to try to make it funny, we get to know more about each other in little bits. But such happy breaches of the rule are rare. It's a different culture in the group, a different social contract. Rather than popular culture, an anti–popular culture prevails here, which is a reflection of Jan's nature, his deeply reflexive "no" response to whatever everyone else does. So instead of joining the trending wave of confession and expression, we invest in this alt-culture, in which you never say much about yourself.

Instead we learn about each other and become bound in friendship through here-and-now experience in The Work. And through some of the Tasks, we learn more from each other and about each other than we ever would through self-explanation or self-definition. The Tasks Jan continues to conjure flow from an apparently endless reservoir, and they always emerge well-formed and surprising, and the benefits accrue.

One week, Jan says everyone must send him a note listing areas of personal expertise, talent, and accomplishment. The next week, Jan says we're going to have classes, taught by people in the group, on an unpredictably wide array of subjects.

Jan doesn't attend the classes, and without him, we attend to the material seriously and curiously and pleasurably. Probably better that he's not there, because people act pressurized when he's around.

In the massage class, everyone pairs up, sprawls on the floor, and we learn how to stroke toward the heart and how to approach cheekbones.

In horticulture, Jim Davie spreads a big drop cloth on the floor and manhandles a potted plant, insisting that the plant loves it. "See?" He points to the roots. "It's pot-bound. You gotta cut this tangled mess and leave the tips cut clean, because that's where the new growth will come."

Dustin and Dale hold forth on computers at a time when nobody has one. They take us back to Charles Babbage and Alan Turing and all the way forward into a CPU before anyone has heard the term "central processing unit."

I find the most surprising class to be boxing. Boxing? Boxing! Leave it to Jan Cox to require boxing classes for a bunch of would-be pacifist mystics who swear they'll never express any hostility whatsoever. That's the first surprise. Maybe it's Jan's way of telling everyone you can withhold hostility without being a pussy. Find some backbone. One night he says, "You can't accomplish anything without putting your back into it."

So we don the head protectors, snug down these puffy

boxing gloves, and our boxing instructor, Joseph, insists we lock our jaws tight to minimize damage if we're hit in the face. Then into the ring, and—pow!—the second surprise is how damn good I am at something I've never done before. Dancing on my toes, shifty, quick, these toes and snappy legs eager to pack extra lumber in each jab. I'm neither here nor there, so you can't hit me, seeing quicker than the other guy moves, fast hands flying, and POW! My electric left hand tags the other guy's jaw. The brute satisfaction of contact registers solid in my spine and spirit, and POW! I tag his jaw again. I am brutally alive, inevitable, hydroelectric.

≈ ≈ ≈

The third surprise is Grandpa. He says, "I boxed for a time." He laughs a little. "I was

    good. I could handle myself."

    He must have been a lightweight, small, around 135 pounds, but his gravitational energy could take over a room. I can see him snapping around the ring. Long arms for a short guy, coiled in close and ready to pow! I get it, Grandpa: I can see you acting cautious and then shocking people. Just as you did in business.

    He likes this.

    He laughs a little more. "Then I got hit in the nose." He grimaces. "I didn't like getting hit in the nose. So I quit."

    He continues. "Then I needed something to replace it. That wide-eyed animality. Not staring—it makes me think of your exercise, because in the ring you are not staring. Your eyes and your hands see in unison."

    Well said, Grandpa.

Grandpa says, "That's when I took up riding."

A framed photograph of him stood out from the others on Mom's dresser. He sat tall in the saddle, looking like a military hero on his favorite steed. He looked younger than Mom and Dad, and his eyes were shining. He wasn't smiling.

"I had some moments on horseback," he says.

Huh?

"I was an accomplished rider," he says matter-of-factly.

It strikes me that he must have grown up around draft animals in the shtetl, as a kid in the 1880s. I had never thought about that before.

He continues. "I don't know if I could have ridden rodeo with the cowboys in St. Louis, when I took the train out there to buy pelts. But I could handle myself in the English saddle, the way we rode in New York. One day when your mother was a little girl, I went riding up in Sleepy Hollow." He catches himself and laughs at the name. "In the woods on a bluff above the Hudson River. They said, 'Philip, you can handle the stallion.' And I felt that I could. Even though he was strapping big, about seventeen hands, and I wasn't. I was small but tough, like a jockey. I got up in the saddle easily, and I felt good, good like a giant. We rode along in a group, on a trail in the woods, where towns are now, and suddenly my big stallion bolted. I gathered in the reins to say 'Whoa!' But he had such strength, and not just physically. He had a kind of majesty about him, and I said to myself, 'All right, then,' and with my body I said, 'Yes.' My weight dropped in the stirrups and my legs hugged his belly and I let the reins follow his motion. I gave him what he wanted. Freedom. His neck stretched out. His legs were churning. His mane flew in the wind, and the wind blew tears from my wide eyes in straight lines back to my temples."

And then Grandpa Phil says, "I lived for ninety years, and that was one of the best hours of my life, when the horse took off and I gave him the reins. I lived more in that hour than I did in entire years. Everything happened all at once, and I knew what I was doing."

He chuckles and his eyes go far away and he nods to his secret self. I imagine Grandpa wearing a tallith and a yarmulke, sitting cross-legged in a lofty crag on Mount Sinai.

And he says with a twinkle in his eye, "I was wide awake in Sleepy Hollow."

≈ ≈ ≈

Never thought I would hear Grandpa talk about being wide awake in that way. Then I remember the words in my prayer for him at the Wailing Wall. *May the yearnings he honored in transforming his life be further honored by his grateful, admiring grandson, that the yearnings may serve further transformations.* Maybe the gap between us is no more of a gap than the space defined by the links of a chain. Without the space, the chain wouldn't work.

"Being wide awake" acquires new meaning in the days following the mad dash to the hospital after Cara says, "I think my water just broke."

Wasn't supposed to happen yet. But it is happening, at seven and a half months. Maybe it's all the sex and all the dancing, all the fun out there in the world of Mom and Dad, so the kid figures, why wait?

This kid isn't waiting and emerges into the world tiny and healthy and full of force.

We had discussed only son names, no daughter names, because I was so sure that the kid would be a he. And here I am thrilled to be wrong. And amazed at a daughter. The next day, Cara asks, "What do you want to name her?"

The answer came just like the "decision" to live together did, an arrow from a quiver you can't always reach.

"Rose. Let's name her Rose."

Named after Grandma Rose. Grandpa will tear up when he hears her name.

Cara makes me wait a beat, the way she does. Then she says, "All right."

I will tell Grandpa, "Rose said everything without saying anything."

It takes a few hours from the moment of her birth to figure out who's in charge.

She is.

It is.

It.

The force of life.

I'm only a steward. A sluice for the raw energy.

The way her arms wave in the air. Motion is bliss.

What is air? What are these things called hands? Who or what is moving them? They stop moving. Whoa: everything just stopped moving, everything being my hands.

Out of coat hangers, thread, and glued-up polygons made of brilliant color swatches from an art supply house, I fashion a mobile and hang it above her crib.

Whoa! Look at that thing flying around! Whoa! What is that other thing flying around?

She spends the better part of a year lying on her back dealing with light, shapes, space, and the eternal now . . . while faces lean in and out of the ceiling.

Sometimes I blow on the mobile floating above her face. Slivers of pigment rotate randomly in the rapt pools of her shiny eyes.

Direct perception. "I want to see things as they are," I told Jan way back when—the first time I met "Dr. Cox" at the Miller Building.

Now Rose is a guide in another way.

She alters the landscape of where the power lies. Power of life, force of truth.

Direct perception. Here she is guiding me to it.

She changes the meaning of the words "wide awake."

If what she's doing with these colors floating into her mind isn't *wide awake*, then I'll give everyone fifty bucks.

Rose commandeers a chunk of Jan's real estate, his land in my mind.

1984

Jan institutes a practice he calls *equalization*. You wouldn't expect something so subtle and personal to radiate from Jan's pervasive certitude, bluster, and—especially—lack of interest in anyone else's life.

Equalization takes place in a three-by-five-inch spiral notebook. He tells everyone to buy one. Says this is strictly between each of you and me. You go first. Write something, anything. Ask a question. Share a thought, an observation. Anything. "And I will respond to you in a particular way."

So I write to him, on pure impulse, that I have recently read that until the 1300s, people in Europe didn't have chimneys. They had fire, but they didn't have chimneys. So basically they're all huddled up in cramped, one-room hovels that fill with smoke, and they all die young of smoke inhalation.

At the weekly meeting, all the notebooks are picked up and

delivered to Jan. The next week, the notebooks come back with answers in Jan's big script.

Jan answers my first foray into equalization by asking, *At what stage of refinement is your own inner domicile? Is your revolutionist's brain feasting on oxygen-enriched air? Or are you misfiring in an atmosphere of foul, recycled fumes?*

Ah, yes, Jan in action: transmuting an external observation or fact into a nifty, internal judo move that you may apply as you wish.

The next week, I ask in my little notebook, *Can you change the past?*

And he replies, *The question contains the answer.*

The question contains the answer? That's his answer? At first, I feel shortchanged by New Age blather.

But the next day, as I reconsider it, *the question contains the answer* strikes a different chord. Translation: if you're asking a question like that, you already know the answer, so don't look at me for an answer.

And then *blam*, the answer couldn't be more obvious. The past changes the day you learn how to ride a bike. The past changes when you buy a one-way plane ticket to Glasgow, Scotland. The past changes the day you are born and the day you die. The past changes the day you mouth a heartfelt prayer for your grandfather. Your past flexes and fluxes with your present.

I'm glad I asked him the question.

I'm glad he threw me a curveball instead of an answer.

So from that day forward, my future changes: I quit asking him questions. Instead I collect my own questions and wrestle or tease or meditate or beat the answers out of them.

Or to hell with the questions. Instead I play in the backyard under the giant poplars with Rose. I build her a sandbox. The sand is full of life. You can tell by the way she grabs it, lets it sift through her fingers.

≈ ≈ ≈

If equalization exemplifies the subtle end of this endeavor with Jan, well, at the other extreme we have Saint Quantum's Day. Not subtle in the least.

Who would have thought up such a thing?

Saint Quantum's Day. You gotta love the name.

Jan announces "our own holiday." Here's the deal: we celebrate twice a year, starting on the Friday night after both the vernal and autumnal equinoxes. For forty-eight hours, do anything you want. Anything. Anything goes. Anything except casual sex with people in the group and expressing hostility. Those two rules always remain in force, he says.

But anything else goes. *Anything.* So go ahead. For forty-eight hours, go ahead and do whatever it is you're not supposed to do. Just don't get caught. That's one of the rules, part of the deal. Don't ever get caught. Actually, I guess that's the only rule.

I never would have thought of *this.*

Some people break some rules, others break others. Makes me realize that we have pages of rules. I laugh out loud because this is starting to resemble Judaism, in which the Orthodox abide by six hundred and thirteen rules. I don't think Jan has instituted that many, but I'm not going to count them all.

Some vegetarians celebrate Saint Quantum's Day by eating meat. Some go on shopping sprees or movie sprees. Everyone indulges guilty pleasures without the guilt. Saint Quantum's Day is a modern-day pagan rite, a right to do wrong and enjoy the hell out of it.

Most of us rediscover drugs. Or discover drugs for the first time.

The whole thing sounds insane. It *is* insane. You can't turn a hundred people loose on a two-day carnival drug binge without something really bad happening. The rule has always been: no drugs whatsoever. Now it's no drugs whatsoever except all drugs whatsoever for forty-eight hours twice a year. What kind of sense could that possibly make?

None.

Saint Quantum's is not about making sense.

On the Friday night of the autumnal equinox, with a fresh chill in the air and the brace of seasons changing, it's about swallowing stuff and snorting stuff and smoking stuff while smashed into the tiny intensely solar yellow kitchen at the little stone house of Perry the physicist-framer. That's where the party ramps up.

A small house of big stones. Ha-ha, that's really funny. Everyone's laughing. Because we're all small and stoned. Ha-ha. Everyone's laughing one laugh. We are one larynx and one eardrum. All packed in. Packed into euphoria. Smoke clouds. White powder on the kitchen counter. Powder in your nose now. Yes, you say to the ceiling.

Yes, you say to the person next to you and next to that person because you are saying yes to everything, which leads to conversation about how to put the fizz back in fizziology, which could bounce to another conversation about the subtle practice of equalization.

Ken Lee confides that equalization is the only way he communicates with Jan. Ken Lee, whom everyone calls Ken Lee, does not want to talk to Jan, ever, but he gets what Jan talks about, and he doesn't trust him, and then he looks at me as if to say he shouldn't have told me that, and I break the silence and say out loud, "Yes, you should have." And he gets it, and we laugh.

Yes, you say later, when the party moves to Joe's loft in the wee hours. I'm on my way.

Driving alone down DeKalb Avenue. Don't worry, I can

always drive—that's what I tell myself, even as I am now a wolf riding a comet with a beefy internal combustion engine.

The road undulates alongside the railroad tracks, each incline spectacularly, ridiculously enjoyable. The amber lights on the instrument panel match the amber streetlights. Everything is happening at once. The pipes rumble softly while the motor loafs at just a thousand RPMs. Gliding up and down the inclines. The luxury of locomotion. The gilded illuminations. It's simply thrilling. Gilded and gliding.

≈ ≈ ≈

The hangover is brutal, way worse than a booze hangover. Because you just sucked and burned next week's life force. But the ache from that hole doesn't keep anyone from taking the plunge and flying in headfirst next time. Saint Quantum's Day weaves its way into the annual calendar, each year studded with a pair of off-season psycho Christmases from another reality: a quick crazy cleanse with poison. A blast of *Wha!* while the rest of your life hinges on struggle, fruitful or not.

Saint Quantum's Day, though, can enrich revelers unexpectedly.

Reminds me of that overused statement about the Sixties: if you remember it, you weren't there. That is not true. If you were there, you were given gifts of volatility, exuberance, and expansion—and if you thought it was all about the drugs, then you missed the gift.

Same with Saint Quantum's. The takeaways include conversations you'd never have any other way, such as Ken Lee saying he can't stand Jan Cox but he cherishes the intimate, respectful, intelligent gateway exchanges with him. Ken Lee adds, "Jan knows I'm smart, and I get what he's about." Surely Jan knows that Ken Lee and a bunch of other people want nothing to do with him, so Jan invents a safe avenue of connection and exchange and quiet validation woven with counterpoint.

This in turn reminds me of one of Jan's statements that makes me squirm every time he says it, maybe once every year or two: *Some of those who keep the greatest distance from me personally get the most out of all this.*

For those of us with the right-hand-man syndrome, this is Jan's sucker punch to the gut. It's a good one, and it's the truth: he doesn't care about anyone personally. I wouldn't say he has friends. He's drawn to whomever is drawn to what draws him.

And while slogging through the Saint Quantum's hangover, I gotta give Jan credit for one more thing. Whenever the group practice seems to attain stability and predictability, conditions around which followers self-organize, Jan shakes it up, upends the patterns, and rewrites the rules.

≈ ≈ ≈

After most of the Ron Ramos group from Eugene moves to Atlanta—without Ron Ramos, who is left alone in his garage— other groups from around the country who have discovered us through Jan's *Death of Gurdjieff* book move here from Miami, New York, Los Angeles, and Boston.

And then a guy shows up at public meetings who speaks no English. He smiles all the time and is inordinately happy to be among us—happier, it seems, than all of us who have been here the whole time, deeply committed. The guy is named, improbably, Jesus, and after a few weeks Jan admits him to the group. One of the Cubans from the Miami group translates his story, which would never make good fiction because it is not credible: he read about The Work in his native farming village outside Durango, Mexico, determined that this is what he'd been looking for and that he could find it only in America, so he left home, crossed the border, and asked people in Texas, "Where is The Work?" Assuming he was looking for employment, they answered, "Go to Atlanta." So Jesus comes to Atlanta and somehow finds the same announcement that Cara found in *Creative Loafing*, the free local paper: a public lecture series about The Work. So he shows up at our meetings . . .

The story of Jesus is fantastical and true and driven by pure desire. But all the people arrive with a story and desire and a longing, and many are exceptional. Matt studied neuroscience but lost interest when he realized that science would not be able to answer elemental questions about consciousness, so he looked elsewhere for answers. Jack studied philosophy but lost interest in endless discussions that never approach the verve of a racquetball game. Calvin was a committed pothead until the night his six-foot-tall red-haired aristocratic beauty girlfriend, whom I had admired in the steam room, brought him to a meeting, after which he stayed up all night on the raw energy.

In very broad terms, the women who find The Work, in numbers approximately equal to the men's, do not usually arrive with such specific agendas. Cara would be a case in point. She did not have a bookshelf packed with Gurdjieff books—she hardly had a bookshelf at all, for that matter—but she wanted something, and when she found something, she wrapped into it.

Jan would often share with me what he deemed exceptional notes and letters written by group members, and one night he handed me one written by Cara. It included the following passage addressing the subject of what we in the group might represent to the general public: "Instead of appearing to be this secret, separate organization, we can bombard people with the feeling that this passion is inseparable and flows through the veins of all humanity. And that we are here to, instead of spreading the word, spread the passion. We are not here in the name of God but in the name of Life, our growth in Life."

In one way, the new people from near and far do follow a pattern: each arrives with a furrowed brow, convinced that this is the most serious endeavor ever, ready to hunker down on the holy path to enlightenment; yet within a few weeks, if he or she survives Jan's assaults on various gods and everyone's personalities and shattered expectations of a benign, loving guru, then the furrows melt from brows and are replaced by some much-needed belly laughs, as welcome as rain on dry fields.

1985

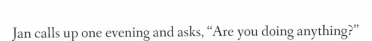

Jan calls up one evening and asks, "Are you doing anything?"

This is a formality, because it's expected that if Jan wants to get together, you get together.

Usually, after I say yes, he tells me where to meet him. Usually it's a bar.

This time he says, I'll pick you up at your place. In an hour. Well, okay.

Usually I drive—on account of his multiple DUIs. I guess he's feeling confident about drinking and driving tonight, or perhaps we are not drinking.

We are drinking. He hands me a beer in the car and drives straight to a strip club on Cheshire Bridge Road. A strip club? Jan mentions strip clubs at parties sometimes, as if every guy and maybe half the women love the places. I don't.

I follow him in as if this is great fun.

Nursing my second beer, I ogle breasts while realizing,

again, that hanging out with Jan is just not that much fun. Why is this so hard to remember? This particular pair of breasts is gorgeous, though, and so is her ass, but the red lights and the yellow lights and the disco music aren't, and what am I going to do while pretending to have fun? I hate the smile stuck on my face, but maybe it makes me look like all the used-car salesmen surrounding us.

Jan and I get into a conversation about cars, which is always fun, and I tell him about my new pristine antique convertible, a 1966 Dodge Polara with a 383 V-8. "Bought it from the proverbial little old lady," I tell him. Actually, her sister. The woman practically never drove it, and after almost twenty years, it has only 43,000 miles on it. He's impressed. But not as impressed as I am.

So I ask, "How d'ya like your car?"

It's a 1982 Camaro, black with gold racing stripes, with T-tops and a big motor. Jan thinks it's God. I think it's Judas. I would never have that car. It's a truck, really, in a late-period Elvis jumpsuit. For that money, you could have had something bloody good.

But I don't say that. You don't tell Jan that he's, um, stupid.

Soon enough, to his credit, Jan figures out that I don't love hanging out in strip clubs. He pays the bill, and we leave. He says, "Got a beer at your place?"

Sure. C'mon over.

I open the beers. He asks, "Where is Cara?"

"She's sewing at her sister's, until tomorrow afternoon." Jan doesn't ask about Rose. Rose is with her.

He swills his beer. He looks at the furniture. He looks at me. He says, "You wanna fool around?"

Do I wanna fool around? Does he mean *sex*?

If it weren't my house, I would leave.

No, I don't want to "fool around."

But I don't say that. I shrug. I guess he takes the shrug to mean "Why not?" instead of "What the fuck! Would you just go away? Now!" So he walks over and puts his arm around me. I have no interest whatsoever. My only thought is, *how do I get out of this?* I don't know how to get out of this. He leans in for the kiss. Don't want to. I don't have a plan. My body takes over as it did the night he was "dancing" with Madeleine in the farmhouse kitchen. I whip the other way with unintended force, knocking his arm off my shoulder, which I don't mind at all.

Jan handles the tension with aplomb. Somehow he manages to get out of my house without either of us feeling too strange. Except me.

As the bullshit Camaro rumbles up the hill, I wonder if this is one of Jan's recipes: take a guy to a strip club, buy him a beer, talk about cars, and then—supposedly horny after looking at naked women—have sex. I don't care if Jan has sex with men. The sleaze factor, though, with the garish strip club and the sense that "this sequence works," sticks to me like fryer grease, and I need a shower. I wonder if women in the group feel the same way. Yuk.

≈ ≈ ≈

Jan says the Task for this week is to pop into any place of business that does not make keys and ask, "Do you make keys?" Everyone in the room laughs except Jan. He says do it once a day—just ask the question. Ask at a shoe repair shop or a law office or a pawn shop. He offers no further explanation and leaves it at that.

So it happens that I'm working on a restaurant renovation, a job that entails hanging horrible wallpaper on one long wall, "horrible" being an easy assessment because all wallpaper is horrible. I'm up on the ladder, starting a strip, when the owner walks in. His standard greeting, since he saw me reading the *New York Times* one day, has become, "How's the Communist today?" He laughs. He loves his joke.

So I say, "You guys gonna make keys?"

He says, "What?"

Everyone I've asked so far has been unable to hear the question the first time.

"You know—are you gonna make keys for people? Here at the restaurant?"

His face scrunches up as his brain struggles to metabolize the question. After long seconds, his face lights up, and he says, "That's a great idea! Make keys! Yes, by God, we should make keys! We could set the machine up right here by the front door!"

The Tasks continue to surprise and to reveal unnamed, unseen edges in this life that we all accept at face value. Edge by edge, week by week.

Jan says, *"Move your hands more slowly—just enough so that only you can tell the difference."*

Agree with everyone this week.

Use this as a prayer: Superman is fearless, mysterious, and does not complain.

Pick a thought worth remembering, and make it your last thought before going to sleep every night and your first thought upon awakening in the morning.

For a week, record observed examples of people exchanging counterfeit currency in the form of emotional funny money. Write them down and turn them in.

For the rest of your life, say something humorous to yourself in the mirror every morning.

Every day for the next week, walk for ninety minutes. On the first half of the walk, chant a common refrain, such as "Two, four, six, eight, who do we appreciate?" On the second half of the walk, continue the chant while periodically checking to see if your thoughts come in words or pictures. Observe how many things the mind can do at once under ordinary circumstances.

The Task for this week is a question: What are you going to say next?

There he goes again: Jan throws another ringer, as resonant as "What's the first word in dictionary?" and "Where is a tree's brain?" The honest answer to the question, "What are you going to say next?" is, most the time: I don't know. People don't know what they're going to say until it's said. Hmm.

And it doesn't stop. *Later, he says make a list of what you actually know—not what someone told you, but what you absolutely know for certain.*

And: Walk on a single rail of the railroad tracks for twenty minutes without stopping, unless a train wants the same track. That's it. No other explanation.

≈ ≈ ≈

Often, after a Task is put forth, we never hear about it again, and it weaves into experience, so the fabric of experience is rewoven.

Occasionally the Tasks reappear like pop-up ambushes on our bumper-car path to enlightenment. Such as the night Jan asks me before the meeting, "Are you ready?" He's smiling. Don't know what he's talking about, but I tell him, sure, I'm ready. He smiles some more and says, "Better get ready!"

I answer back, "I'm getting ready!"

He can't stop. "Well, then, get ready some more!"

The meeting starts. He walks to his customary place at the front of the room. And everyone's ready—for Jan's routine hour-long delivery. But instead of jumping right in, he says, "Jon is going to tell us about astrophysics." That's all he says. Jan walks to the side of the room, and with his head, points me to the front of the room.

Shit. I said I was ready, but I wasn't ready for *this*. And why me? Everyone else on the astrophysics project knows more than I do. Don't they?

I walk slowly to the front of room, all cool like I know what I'm going to say next. But I don't. My face is hot. This heat on my face is a good place to start.

I am up there in front of everyone, saying, "The sun is very hot." Nobody is sure if this is supposed to be funny or not, but I am not laughing, so neither is anyone else. "The heat you feel on your face might be a full hundred degrees, while the heat on the face of the sun is millions of degrees. So the sun is over here at millions of degrees, and most of the universe, meaning practically everywhere else, is approaching four hundred and sixty degrees below zero, which is the state of entropy, wherein so little energy exists that nothing happens, and subatomic particles lose their joie de vivre."

I get that far, take a breath to organize myself, and continue.

"In the context of the universe, we here on earth live in an environment extremely close to entropy. We are more than ninety-nine and ninety-nine one hundredths closer to the temperature of entropy than we are to the temperature of the sun. So . . ." I pause, wondering what I am going to say next, and continue. "So what does that have to do with any of this? *This*. What we're doing here."

In this way, I am broadly following Jan's approach of reaping information or observations from the world and fashioning them—or cooking them, you could say—into flavor notes and micronutrients for our ever-enriching stew.

I find my pace with this angle, follow the raveling threads from our astrophysics studies, and wind up connecting the energy extremes of the universe to the energy extremes that one human mind can harness intentionally, such as: you benefit from *cool,* as in the practice of slowing your hand gestures just enough so that only you know the difference. A hidden-in-plain-sight window opens by this mindful reduction in a mindless habit—your own hand speed.

And just as the universe is packed with opposites, such as black holes and pulsars, so are the possibilities for what we're doing here. Such as, consider *heat,* in the form of boxing, when your hands flick faster and quicker and with more whiz-bang than thought.

My ambush Task-Talk continues as I think and speak simultaneously, speaking what I never thought before, and I am enjoying listening to it, *discovering what I am going to say next,* and so is everyone else. I weave in questions, such as: If the universe has no center, how can you? Everyone laughs. And I throw in one from our study: What force holds the electron away from the nucleus?

When I finish, Jan says, "I can't follow that." And he means it. Jan asks for the drums, the staccato beat fills the room, and people are dancing. The after-the-meeting party starts now.

I get that big feeling. That big feeling, feeling big, like it's more than you know, and you know it, and IT knows you know it, and IT is BIG.

And IT gives me an inside-the-brain-snapshot of Jan. Some years ago, he quit using notes at the meetings. He just starts in on something and finds a way to dig in. He dig-talks his way around it until he gets through to IT.

And all this bigness makes me wonder how Jan can make

statements like "All this comes from me." I don't feel it that way and would never frame it that way. It's more accurate to say, "All of me comes from IT," and I am abundantly pleased to be a conduit for the raw energy, as I would aspire to be for Rose.

And IT suffuses me with more questions. More is good, and so are questions. Although I don't have any questions at the moment. All I have is a delicious affirmation in the form of a giant grin on the inside of my entire being.

$$\approx \approx \approx$$

Questions. Questions about enlightenment.

The questions are not theoretical, and it's not about beating answers out of this one confounding word, "enlightenment," chained to a chair under a bare bulb.

Funny that "enlightenment" is a word from which you expect perfect behavior. But it turns out that enlightenment can't behave, because containment is not its true nature.

It's about starting in on something, and trail-blazing your way, with jazz questions and riff answers, to the sunshine scales.

Jan would never condone questions about enlightenment. He would consider it an off-limits subject, and I get that—in the sense that you're not gonna get enlightened sitting around theorizing about enlightenment.

But so what?

He says not to: that's all the reason I need to ask the questions anyway.

Not that I need reasons or have reasons, exactly. I do have urges and curiosities embedded in my bloodlines, in the form of Grandpa's quest for a new world and continuing in the form of

Rose's exploding enlightening being making the world new, day by day, neuron by neuron.

Jazz. Music is a language. Hmm: language. Humans learn language only when immersed in language. It's true with spoken language: if you don't learn it by a certain stage of development, you probably never will. Music, another language, is inculcated similarly. One tribe's harmony is the other tribe's cacophony. And it's true of money. If you're not conversant with it, you won't have much of it.

We have these propensities and potentialities, but they never develop without traction, without engagement, from culture.

Isn't this dynamic true of the enlightenment quest as well? You can't get there without a certain kind of immersion, the right kind of growth medium to foster a newer, broader-beamed being.

People around me have experienced the extraordinary in the solar time machine.

Weirdly, some of them become even more annoying. Not as annoying as Jan, though. He'd throw anyone half as annoying as himself out of the group for being too goddamn annoying.

Other people in the group, though, elegantly weave the extraordinary with the ordinary and lead rich, rewarding lives.

But some of the people now seem even more separate from everyone else, which raises the question: How can union separate you? How unifying was your enlightenment experience if it results in your separation?

And another question flies in sideways: How can entropy and sunshine coexist in one person?

≈ ≈ ≈

When Jan calls five of us into his office one afternoon—no group meeting, nobody else around—he blows any enlightenment question out of the firmament when he says, looking like a tornado, his sky black, "I'm throwing Madeleine out of the group."

Oh, shit! Oh, no! I know exactly what happened before anyone else does because Madeleine told me that she and Rob, this guy in the group—they've always had the hots for each other and are finally having a torrid affair, which seemed like a good idea to me since Jan was fucking everyone in sight, even coming after me, so why shouldn't she have some fun and do whoever the hell she wants?

All five of us squirm. Madeleine lives with Jan. They have been living together for—what? More than twelve years? Now he's gonna kick her out of the house *and* out of the group? After she's done once what he's done a thousand times?

Jan continues. "Rob is out, too." He hardly pauses. "They have broken one of the primary rules here."

Everyone knows what he means. No casual sex between group members. My first flash thought is, "What if it wasn't casual?"

My second thought is, "Fuck you, asshole. After all the fucking around you've done?"

Makes me sick. Gotta get out of the room. Not that he fucked around. The cold-blooded, bold-faced, narcissistic hypocrisy is what sickens me.

Two days later, Jan tells Madeleine and Rob they can come back to the group.

Most of the people in the group never knew it happened. But the five of us help Madeleine move out of the house on Memorial Drive, where she's been living with Jan.

1986

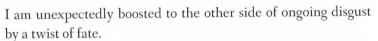

I am unexpectedly boosted to the other side of ongoing disgust by a twist of fate.

Through a business friend and client, I had been negotiating to obtain a new meeting place for the group at what is probably the best commercial intersection between Washington and Miami. For free. Seriously. At the corner of Peachtree and West Paces Ferry, right in the heart of Buckhead. The building is slated for development. The owner wants somebody to occupy it until the renovation. It might be a while, like a couple of years.

So Jason, the owner, says, yes, take the space, plus you can rent out the other vacant storefronts and keep half the money.

Free real estate, with income potential and no risk, might possibly interest Jan the cheapskate more than a harem.

My wrangles with Jan's hypocrisy are immediately swallowed by the excitement and exertion of whipping this prime location into shape for our meetings. Seems crazy that we outliers have scored a turn in the bull's-eye of Buckhead. It's all we do for the next few weeks. We convert one of the vacant storefronts, the one with a marquee over the door, into our lobby, and we use the existing gracious staircase to access the cavernous upstairs, where we build a large meeting room, more than big enough to accommodate the hundred people showing up for every meeting.

As soon as the build-out is done, you can hear an audible sigh as the group relaxes into the new normal of meeting in the sexy commercial heart of Atlanta.

But Jan, true to form, shocks the shit out of constantly creeping complacency when he announces the new program: we are going to open a theater. Our own theater. With all original scripts. We will write our own plays, build our own sets, score and play our own music. We will be the production company and the ushers and the stage hands. Every six weeks, a new play, entirely original, scripted and produced by a different crew of group members.

Then he says, "Beyond those parameters, I'm staying out of it. You people name the theater, you write the plays, you do the work, and I will show up on opening night prepared to be surprised and delighted." He names six people who will produce the first play, opening in six weeks. And in another break from the norm, none of the six is from the group of us he holds the closest.

We brainstorm the name and agree on Evoteck Theater, as a play on "evolution" and "technology" and mainly just because we like the sound of it, and on top of the prominent marquee out front, we mount a ten-foot-tall space monster straddling a rocket.

Evoteck Theater. Revolutionists, as Jan calls us, in the heart of Buckhead.

≈ ≈ ≈

"Did you charge for tickets?" Grandpa asks.

Yes, we did charge for tickets.

Grandpa nods. "Did people show up?"

I love that he measures our theater experiment as a business-man. And I'm pleased to tell him that it measures well enough, especially because the people behind it are a bunch of over-talented, underpaid wannabe mystics. "Well, yeah, Grandpa, we had a lot of sold-out shows. The room filled with people guffaw-ing, surprised, entertained. We developed a following. The plays were reviewed in the paper. They interviewed us on the college radio stations. And other theater—"

"Were the plays good?"

"Were they good?" I repeat the question.

Mainly, I'm pleased that he's interested. Grandpa had some stage experience at the Daytona Playhouse. Of course. Singing. His baritone. He sang to the sea.

So I say to Grandpa, "Not as good as they would have been with you. Singing opera."

He likes this.

His face gets serious. "Tell me some of the plays," he says.

"About them?"

"No, I just want the names. I want to hear the names."

So I tell him some names.

The Astro Pups: Journey to Alpha Nine.

The Rehearsal.

Zoombox to Zargon.

Simon and the Big Seed.

Rosa's Hyperauthentic Cantina.

The Tomorrow Show.

Nick Anvil: Private I.

He puts up his hand, as he often does. "That's enough."

We're both silent.
Now he's nodding.
And Grandpa says, "This is good."

≈ ≈ ≈

You could call it the golden age of the group.

Each show jolts toward opening night. Scary as crap. Every single time, every single person working on every single show swears this one is gonna be the ultimate fiasco. But it never fails: every show succeeds. Funny. Smart. Jarring. Quotable. Above all, alive. Animated. Kicking ass.

I love being involved in the productions, especially on the script side or live on stage. Most of us do. Everyone crackles.

But my favorite part of Evoteck is peeking through the curtain in the back of the room during a play, watching people in the group performing on stage or playing live music in the wings—people who had been all locked up with heavy brows and stiff shoulders coming alive on stage and lifting the audience from wild laughter to wide-eyed silence.

Weather systems ripple around the room.

I imagine an Evoteck opera, starring Grandpa Philip Rothenberg as Enrico Caruso. People would pay a lot for tickets to that show. We could triple our prices.

≈ ≈ ≈

You would think we'd have taken Sundays off. You could have made a case for it. We all have jobs. (Well, most of us, anyway.) And we attend group meetings a couple of days a week. And we're running a theater. And Jan hardly ever bothers anyone on Sunday, unless we're overhauling the building in Buckhead. We could have taken Sundays off.

But no. On Sundays, around twenty people usually show up for touch football at Medlock Park, in Decatur. This is not Jan's doing. We just want to. Men and women both, playing serious hilarious touch football. At all skill levels, on one field. Some of the guys played in college, they're that good, and some have never played before. What a riot. A riot of quickness and great grabs and horrific blunders, enough to drive a coach batshit crazy. Good thing we have no coach. He would douse the vibe. We're just out there to spiral the pigskin into open palms sprinting west at twenty miles an hour. We are drawn to connect on the green grass in the sun.

≈ ≈ ≈

Saint Quantum's Day at Evoteck in Buckhead automatically, by dint of the uptown vibe, clicks up a couple of notches and unofficially becomes the Over-Talented, Overdressed Wannabe Mystics' Equinox Ball. With some drugs, meaning as much as anyone wanted. Not that everyone wanted, but those who did made up for those who didn't.

People dress up crazy with top hats and coats of many colors, and the band plays music of many colors. I have no idea how they play under these mind-space conditions, but I am glad they play, because sound waves are crashing.

After that Saint Quantum's Day weekend, I notice that I have managed not to notice that Cara can't stop.

It's not that hard to notice.

She already wrecked one car this year.

And sometimes in the middle of the day, she rushes out of the house, like she's gotta get something *now*.

And now she wrecks another car.

When you're driving a motor vehicle, it's just not that hard to steer clear of stationary objects, such as other cars. Other cars that are not moving. But it's hard for Cara. When she's drinking. Or whatever.

Snuck up on her, and not just on Saint Quantum's Day. Pretty much every week we have a party after the Friday meeting. Yes, we drink, and yes, it can be a beautiful thing. But it is not always beautiful. It snuck up on me that it snuck up on her. But now I notice. Half-empty bottles disappear, with dumb explanations that I don't even ask for.

When I bring it up, she doesn't want to talk about it. The ethos of the group holds sway. We do not "put our hands on other people"—meaning putting the hands of your mind on another's mind—so we do not confront each other much. This can be beneficial. You let people do what they do and see them with new eyes. It's pleasurable to see with your eyes and mind wide open. But the same practice can also wreck your life when your significant other is a drunk and you do not press the issue.

Maybe she hides it well. Some weeks I forget about it. But some weeks I can't.

She's not the only one sliding around like this. But she's the only one I'm living with, the only one who's the mother of Rose.

≈ ≈ ≈

After the Evoteck plays have been running for more than a year, Jan announces that we're going to do something.

"Do something" usually means do something big. So my first thought is that we're already doing something big. When you add up the theater two nights a week, plus the meetings two nights a week, Evoteck is a brimming lifestyle. A lot of us are in the building four, five, six nights a week, plus we have jobs and run small businesses and—oh, yeah—we have lives, too. And he doesn't even know we play football on Sundays.

None of that seems to register with Jan, and he doesn't ask for opinions. He announces that we are going to offer public presentations two nights a week. "'We' meaning you," he says. "All of you. None of me. You people split it up, do it however you want to do it, name it what you want to name it. Just do it. I want people in here listening to you."

Well, okay. We've done the impossible before. Maybe we can do it again. Here goes.

We call it Paradigm.

It's free-form. It could be a skit. It could be a monologue or a dialogue or our own invented form, the trialogue, in which three monologues intersect or converge or explode.

It could be a song followed by an interpretation of a completely different song, neither of which anyone has ever heard before.

But all those forms—song, skit, trialogue—are mere tropes for how far we reach in monologue. Because that's what Paradigm is: people talking. One at a time. On stage. To people out there, in the chairs, willing to let a bunch of non-entertainers entertain them. Because the truth is entertaining. Great comedians strip bare the truth in a way it's never been stripped, and this is highly entertaining. Not that we're trying to be standup comics. It's about standing up and being who we are. Paradigm will succeed when it draws on the truth, and expresses it well.

The truth of our collective experience, the truth of insight, the truth of ha-ha-we're-all-idiots.

And what is success? Well, we never break it down this way, but you could say success occurs when the activity pays more than it costs. Energetically speaking, that is. You expend energy telling the truth this way. And if the people you address benefit in some way, that benefit accrues to you. And multiplies.

In a couple of weeks, the room does fill up. People do want to hear fresh takes on how a human brain may enrich a human life.

In a broad sense, a portion of the Paradigm talks follow Jan's general model: he shares a sharp observation of something that might be ripe for further consideration, which includes everything happening at once. Then follows a cool intellectual judo move on the matter at hand so that what seemed to be external becomes internal in a most challenging, stimulating way. I followed this broad model when he threw me in front of the room to talk about astrophysics: entropy exists in your own nervous system, and so does solar energy. So it's not about astrophysics *out there*, as interesting as that may be in its own right. It's about *in here*, about how your brain might work best and how it barely works at all sometimes and how someone would make it work better if someone had the raw desire to do so and how funny and freshening and profoundly un-serious it is when you actually get somewhere with all this.

But the kernel of the appeal in our Paradigm presentations is not really in whether or not we follow Jan's general model. The kernel is wrapped in the pleasure of joining the ascent to a summit atop someone else's mind.

One night while listening at Paradigm, I am struck by the most delightful blasphemy: I like listening to Paradigm—people in the group—more than I like listening to Jan!

This is a shocking, practically "illegal" thought. We are not supposed to think this. Yet it's undeniable. I enjoy listening to what fellow group member, Erin, is saying about managing environmental waste. She slides easily from environ*mental* into mental waste and how to process it. But the kernel of it is more than the deft judo move pivoting on the "mental" in "environmental." It's the smile on her face, her enjoyment in escorting us on this hike up her mind.

Without Jan's baggage. Without his edge.

Feels good and free and clean and open and happy and new.

≈ ≈ ≈

One of the Paradigm audience members who persists his way into the group is Ray LaNeer. Ray is only nineteen. He's around six foot four and lean and supple and he gets it. He gets what this is about, and it doesn't matter that some of us might be his parents' age.

At the next Saint Quantum's Day, I'm going to ask Ray if he's related to Sidney Lanier, Georgia's de facto poet laureate, after whom a street in my neighborhood is named. It's a poetically winding hilly street with islands of magnolia and ginkgo overwhelming the asphalt.

But I never have the chance.

During Jan's talk at one particular weekly meeting, Ray sits in the front row, off to the right side.

Jan is framing everything, as he often does, in terms of "the Life of Life," as he puts it. That is, Life itself (he always capitalizes "Life") is alive and growing—and human consciousness is the primary outlet through which life's growth takes form.

Then Jan states with force: one method for understanding the reality of this is to think another person's thoughts.

Jan does not solidly connect these thoughts—not in any linear progression—but he sketches them in quick verbal strokes to facilitate the leap. Another person's thoughts are portals. If you are going to get anywhere with all this, you must optimize the portals that are available to you.

And speaking of thoughts, he says, new ideas are holes for people to look through. He says, "New ideas are peepholes in the fabric of what you already know."

This is a stunning image, delivered with the full force of Jan's certitude. I'm instantly savoring these peepholes. But I'm interrupted.

Ray LaNeer erupts.

First, the laughter.

Laughter is common at the meetings. People laugh all the time. Jan is funny. Not ashamed to be goofy. And cynical, ridiculously and bitingly cynical. And sometimes people laugh at a heretofore unstated but suddenly obvious truth, little chuckles like bubbles rising from the froth of liberation.

But Ray LaNeer's laugh is different from what follows a punch line or an insight. Bottomless, emancipating. From the substrate. This kind of laughter is not a normal part of the scene here. A laugh we all want.

Jan glances Ray's way and keeps talking.

Ray's laugh arcs into crying.

Jan keeps talking.

Ray is sobbing with his shoulders and his long torso.

The weeping is a first. Nobody ever sobbed out loud in the middle of one of Jan's talks. But Jan tacitly affirms it, he's easy with it, as if a fellow traveler just joined him at speed, and he keeps right on going. The laughter and weeping merge and separate, then soften and subside, as Ray surfs waves far away.

The cycle of primal sounds reemerges from Ray as Jan winds down his talk.

As Jan steps away from the podium at the front of the room, he blows a big kiss to Ray LaNeer. Jan smiles a gleeful smile that lights his face, just as it did on the night he told us about Wade's big breakthrough.

The next week, Ray LaNeer performs on the Evoteck stage a kind of otherworldly rap poem punctuated by his long rubber body. The crowd loves it. Everybody is happy. And then Ray disappears. A few months later, we hear he's in Alaska.

I never get to ask if he's related to Sidney Lanier. Not that it matters. What matters is the ray of solar energy I get from Ray LaNeer.

1988

Jan looks at me and says, "I'm shutting it all down."

Before the meeting, I always stop by his office to see what's up. Depends on his mood. I like to make him laugh, and if he's not wearing that frown of his, I'll usually give it a try, and I'll usually succeed. Sometimes he'll run a plan or a question by me. An intelligent conversation with him always sits well. But—what?

"Shutting what down?"

He says, "All of it. Paradigm. Evoteck. All of it. No more public stuff. Immediately. As of tonight. I am shutting it all down."

What? Why?

I want to tell Jan that this is a bad idea. Don't do this. You always said that everything is either living or dying. Expanding or contracting. You're not in the room to see people in the group hold forth at Paradigm. You're not there to see the way they light up. I want to say, *I like listening to them more than I like listening to you! And you're gonna shut them up?*

But the walls are up, the walls around Jan's face, and I don't say anything.

He doesn't look up. I can't stop looking down, staring at him as I've never done before.

Is the man jealous?

Jealous of us? We're running and funning and punning and gunning beyond ourselves without him. And it pisses him off?

Hmm.

Here's the guy who claims all the answers to all the questions about human consciousness. He claims all the recipes for extraordinary development. And he's jealous of the people he's leading? Is that it? Is the alpha dog jealous of other dogs in the pack when they dance and flourish?

But Jan doesn't brook discussion on any of his fierce decisions, and as soon as the meeting starts he tells the group, just like he told me, "I'm shutting it all down."

Evoteck Theater disappears. The name and the space monster are dismantled from the marquee. The group activities now consist exclusively of listening to Jan hold forth three nights a week.

Nobody says anything about it. But the energy dissipates. The buzz and hum of wannabe mystics polishing scripts and rehearsing the next play and conjuring a presentation for Paradigm—it all shrivels and dies. As if we are a small town, and the mayor just shuttered the factory and closed the union hall. And in place of all that, Jan decides we need to listen to him three nights a week?

Shit, Jan just slammed the door on a golden age. He didn't have to do that. I feel like a wizened old seer who knows the man is losing his way.

≈ ≈ ≈

Cara wrecks the car again. Same thing. Woman smashes two-ton machine into stationary object. Woman drinking.

This is not going well. But it's not every day, her drinking. The days of sobriety replenish her magnetism, and the pull of it squelches lingering questions about how long this glow will last, and you suck on the myth of It Will Be Just Like It Is Now Forever.

≈ ≈ ≈

I catch up with my old friend from high school, Rick Roth, now an attorney in Savannah, Georgia. Haven't seen him in more than twenty years. But we reconnect instantly and joke about our underachieving Jewish Boy Scout troop. None of us made it to First Class, but we went camping every month with Mr. Jacobs.

Over a bottle of wine, Rick leans in and says, "I know something about your past that you don't know."

That's a statement you hardly ever hear.

He leans in closer and tells me, "During law school at the University of Georgia, in the summer of '72, I interned at the federal prosecutor's office. I was told to review a stack of draft dodgers the government was going to prosecute for evasion. I start thumbing through the file folders to see what I'm up against, and I come across one with the name Jonathan Marcus on it. I'm thinking, 'There can't be two of these guys.' So I open the folder and see your picture. I close the folder. I look over my right shoulder. Look over my left shoulder. No one sees me. I take your entire file and slide it into the wastebasket."

So that's how I got out of the draft! Crazy! Rick tossed my file!

Wow. Thank you, Rick.

Wow. Had nothing at all to do with Jan's supposedly amazing letter. The one he was bragging about. Shit. For all I know, they read Jan's letter and dumped me into the *prosecute now* pile.

Hmm.

≈ ≈ ≈

"In Judaism," Grandpa says, *"we didn't measure everything in terms of enlightenment, as you people seem to do. In Judaism, we argue about the laws while we obey the laws, at least some of them, and we argue with God. We argue with each other. We argue with the rabbi. We argue about Moses and Jacob and Esau and all the rest of them."* I think he's talking more to himself than to me. *"To put a word on it, I would say that we were trying to cultivate wisdom. Wisdom. Is wisdom different from enlightenment?"*

He looks at me and asks, *"Is wisdom different from enlightenment?"*

Damn, Grandpa. That is a great question.

That is a damn good question. I never thought about it that way before. Probably because Jan never talks about wisdom, except maybe to make fun of it. And if he isn't explicit very often about enlightenment, well, it's woven into the process. Wisdom isn't.

I want to say yes, wisdom is different from enlightenment.

But Grandpa continues, "By either measure, by the measure of wisdom, or the measure of enlightenment, self-aggrandizement fails."

I love Grandpa. I want to be like Grandpa.

"You're right," I tell him. "I don't know why Jan had to claim credit for the success of my draft avoidance. What a bunch of arrogant bullshit! What the hell? Even though Jan doesn't go around saying, 'I'm enlightened,' everything is based on that assumption, which Jan certainly reinforces . . . So what is this immense pile of bullshit that impels a supposedly more enlightened being to take wrongful credit for writing a letter?"

Grandpa listens but doesn't say anything.

I tell him, "One night Jan and I were out drinking, and he began a sentence with these words: 'If I became an egomaniac . . .'"

Then Grandpa puts his hand up the way he does and says, "The promised land. It moves around."

Grandpa should know. He came to the promised land alone as a teenager, and here we are, Grandpa and I and everyone else, still clambering our way toward fulfilling the promise of that land, that promise.

I don't know why Grandpa cut me off. But I don't care. The question he's posing is way bigger that what I was saying. What an epic question. Wisdom as opposed to enlightenment. Thank you, Grandpa. We're not done with this one. We're just beginning.

≈ ≈ ≈

Middle of the week, way after dark, Perry and I go to Jan's house to do a small carpentry repair. We get done before midnight. Jan says, "Want a beer?"

Sure, we want a beer.

We're sipping—or gulping—in Jan's "music room," a carpeted quiet room with no windows. Completely carpeted: walls, floors, and ceiling. Shag carpeting. Maybe Jan conflates shag carpeting with shagging. Or maybe he just likes to shag on shag. Whatever, the carpet on all surfaces is navy blue. The navy blue cube effect mutes the shag effect. But still. It's hideous. And quiet, almost. You can hear trucks on Memorial Drive when the stereo is off. A cheapskate's sound studio.

The beer makes the blue shag cube more tolerable than it deserves to be. But who's counting? The empties line up in a row by the door. Jan likes things in rows. And books by height.

Not that the conversation is especially organized. Anything but, actually. More like happy sloppy. When Jan hangs out with just a couple of people, he eases up on the I-know-everything-and-I'm-the-big-dog syndrome, and he's maybe halfway to being a regular guy.

Jan keeps changing LPs on the stereo, the way he does at parties. Howlin' Wolf comes on. "Smokestack Lightning." He doesn't know I love Howlin' Wolf. Jan connects with anyone's connection with music. Howlin' Wolf sings right up my spine. Delta blues growling, note by note, syllable by syllable. Sparse, swanky instrumentation.

I tell them, "I saw him at Richards on Monroe Drive a couple of years ago. Turned out to be one of the last performances before he died."

Jan and Perry, both musicians, look at me as if to imply, "You're not so dumb for a guy who can't play a lick."

Jan calls him Chester Burnett, acts like he knows him personally, not sure I believe that, but Jan's eyebrows rise when

I say, "He looks just like he sounds. An NFL-size guy who's crushing the microphone as if it were Jericho . . . and then this tender falsetto sweetens the room, and you don't know where it came from."

Jan likes the Jericho reference.

Then we talk about falsetto voices, which ripens into all of us talking in our falsettos, at which point I chide them both by saying in falsetto, "Your 914 is a falsetto car."

They both have a Porsche 914s, "which are really Volkswagens, guys." I have made this point before, and it never fails to get them going.

I always concede that, yes, your 914s have the ideal center of gravity and a removable roof. All good. But what's with the grandmommy motor and the transmission made out of rocks?

Perry and I get in a jag of falsetto arguing about 914s, and it escalates until neither of us can stop falsetto talking, and we giggle like schoolgirls. Jan seems mildly amused and keeps changing the music.

Robert Johnson's guitar riff fills the blue shag cube. Then comes his voice-from-the-tomb mojo chanting to his guitar, and you forget falsetto. This is not a giggling matter. We are three solemn men peering into the campfire, and the campfire is fierce. The campfire is Robert Johnson.

As Robert Johnson's last chord fades, we stare into his audio embers. Dust motes click on the needle and are broadcast through the giant sound speakers.

I ask Jan straight up, "Why are you doing this?"

Jan and Perry both look at me.

"This, what we're doing. The group. Why are you doing this?"

Jan gets that half grin on his face.

We keep drinking beer.

He keeps changing the music.

Perry joins me. We keep asking Jan why is he doing this.

He likes the question, pretends to start answering, but never does. We keep asking.

When we step outside to go home, the sky is getting light and traffic rumbles. Oh, shit. We have to drive home in morning rush hour after drinking all night.

≈ ≈ ≈

Rich Kidd—is he a major now? A colonel? Is he right-hand man to a general? Does he think he's in the center of everything happening at once? Has he attended Joint Chiefs of Staff meetings? Has he played golf with defense contractors and made back-door deals?

Does he have a kid?

I hope he is learning from his child. The wide-open gemstone eyes. The world is starting over, right here, right now, in this brain and spirit. The first steps. The first words. The first sentences. The first time his kid says, "This is an interesting area."

The first steps and the first words and sentences have currency in a world aborning, as much as Grandpa's first double eagle, solid-gold American, in the safe of his palm.

I wonder if Rich Kidd is itching for a dollop of free-form.

1989

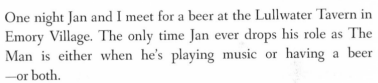

One night Jan and I meet for a beer at the Lullwater Tavern in Emory Village. The only time Jan ever drops his role as The Man is either when he's playing music or having a beer —or both.

While looking around the room, Jan says, "Look at that double reflection in the window. Ever think how strange that is?"

And I tell Jan no, it's not strange at all. That's double-paned glass, and because of the small difference in the distance of the two panes from us, they reflect slightly different images.

As soon as I say it, he gets it, but he doesn't like it at all: doesn't like that I get something he didn't. His face hardens, and he freezes.

After a few minutes and another pint of beer, he relaxes and we resume chatting. He glances at the menu, locks on a detail, and says, "Some words just seem to come from nowhere. A collection of letters that have hardly anything to do with any others. Like the word 'delicatessen.' Where would that bunch of letters come from?"

I look at him and answer, "Delicacy." Jan doesn't say anything, and he freezes up again. Soon he leaves.

I stay and chat with my beer about how Jan has a stick up his ass about acting like he knows everything. Nobody knows everything. Human knowledge is far more capacious than any one brain. Wish he would quit pretending. And besides, if you think you know everything, how do you learn from anybody?

Hmm.

≈ ≈ ≈

Seems that talking to Cara about drinking makes her drink more. Certainly doesn't make her drink less. I have seen this Cara before. Eight or nine years ago, when she'd show up late at night, half drunk, smelling bad, liquor stains on her fine wool coat.

Just as she does now.

Then it goes away. Again. She stops. Then it seems, as it always does, that it will be this way forever all over again.

But it won't, and it doesn't.

Reminds me of the double reflection Jan saw in the window at the Lullwater Tavern. Everyone in the group stutter-steps up and down the ladder of evolution. Everyone's got multiple reflections.

A bunch of us in the group are addicted to these expanses of arrest, amazement, completion. These transcendent passages seem far more important than a job. Anyone can do a job, right? But how many people can *do this*?

Aided by sharpened minds and opened spirits, a lot of people in the group do succeed in careers . . . construction, law, education, software, entrepreneurship, craft. The other half can't quite make it click on a getting-through-the-day basis. And the third half includes a couple of bums, some cheats, a reprobate, a few loons, and the damned.

Cara's bloody muddle with booze rips "the group is great" blinders from my eyes and lays bare everyone's addiction: we're all addicted to being ourselves.

The enlightenment experience soars above the channels of self, yet the channels and self are one and the same, no matter the height of the flight. Some selves prove compatible with enlightenment flights. Some don't. Grandpa's question comes to mind. Maybe wisdom blooms when enlightenment harmonizes with these idiosyncratic channels.

Addictions, to booze or self or enlightenment, have side effects.

And everyone's got them. Addictions. Side effects. And you don't get to choose them. They just show up and glom on.

One side effect of my addiction to "higher consciousness" shows up blatantly, inexplicably, ridiculously, embarrassingly, as bad work habits. Such as being late for business meetings, late to the job site, constantly. Flaky stupid shit.

So stupid. Before Jan, I used to have, well, damn near perfect work habits. And now, immersed in this path to *higher consciousness*, I am unable to just show up for work on time. Despite guilt and efforts to correct it, I can't control it. Which is horrible. And exacerbated by the fact that if Jan Cox says be somewhere on time, I'm there. Right on time.

I don't want Grandpa to know about this idiocy of mine, because he worked his ass off so we wouldn't have to.

Grandpa nods solemnly and says, "*I know what it is to lose control of something.*"

His melancholia.

Wow. That's a problem of another magnitude.

≈ ≈ ≈

I scrub my fingers across the limestone facade of the Ethical Culture society building at the corner of Central Park West and Sixty-Fourth Street. Whenever I'm on the Upper West Side, I make sure to pass that way.

"You went there," I say to Grandpa Phil.

He nods.

"Well," I tell him, "I like the building. I like it just because you went there. I try to feel you in there, wondering."

Grandpa nods again. "It was founded by the son of a rabbi. He worked on establishing a kind of nonreligious Judaism based on ethics—the essence of Judaism. Based on the teachings of the Talmud but without all the rigmarole, accessible to everyone."

Grandpa likes the concept.

"We lived in the neighborhood for a time. It was after the girls left home. We didn't need the big house in Mount Vernon anymore, so your grandmother and I moved into a very nice apartment facing Central Park."

An apartment overlooking the park sounds, well, pretty fantastic, but Grandpa doesn't rave about it.

"The doorman bothered me," he says. "I didn't want the man

hailing a cab for me. I wanted to hail my own cab. I was itchy to connect with common things."

Wow. Most rich guys pay a lot just to be in the company of other rich guys. Grandpa could have been a pompous rich guy who treats the help the way his abusive brother-in-law treated him. But Grandpa just wants to hail his own cab. He cherishes his own humanity, and he doesn't want anyone kissing his ass.

I love Grandpa for this.

He continues. *"Finally I had some leisure time, as you have had your whole life."*

He says this without a trace of rancor.

And I can't get to work on time?

"And I didn't want anyone serving me like that. He called me Sir and Mr. Rothenberg. So I found myself leaving the building through the alley door. It was during this period that I sought out the Ethical Culture society." He pauses.

"Not because of the doorman." He laughs a little.

"Your grandmother and I supported the synagogue, of course. Our Judaism was never in question.

"But when the melancholia would close in and pull down and sink me, with no warning, it was devastating. Was it an addiction? A side effect? I don't know. I came to the new world, and made a new life, but when the melancholia closed in, I was very old. Sometimes I could hardly move, even as I was desperate to shake it. I spoke to various rabbis about it over the years, but they didn't understand, and they gave me the same general prescriptions. Love God. Obey His laws. Perform deeds of loving-kindness.

"You know," he says, his voice tightening, *"I was not going to become an Orthodox Jew. Obeying more laws was not going to solve this for me. I grew up in the orthodoxy of Augostowa, and only Mendel the shoemaker had bright eyes. And it wasn't*

because he obeyed more laws than the rabbi. The rabbi was given to fits of rage.

"And I was never going to be a true student of Torah.

"But I was a good man."

Sounds like a plea from the Book of Lamentations in the Old Testament.

"And I asked God for freedom from the gloom that stalked me and drowned my spirit. But I didn't get an answer.

"So with your Grandma Rose's support, I tried whatever we could find.

"But still, when the cold dark came, it trapped everything. The way the northern ocean crushes ships in the ice sheet.

"And Ethical Culture? It was another effort to establish a safe harbor from those waves of darkness. And it did lead me to new thoughts and to thoughtful, accomplished people. I appreciate that. But perhaps, after listening to some of your experiences . . . perhaps it was all too reasonable and rational. It became clear that ideas, no matter how illuminating, were not going banish the gloom."

"Grandpa," I say to him, "we are different coils of the same rope."

≈ ≈ ≈

Two weeks after I ask myself how to get out of this goddamn mess with Cara, which is now Cara + Cara's addiction, her cohabiting twin—which ought to be funny because Jan has recently used the term "your twin" when skewering the universal yet unique internal dialogue prevailing in most people most of the time even though most people never talk about it, but it isn't funny because Cara's twin is smelly and expensive—Cara says she's moving out. I try to hide my excitement and say okay, which is tantamount to: Can I help you? Get out by noon?

The big concern is Rose.

And it's not that simple, of course. Yes, whew, it's a relief to be unhooked from the mess of living with an alcoholic. But it's hardly a happy day. Tragic, unable to stop such brains and beauty and goodness shadowing booze into darkness.

And she's the mother of my daughter.

I wonder, at the same time, as Cara gets her stuff . . . how did I get hooked on an addict in the first place? Well, I was like a junkie. I was hooked on the high. Or rather the memory of it.

And, it finally snapped. My addiction, that is. Done. Done with Cara. And only when it snaps do I see it with any clarity.

A declaration from Jan comes to mind: "The only useful change is abrupt change, and even that may be too familiar."

She's moving out. When the door opens, sprint for daylight.

Sprinting indeed, thrilled to be unstuck. While cherishing and honoring and worrying over the divine side effect of our relationship: Rose.

≈ ≈ ≈

Rose is busy making a house under the dining room table when Butch the cat saunters in to assess. Rose lunges for Butch. Butch dematerializes. Rose maintains lunge velocity until her forehead collides with the table leg. Sounds like a drunk banging a Buick into a boulder. She flops on the floor.

The loud sound, then silence. Scary. Is she knocked out?

No. But she can't find her breath.

I remember this from childhood—the dizziness flooding a crack of pain. Inflation of heat and cold and panic. It consumes your brain and disables your lungs so you can't breathe or scream or remember your life. Trying to breathe. Can't. Everything goes red, the world through lenses of blood.

I hoist her up, her head to my shoulder, the way Dad did for me, his giant hands and mattress-like shoulder into which, as soon as I was able, I screamed—just as Rose does right now, so I know she is fine even though she sounds like a crazy person. A very loud crazy person. Screaming in my ear.

In adulthood, you forget that breathlessness and that scream —where do they go? But the same sickening seconds of pain stun me at our custody proceeding. Cara shows up looking healthy and glamorous. The judge awards her custody of Rose. I can't find my breath, and everything goes red.

≈ ≈ ≈

For a month, the Task consists of listening to a radio station you can't stand, every day for an hour. Simple. Good, I get it. I can do this.

Shit, I can't do this. I hate the radio station Task. I hate it because I really hate it—so much that I can't do it.

But I do try. I find a right-wing talk show and love how much I hate how stupid it is. I listen every day, and every day I try to last an hour. But every day, failure. Can't do it. Some days I last maybe four minutes and even then can't wait for the commercial break.

But damn it, I get the idea, and I love the idea. The idea that you *benefit* by learning how to agree with another part of it all.

Learn how to agree with the other, because we're all planets rattling around the same cosmos, and if you wanna become intimate with the larger whole—the cosmos, if you can—then you have to at least consider everything from the other point of view, whatever *the other* might be.

I + Not-I = Everything.

I take this to heart: if you don't agree with it, and especially if you really, *really*, instinctively, deeply, don't agree with it, then *find a way to agree with it!*

That's the radio station Task, in essence.

So even though I can't possibly get through an hour of the goddamn bullshit radio shit and quit trying, well, I can still listen to thoughts I don't agree with and be open to learning from them.

So my new girlfriend attends a couple of meetings, to see what the hell I'm up to all the time, and she says to me *Jan Cox is the angriest man I've ever met.*

Aha! This is an idea I do not automatically agree with.

But I want to find a way to agree with her, because, well, she is part of the cosmos I particularly want to embrace. Plus she has her own take on things. Plus I do not want to get into an argument with her about how great and un-angry Jan is.

So her words stick in my head: the angriest man she's ever met. Hmm.

The next month, following the pattern of life-goes-on-and-do-what-you-always-do, I enter Jan's office before the meeting like a good little right-hand man. Without looking up, he says, "Do you have a pen?" I hand him my pen. He puts it to the paper. No ink comes out. He scowls at me as if to say how could I possibly do this to him—hand him a pen that doesn't write? He throws the pen across the room. It hits the far wall and bounces on the floor.

The angriest person I ever met.

I am finding a way to agree with her.

Look at him. Who the fuck are you to throw my pen across the room? I have been with you since the Miller Building, when you were drawing charts for twelve people huddled around your desk. And now you're whacked out because my pen quit? Like I'm supposed to fret before I walk in here and check my pen because what if Jan wants my pen and it doesn't work? Oh, no! He might have a little conniption fit . . . is that what I'm supposed to be thinking about? Jan and his pouty, pen-hurling petulance? Shit, no, man.

Get over your goddamn self, Jan Cox.

But I don't say a word.

But I do say to myself:

Hmm.

≈ ≈ ≈

Jan gets on a tear bashing Emily Dickinson. He thinks he's funny. People laugh because Jan expects them to laugh. But it doesn't strike me funny. Makes me wonder. So I read her poetry, and a lot of the time, she's got better stuff on her fastball than he does on his. And she didn't parade around with an ego too big for the Pentagon.

I always love the way Jan appreciates all kinds of music and musicians and art and artists, but he never applauds anyone in philosophy or mysticism. That just doesn't wash. You who purport to lead us to the whole enchilada? Can't applaud the shoulders on which you stand?

Hmm.

And what about the way he forbids the expression of anger,

but everyone's always tiptoeing around him so they don't make him angry?

Hmm.

I suppose the tipping point for me is Rose. She has taught me more in a short time than he did in a long time.

But I am not building a case toward a logical conclusion.

That's not how it happens.

1990

It happens in a way I never expected, never imagined.

In the springtime.

Springtime in Atlanta's densely planted old downtown neighborhoods may be the finest anywhere. The light air lingers for three months, and each week or two a new perfume and a new palette decorate the forests and valleys and creek beds, commencing with redbud and climaxing with magnolia. And don't miss the oakleaf hydrangeas. They bloom in May.

So I am sitting on the back deck, reveling in the sky-green new oak leaves, because if the sky were green, this luminous new oak-leaf green is the green the sky would be.

Oh!

A built-in alarm clock rings. I look at my watch. Yes, it's *right now time* to get up and go to the meeting.

Suddenly, just as it happens in the Bible, in the ancient

desert with God, embossed words sear my mind: *I don't want to listen to him anymore.*

Startling.

I don't want to listen to him anymore.

This thought springs into being fully formed, bypassing any process of *thinking*.

Irrefutable.

Fresh air.

Freedom.

I don't want to listen to him anymore! I don't have to listen to him anymore! I'm done! Done listening to Jan!

The giant sky-green, new-leafing, high-reaching oak in the back yard never looked so splendid.

When the door opens, sprint for daylight.

Liberation.

Gazing up at the trees. Green halos glow on the crowns of the oaks. Major springtime. One of a thousand enlightenments.

This one especially delicious: I don't need the teacher anymore.

Ironically, it's Jan who has already described this rejection of him in a deliciously pithy statement: *The mind is the last to know.*

I was already done with him. I just didn't know it yet.

Yes, Jan Cox, you are right: it came from my body. I did not want to sit there and listen to you anymore, ever again.

And then another line of Jan's from some years back follows: *You can't leave a place until you really know it.*

And I say: "Check. Roger that," as if I'm radioing Richard Kidd III while he collects his honorable discharge. Got it. Right-o. I know the place. Am now leaving. Rich Kidd and I exchange knowing winks across the dimensions.

Am now gone.

Free.

That's the moment.

About an hour before the meeting, about twenty years after I met Jan, I quit. I don't go to the meeting that night or ever again.

I never need to hear his voice again.

I knew the place.

And left.

≈ ≈ ≈

The next week, I quit being late. The next week. On time for everything. Suddenly, just like that—snap—the side effect disappears with the addiction. After all the effort I had put into trying to be on time and failing, here I am suddenly reincarnated as Mr. On Time All the Time.

Not all the changes follow so quickly or with such utter ease.

Thinking takes time, as Grandpa says.

I do take time sifting through the experiences with Jan and group, even as I never listen to Jan again.

2005

I won't be able to listen to Jan anymore, because he died. Fifteen years after I quit the group.

The cancer that killed him was practically biblical. It ate him up piece by piece, and because he was such an ornery old goat, it took years and culminated in the loss of his vocal cords, so for the last seasons of his life, he held forth to the shrinking group by whispering.

I knew I'd never hear from Jan again, because he never reached out to anyone who left the group. So when he had Madeleine ask me to show up for a private meeting a few weeks after I quit, I did pause for a moment. She named the time and place, presuming my attendance. A reasonable presumption, since I'd been showing up wherever Jan Cox said to show up for twenty years. But no. The pause endured for only a moment, like the last gust of a withered weather system. I didn't have to think about it: I never wanted to listen to him again. I would not be showing up for any private meetings with Jan.

Not that I was trying to avoid him. I didn't care if I saw him or not, and it seemed natural to me to show up at parties whenever the urge struck. I'd been in the trenches with my tribe for twenty years, and the connections forged there remained even though I never listened to Jan again. So when I encountered him at social gatherings, he saw me yukking it up with people in the group, but he didn't know what to say or how to act around me, because he had only one gear for engagement, and I wasn't following the script anymore.

Some years later, though, he gentled—after the diagnosis, when his time grew short. On the rare occasions when we saw each other, he would kiss me on the forehead. The significance of this was not lost on me, and if he found a measure of love as mortality loomed, well, I'm all for it. But the feeling was not mutual because my feelings for him were all gone.

≈ ≈ ≈

Jan's wake, as he specified, was a huge, joyous party. It surpassed high expectations. Hundreds of people showed up to celebrate his life—people who had been there the whole time as well as people who had been involved for only a year or two and had disappeared twenty years earlier. He certainly did have an impact, and people came to acknowledge that impact, applaud it, and drink to it, including people from every time zone, every decade, every economic level, every sexual preference.

Jan's ex-wife and sons showed up. I had last seen the boys when they were teenagers. All of a sudden they were middle-aged. They uncannily, unwittingly stripped bare the two halves of Jan.

One son was massive—all physical and emotional and insightful. Multiple short jail terms attested to an unfiltered live-in-the-moment surfeit of loving and loathing. He could probably have taken down a horse if it pissed him off and then later married that same mare after they got drunk and fell in love.

The other son—skinny; all cool, cerebral, cynical, smart, and as insightful as his brother. But afraid of horses. And women. A gifted musician. And unemployed.

Click the two together, and you have Jan Cox.

≈ ≈ ≈

Jan was already dead to me at the time of his wake, so I did not miss him or mourn him. But I never stopped appreciating the ideas and methods and Tasks and experiences and the bonds with friends on the path. The good throbs on.

For years, deconstruction followed, brick by brick, as if I were taking apart a wall. Discard the parts that are useless or get in the way. You save the good bricks, use them in a new edifice. Bricks in a new bridge.

I wondered how a guy who spewed and spawned freeways to new skies could possibly have been so angry, so difficult. He would not tolerate his own behavior in others. And he had chances, as we all do, all the time, to come clean right in the middle of everything. But he could not say these simple words: *I don't know everything.* He could have learned from us—about decency, friendship, and humility. But he didn't, and it cost him.

Eventually I gave up trying to figure it out. I had a new life to live. Just as Rose did.

But later, years after I gave up trying to figure it out, a simple picture emerged—what Jan was about.

One of the differences between us and him is that Jan's demons howled more darkly than ours do, and he hated them more than we hate ours. So his geologic thrust was more extreme than ours. Jan fought monsters mightily. He put up a great fight. The fight cracked him in two. That's where his feet were nailed to the floor, right there at the crack, one foot on each side. It's a mesmerizing goddamn crack between extreme forces. Like he was a perpetual gonna-be-a-tornado weather system . . . the collision of ice and steam.

So Jan spoke from the edge of the storm, which is everyone's storm, only his was worse. But Jan talked better than he fought, and he was impaled with an ego too big for the Pentagon.

The demons feasted.

And truths spewed from the vortex.

≈ ≈ ≈

With an impish grin, Grandpa says, "One of my favorite things about Judaism is that you can talk during services."

He continues, "And everyone is always disagreeing with the rabbi. Judaism doesn't belong to the rabbi. Nobody owns Judaism. The Book of Knowledge should be an open book."

Grandpa says, "You were wrong about a lot of things. I doubt I would have made the choices you made had all those opportunities been given to me. Yet still, you were driven by forces I recognize. Forces that drove me."

And then he says, "But you were right about a lot of things, too. The way you fulfilled your youthful prayer in my memory at the Wailing Wall surpasses anything I might have dared to imagine. There are loud accomplishments and quiet accomplishments. Yours is quiet, yet it is already inscribed in the Book of Life.

"You were right to wrestle with demons I could barely recognize. I didn't have an exclusive on demons. Yours were subtler than mine. And you wrestled them well. Demons and desires, you chased them both, as well you should.

"And one more thing," he says. "I want to hear that name Rose some more."

"Oh, you will, Grandpa, you will. We have a lot to talk about. You know, Grandpa, enlightenment should inform wisdom. Don't you think?"

ABOUT THE AUTHOR

Jonathan Marcus grew up in a middle class Jewish family and was draft-age during the Vietnam War. Like many young people during the late Sixties, he craved New Age consciousness and self-discovery. His intellectual curiosity led him on a decades-long spiritual journey with the charismatic leader, Jan Cox, and The Work.

Marcus earned a degree from Emory University. However, he was self-taught in all his careers and avocations: short order cook, welder, ranch hand, awning entrepreneur, performer, photographer and carpenter. For more than thirty years, he designed and built homes in the urban pioneer neighborhoods of downtown Atlanta.

He is happy to live in Richmond, Virginia, as a writer, activist and community organizer.

Email Jonathan at jm@jonathanmarcus.org
*Instagram at jonathanmarcus_*
Facebook at jonathanmarcuswriter
Read his weekly ShortCuts at jonathanmarcus.org

WAIT! THERE'S MORE . . .

EVERYTHING ELSE

We'd love to send you . . . ***Everything Else***, including:

1. A List of Tasks, including all those described in the memoir, plus many others. We welcome any stories you may share about how these recipes are served up in your own life adventures. And when you're feeling generous, we welcome any Tasks you may add to our eager list.

2. Outtakes from *Everything Is Happening at Once*. These orphans might need some attention. Sometimes editors are just mean and throw excellent passages into the void. Here's a short collection from the original book.

Just send your request to jm@jonathanmarcus.org and we'll send you a free link to this e-book or a printable PDF.

And, the journey continues. A sequel is in process.

That's right, it's in production and answers the question: "What happens when your career has been a quest for the ineffable, and your friends and livelihood have rolled up into one tight-knit group for two decades, and you suddenly quit without considering the consequences?"

The same editors who can be so mean have now decided to play nice and include, for your reading pleasure - - -

3. The first chapter (with an appearance from Grandpa Phil) of *Everything is Happening at Once Again*. Thank you, editors!

Wait! There's Still More . . .

Beg to differ, if you dare, with the sideways insights you'll find in regular Short Cuts at jonathanmarcus.org.

Follow us on Instagram @ jonathanmarcus_
(for an interesting collection of feet in all sorts of situations),
and the antics on Facebook @ jonathanmarcuswriter.

Plus, we have a request:
If you enjoyed *Everything is Happening at Once*
please consider leaving a review on Amazon. Everyone will appreciate it, especially Marcus + Myer Publishing.

We'd love to hear from you . . .
Happy Everything from
Marcus + Myer

Fictionary: Words You Need

Nobody knows how many words the English language contains. Estimates range from 800,000 to over a million. Seems that with such gobs of words, every little niggling nuance and every little twisted bitchy emotional stain must be ripe for articulation. But no.

As big as the English cloak may be, we are left bare, chilly, and mute when attempting to clarify all the knots of torment, zaniness, euphoria, and outrage which fester beyond the boundaries of our incomprehensibly huge lexicon.

Therefore, Marcus + Myer Publishing is thrilled to provide desperately needed words—wily, wonderful words to grease the urge-to-spit-it-out among the repressed, distressed, perplexed, and verbally constipated English speakers around the world.

Email jm@jonathanmarcus.org for a free sample.

ACKNOWLEDGMENTS

Thank you everyone in the group with Jan Cox, and thank you Jan, too. We were all in it together in different ways, which is the best way. Thank you especially to Calvin Burgamy and Matt Rosenberger for many happy irreverent boisterous arguments over what in the hell did or did not happen there.

For all your support and attention and belief in the first draft, thank you Veronica Draffkorn, Sandi Curry, and Marene Emmanuel.

Thank you Rosemary Rawlins for your readerly appreciation and for introducing me to Barbara Clark, and thank you Barbara Clark for suggesting a completely different memoir, which is this one.

Thank you Cyndy Myer for embracing me and the manuscript equally, for reading it aloud on the sleeping porch, and for becoming my partner in making life and this book immeasurably more than either one would be otherwise.

65155402R00196

Made in the USA
Middletown, DE
01 September 2019